NEWSPA

A MANUAL FOR EDITORS, COPYREADERS, AND STUDENTS OF NEWSPAPER DESK WORK

BY

GRANT MILNOR HYDE, M.A.

PROFESSOR OF JOURNALISM AND EDITOR OF THE UNIVERSITY PRESS BUREAU IN THE UNIVERSITY OF WISCONSIN; AUTHOR OF "NEWSPAPER REPORTING AND CORRESPONDENCE," "HANDBOOK FOR NEWSPAPER WORKERS," AND "A COURSE IN JOURNALISTIC WRITING"

SECOND EDITION
WITH CLASS EXERCISES

D. APPLETON AND COMPANY
NEW YORK   LONDON
1931

COPYRIGHT, 1915, 1925, BY
D. APPLETON AND COMPANY

All rights reserved. This book, or parts thereof, must not be reproduced in any form without permission of the publishers.

PRINTED IN THE UNITED STATES OF AMERICA

*TO
THE MEMORY OF
MY FATHER*

PREFACE

Much has happened in the newspaper profession and in the schools of journalism since this book was first published ten years ago. The newspapers have "covered" a World War—and war periods have always brought the greatest changes in American newspapers—have wrestled with doubled costs of production, reduced staffs, much merging, curtailed income, and are now deep in the perplexities of reconstruction. Meanwhile schools and courses in journalism have greatly increased in number, enrollment, and branches of instruction.

When the book was presented in 1915, it was the first textbook entirely devoted to the problems and technique of newspaper desk work. It has, therefore, been widely used in classes in copyreading, headline writing, and make-up, as well as in newspaper offices. Its contents have been put to a severe test, and some have been found wanting. The author himself, in using it year after year in class, filled many page margins with suggestions for improvement.

Hence, in preparation for its tenth anniversary, it is well that the book should receive a thorough overhauling—to bring it up to date, to put in some things omitted before, to make it more usable and "teachable." Its general structure has not been changed. Most of the alterations are in the chapters on copyreading, headline writing, make-up, and type, but many additions have been made in other chapters.

"Class exercises" have now been added to each chapter to present in brief much of the technique of teaching, as it has developed in the larger schools. They are intended to be suggestive, not only to the teacher, but to independent students and young newspaper workers. A bibliography has been added to suggest further reading.

In the schools of journalism, the methods of teaching copyreading have developed during the period since first publication probably more than any other branch, and have been somewhat standardized. These ideas are now quite generally accepted: (1) the work can best be done with a small group working around a copy desk at high speed and under strict supervision; (2) thorough knowledge of typography must be included; and (3) extensive practice in make-up, either "on the stone" or with shears and paste pot, must bind together other phases of desk work. Hence, the horseshoe copy desk is now a standard piece of furniture in many schools of journalism, and some schools are installing the "type laboratory" of the kind that was first developed at the University of Wisconsin—"a printshop without a press" where students do not merely stand around and watch printers, but actually set type, plan display, and make up pages on the stone.

Not even now is this a volume on "the ethics of desk work." It seems certain, from the trend of talk in newspaper offices and in schools of journalism, that books will be written on the ethical considerations of copyreading and headline writing. But this book was at first, and still is, principally devoted to technique. Here and there, however, hints at ethical considerations have been dropped in, and the public-service aspects of some particular practices are suggested.

The number of "clipped examples" is still kept down to a minimum—for two reasons: (1) any examples of headlines and make-up taken from current newspapers are so bound up with today's news that they will go out of date and become stale in a few months; (2) search for examples, good or bad, is the best exercise for newspaper students. Through searching for one kind of technique, they see others and learn discrimination—learn to distinguish good from bad

PREFACE

in newspaper work. Instead of reprinting headline schedules of today, the author suggests clipping headline styles from current newspapers.

As before, the book aims, not only to present the tools and methods of copyreading, but to show its interesting possibilities. Too many newspaper men, especially reporters, regard desk work as drudgery and feel that to be placed "on the desk" is to be pushed back out of the firing line. Desk work is fascinating if done in the proper spirit, but it must be more than mere "paragraph marking" and "heading up." That is why many subjects have been introduced that may seem "outside the copyreader's line"—for instance, the discussion of type and printing processes, the detailed study of the physical side of the newspaper under "Make-up." Newspaper staffs are becoming more and more interested in these subjects; managing editors are seeking men who know type and what may be done with it.

For the editor and teacher-adviser of student newspapers and magazines, as well as for the newspaper man or student of journalism who is called upon to edit small periodicals, the chapter on "Small Publication Work" presents some of the methods and short cuts of large newspaper and magazine offices.

The Style Sheet (Appendix II) is offered as a model, rather than final dictum. It was drawn up by instructors in the University of Wisconsin school of journalism, in co-operation with several newspaper editors, and embodies practices of that state. For use in other localities, its rules must be altered to match local usages. In whatever form, however, the style sheet offers a means of developing accuracy in small details.

Just as in typographical style, the greatest problem in a book on editing is the selection of average methods from the varying practices of newspaper offices. Desk-work methods and terms differ greatly in various localities. In his work on a New York City newspaper, the author learned methods rarely seen in the Middle West; he has heard newspaper men in one city laugh at the methods of another. Out of all this, he has tried to select the average, discarding the more slipshod methods of smaller offices in favor of the systematic practices of metropolitan offices—in some cases suggesting the highly systematized methods of magazine offices in which he has worked.

The method of presentation throughout is drawn from fifteen years of classroom work in a large school of journalism. Little attempt is made to lay down rules. Rather the effort is to present fundamentals, to encourage analysis of current practices, and to answer the questions that arise in students' minds. In many cases, it is hoped, the answer is one that will open up the broader, ethical aspects of the matter.

For valuable suggestions for the revision of this book the author is indebted to his colleagues, Prof. Willard G. Bleyer and Prof. E. Marion Johnson, of the Course in Journalism of the University of Wisconsin. To many another journalism teacher and newspaper man, the author owes credit for ideas.

G. M. H.

CONTENTS

PART I

PREFACE vii

CHAPTER
I. THE COPYREADER'S PART IN NEWSPAPER MAKING   3
II. COPYREADING 24
III. HEADLINE WRITING 95
IV. PROOFREADING 170
V. NEWSPAPER MAKE-UP 187
VI. SYNDICATE AND ASSOCIATION MATERIAL . . . 231
VII. REWRITE AND FOLLOW STORIES 248

PART II

VIII. TYPE 261
IX. PRINTING PROCESSES 282
X. SMALL PUBLICATION WORK 328

APPENDICES

I. LIST OF SIGNIFICANT DATES IN THE HISTORY OF THE ART OF PRINTING AND THE DEVELOPMENT OF THE NEWSPAPER 373
II. TYPICAL STYLE SHEET 387
III. BOOKS ON JOURNALISM 395
INDEX 401

PART I
THE NEWSPAPER COPY DESK

NEWSPAPER EDITING

CHAPTER I

THE COPYREADER'S PART IN NEWSPAPER MAKING

The copy desk in a city newspaper office is one workbench in a great manufacturing plant, and a copyreader is one of a large group of workmen engaged in the manufacture of a finished product—a newspaper. The copy editor is, from one point of view, the most important workman in the entire plant, since he puts the finishing touches upon the raw material that goes into the product. From another point of view, he is only one of many skilled workers, many of whom are responsible for work as important, if not more important, than the copyreader's. That paradox is one of the things that differentiates the organization of a newspaper plant from that of almost all other manufacturing businesses—and one of the things that makes newspaper work as fascinating as it is.

The copyreader, while occupying a comparatively subordinate position among the newspaper's other workers, bears part of the responsibility of making the newspaper good. Carelessness or inexperience on his part may ruin all the good work done by others; excellence in his work may cause the newspaper to win the coveted reputation of being "well edited." Every stroke of work he does shows in the finished product. There is no one between his desk and the purchaser to gloss over the good or bad quality of his work. The same is true of many another worker in the newspaper plant; his work shows in the finished product with all the good or bad workmanship that he puts into it. There is little chance for the inspection and grading employed in other manufacturing enterprises. Criticism must come after the work has gone into the product. Criticism of bad work done today may improve tomorrow's output in the newspaper plant, but it cannot help the fact that today's bad paper has already gone to the buyer.

The copyreader, when he takes his desk in a newspaper office, must know the relation of his work to the work of others in the office and at the same time must realize thoroughly the responsibility of his work and its effect upon the finished newspaper.

I. Newspaper Organization

The average American citizen thinks of a newspaper office as a hive of peculiarly unbusinesslike men, assisted by some printers and machinery, engaged in the somewhat doubtful occupation of disseminating more or less reliable information and opinions. That they should desire real money for their work, or for its by-product, advertising space, is often to him a humorous thing. Some newspaper men have the same conception of their work.

The modern newspaper plant, however, is in reality a highly businesslike manufacturing enterprise engaged in producing a salable product—and endeavoring to make a legitimate profit out of its manufacture, like any other business concern. The product is a few or many thousand printed newspapers to be sold each day at a specified price per copy. The raw material that goes into their manufacture is paper, ink, and current events. The only differences between this product and any other are (1) that much of the raw material is composed of an illusive substance called "news," whose production is a mental rather than a physical process; and (2) that, because the public bases its opinions on this "news," the newspaper has a public service or public utility function. If the newspaper is bad, its owner should be classed with any other manufacturer of bad wares. The ethical conception of the dishonest newspaper publisher is much the same as that of any other dishonest manufacturer. If he does not put pure raw material into his product, he is selling mislabeled goods. If he colors the news, he is an adulterator—but, more than that, his dishonesty is poisoning the public mind and conscience. It is easy enough to apply this conception to the quality of paper, ink, and typographical impression, but it is hard to apply it to the rest of the raw material. Every newspaper worker, including copyreaders, should, however, have this idea of his work. He should feel that he is a manufacturer who must deliver honest and pure wares to his customers.

To carry on the manufacture of newspapers, a publishing plant has a mechanical department, a business office, and a sales department, like any other manufacturing concern. It also has another staff of men engaged in the production of the raw material—news. Ordinarily the plant is organized on exactly these lines. All sales and other business relations are managed by a business office; the physical production is carried on in a mechanical department; and the raw material, news and opinions, is handled by an editorial staff. All newspapers, large or small, contain the three separate departments, whether they employ a thousand men or one man, like the country editor who embodies the three departments in his own person.

1. The Business Office

The business office of the average newspaper is in charge of a business manager, who is primarily a financial expert responsible only to the owner or owners of the newspaper. His duty is to make the enterprise financially successful. He is independent of the other departments and has no authority over them except through the mediation of the proprietor. A few newspapers, to be sure, have a general manager who guides the work and policy of all three departments and welds them together into a working whole, but he is really a newspaper expert whom the owner employs to exercise general supervision in his stead.

Besides a staff of clerks and bookkeepers, the business manager has in his office several other men to take care of the various branches of the financial work. (1) One is a circulation manager who has charge of the sale of finished newspapers. Under him are subscription clerks, mailing room men, newsboys, wagon drivers, and other agents of distribution. (2) Another is an advertising manager who has charge of the sale of advertising space—both want-ad and display. He has a number of advertising solicitors to assist him in his work. (3) Another is a cashier who has charge of all the newspaper's money, paying all salaries and other expenditures and

THE COPYREADER'S PART

receiving all money paid to the newspaper for advertising, sales, or other purposes.

2. The Mechanical Plant

The mechanical branch of the newspaper plant is in the same way in charge of a single man responsible only to the owner or his representative. There are ordinarily four or five separate departments in his branch. (1) One department is the composing room, in which typesetters, printers, linotype operators, copy cutters, bank men, proofreaders, etc., convert manuscript into type and make it up into the form of the finished pages. (2) Another department is the stereotyping room, in which the flat page forms, composed of type and cuts put together by the printers, are reproduced in curved metal plates for the rotary presses. (3) The third department is the pressroom, which contains huge presses for printing newspapers at a high rate of speed. Each of these departments has its specialized workmen who are hired to do various mechanical work. (4) Sometimes the newspaper has an engraving department whose work is to make plates for the newspaper's illustrations—cuts, as they are called. (5) When the newspaper has automatic mailing machines for wrapping and addressing subscribers' copies, the mechanics in charge of them are a part of the plant's mechanical force. The machinery used in the mechanical plant is among the most ingenious and costly known to modern industry.

3. The Editorial Department

The third and most important division of the newspaper's plant is the editorial department which prepares all the reading matter, except advertisements, that goes into the printed paper. Whether the paper be large or small, the work of this department is divided into a variety of separate and distinct branches of work. Perhaps all the branches may be taken care of by a few men, or, if the staff is large enough, each branch may be in the hands of a specialist. But, however great or small the extent of the staff, the various kinds of work are entirely separate and specialized.

Since the reading matter of every newspaper is distinctly separated into two classes—news and comment—the main division of the editorial department is along the same lines. (1) One staff of men, commonly known as the news staff, is employed for the special work of gathering and writing news. (2) Another staff, usually designated as the editorial staff, is engaged in the work of interpreting the news. The one staff prepares the news pages; the other prepares the editorial columns. So distinct are the two staffs, that each requires of its men a different kind of ability and experience. Whereas one group is engaged in the specific task of drawing conclusions from facts and writing comments on the facts, the other group is usually forbidden to show the slightest evidence of an opinion on anything.

The Editorial Writers.—The news interpreting, or editorial staff, is made up of a group of men called editorial writers, working under an editor-in-chief. This editor, usually the only person whom the outside world recognizes as editor of the paper, guides the paper's editorial policy and dictates the paper's point of view on passing events reported in other pages. He deals out editorial topics to his small staff of writers and passes upon the acceptability of their editorials. He bears entire responsibility for the character and content of the paper's editorial columns and sends all his copy directly to the printers without any corrective editing by any other member of the staff. His group of editorial writers may consist of one or two men, or it may include as many as a dozen, some of whom spend a large part of their time at the state or national capital and have an extensive library to use in their work of molding public opinion.

The News Staff.—The news staff, which prepares the news columns for the paper, is ordinarily larger and composed of many branches. Its head is called the managing editor. Under him are (1) one group of men designated as the local staff, (2) another as the telegraph room, and (3) others known as department editors. Perhaps there is also an art department and a library.

The Local Staff.—The local room, or staff, is concerned with the gathering and writing of all news of the city in which the paper is published. It is entirely in charge of a city editor—or day and night city editors, if the men work in two shifts—who hires and directs all the men in the department. The staff usually consists of a number of reporters and a few desk men. The reporters, all working under the city editor, gather the news and write the stories that make up the news columns. Some of them are department men, making regular daily rounds on a run or beat of news sources; others are assignment men, employed to work up special assignments under the city editor's direction. The desk men, on the other hand, are not writers or newsgatherers but correctors of the reporter's work. They are usually called copyreaders and, if there are several of them, they are organized into a small staff under a head copyreader. Their work is to take the stories which the reporters have written, correct them according to the paper's style and practice, write headlines for them, and prepare them for the printers. Since the telephone has come into common use in newsgathering, certain of the desk men are employed as rewrite men to prepare stories from facts telephoned in by reporters. All of these desk men are assistants of the city editor and work under his direction. The table at which they work is the "copy desk." Another subeditor is the news editor whose work it is to make up the newspaper just before press time.

The Telegraph Room.—All news from outside the city, distinguished in the printed paper by datelines, is handled by the telegraph editor and his assistants. This staff usually comprises one or more telegraph operators, besides the editor and his assistants, and in many cases one or more copyreaders to edit and write headlines for telegraph copy. Some papers, however, have one force of copy editors to handle both local and telegraph news. But, however the staff may be organized, it handles all news that comes to the office by telegraph, mail, cable, or long distance telephone. It has its staff of reporters, also, working under the direction of the telegraph editor, but they are located in distant towns and cities and are known as correspondents.

Department Editors.—These two departments, the local and telegraph rooms, comprise the greater portion of the newspaper's news staff. Others are mainly specialists in charge of small departments of the paper. One is the sporting editor, who, working alone or with assistants, prepares the contents of the sporting page. Another is the society editor who gathers and writes social items. Other special editors, varying in number and importance, are the financial and market editor, the railroad editor, the dramatic and musical critics, and real estate editors, and the exchange editor. Each has his own small section of the paper to fill but whenever he obtains any news too significant to be buried in his corner he turns it over to the local staff to be played up in the more prominent news pages. Each of these various department writers is called an editor because his copy goes to the printer without passing through the hands of a copyreader or another editor.

Other Branches.—If the newspaper has a Sunday supplement or a special Sunday edition, it has a Sunday or supplement editor who devotes his time to preparing the content of the special pages that are folded in with the regular news pages. Many city papers also have an art department, composed of artists, cartoonists, and photographers who prepare illustrations. Another very important member of the editorial staff is the librarian who keeps up files of information easily accessible on a moment's notice. One part of his files, called the "morgue," consists of a collection of biographical facts and photographs of prominent men that may be put together into an obituary sketch whenever the prominent man is in any way connected with the day's news.

II. A STORY'S COURSE THROUGH THE OFFICE

Perhaps the copy editor's part in newspaper making will be clearer if we follow the career of a story through the various parts of the office of an afternoon newspaper.

The story was suggested to the city editor, let us say, by a morning paper's report to the effect that the state legislature was considering a bill for the authorization of paid "civic secretaries" to look after "social centers." He entered the idea in his day book and gave the assignment to Jack Robbins, one of his reporters: "Robbins, go and ask the mayor what he thinks of the appointment of civic secretaries. Ask him if he thinks it will aid the social centers. You've been out to the Webster School at every meeting and know all about it." That was the way the story began. It might have originated in some other way; some reporter might have picked it up on his run or some social center worker might have telephoned it to the office. Robbins went to the mayor's office, at any rate, and after a while returned with the tidings that the mayor thought it a fine idea. "Did he have much to say?" asked the city editor. "A barrelful," answered Robbins and he briefly outlined the mayor's ideas. "Write half a column on it, playing up the mayor's point that it will increase fifty per cent the public's use of public property."

Robbins wrote the story and placed it on the city editor's desk. Other stories were coming in with it from other writers, some from other reporters, some from rewrite men sitting at the telephone, some from the telegraph desk, and even some from outsiders seeking needed publicity. The city editor glanced at Robbins' story and handed it to his head copyreader with the instructions "Cut it to five hundred words; put a little more punch in the lead; give it a No. 8 head." The head copyreader, whose desk was piled high, passed the story and the instructions to one of his assistants. But first he made a record: "Civic Sect. Mayor—500—Robbins—No. 8—10:15."

The copyreader read through the story, correcting a misspelled word here, straightening out a grammatical construction there, consulting the telephone directory for the initials of a social center worker mentioned, toning down an overenthusiastic paragraph, brightening up a bit of summary with some new verbs, and changing the typographical style to suit the style sheet over his desk. The editing finished, he turned back to the first page and put more punch into the lead by incorporating a striking expression that he found buried in the last paragraph. Then skimming through he crossed out sentences here, paragraphs there, useless words and phrases in other places, until he estimated that what was left was about five hundred words long. On page 3 he sliced out a long paragraph by cutting through the manuscript above and below the paragraph with his shears, pasted a blank sheet of copy paper in its place, and wrote a summary of the paragraph's contents in one-third as many words. When he had finished the editing, he took the first page again and wrote in the blank half above the lead the content of a three-deck headline of the style known in the office as No. 8. Beside the head he wrote "No. 8" with a circle around it. At the top of the sheet he wrote "Civic Sect. Mayor," and folded the sheets together ready to hand to the copy boy. Just then the city editor called, "Who's got that interview with the mayor? Here's one with the president of the school board to add to it." The copyreader turned to the last page of the manuscript, crossed out the mark—"# # #"—that indicated the end of the story, and wrote in its place, "More." After the copy boy had taken the manuscript to the composing room, the second interview reached his desk via the head copyreader and his first move was to write at its head "Folo Civic Sect. Mayor."

When the copy reached the composing room, it was placed on the desk of the copy cutter. After glancing at its length, he pasted the five sheets together end to end in a long string and cut the story up into three pieces, or "takes," more or less equal in length, taking care in each case to cut at the end of the paragraph. The headline constituted the fourth take. At the head of the first sheet he wrote "C. 1," on the next he wrote "C. 2," on the next "C. 3." As the boy took it from his hands, he wrote in his record "Civic Sect. Mayor—10:33—C. 1—4." The boy took the three takes to three linotype operators designated by the copy cutter and in a few moments each of the three was setting up his part of the story. In this way, the entire story was in type in the time it took one operator to set one-third of it—one-third of the time it would have taken one man to set the entire story. Take No. 2 was finished first and the operator sent it to the "bank" man who makes up the stories. While the bank man was placing take No. 2 in the center of a galley, chalked "C" according to the copy cutter's schedule, take No. 3 came to him and he placed it below take No. 2; then take No. 1 and the headline came for the head of the galley. At the bottom of the galley he turned over the slug to indicate "More to come." The bank man therefore held the galley until the interview with the president of the school board came along known as "Follow Civic Sect. Mayor" and labeled C. 5—7. As this was marked "End," he turned the galley over to another printer and cleared his bank. The galley was then taken to a proof press and a printer "pulled a proof" of it. In a small glass-inclosed office in the corner of the composing room a proofreader read the proof aloud to an assistant who followed the reading with the original copy. With the corrections marked on the margin, the proof went back to the original operators for revision. They set up the new lines to be inserted in the galley in place of the faulty lines. The galley was then "revised" and revised proofs were pulled. One copy of it went to the proofreader for a second reading, another went to the news editor, and a third to the managing editor.

Meantime many other stories had followed the same course and were in type and proof form. By one o'clock several of the back pages of the paper had been "made up" and "put to bed" on the stereotyper's stone. About two o'clock the news editor gathered up a bundle of proofs marked "Front Page" and started for the composing room to "close up." Just before he left his desk, the managing editor stepped out of his office and said to the city editor, "Kill that interview with the president of the school board; he just telephoned me that he'd give us some better stuff tomorrow." The word was passed on and the news editor drew a line through the "Civic Sect. Mayor Follow" on his proof. Then he went on to the composing room and with the guidance of a "dummy" diagram he had made up beforehand he started taking the first-page stories from their galleys and directed the placing of them in the front-page "chase." He was nearly through when a copy boy came down with the instructions from the editorial room, "Hold front page for fire story." A reporter had just telephoned in that a leading hotel was on fire. It was fifteen minutes before press time but that was time enough for a rewrite man to dash off two hundred words about the fire while a copyreader wrote a headline for it. Ten minutes later the story was in type, revised, and on the make-up stone. But this was more copy than the news editor had counted on and he had too much type for the page—about three stickfuls. As the other pages were closed and there was no time to open them up for a "break-over" of any front-page story, the news editor quickly threw away the last paragraphs of three of his stories. One of them was the interview with the mayor. It is now down to four hundred words. He locked up the form, leaving the upper six inches of the two right-hand columns empty for sport "fudge," and sent the page to the stereotypers.

A stereotyper quickly laid a wet papier-mâché matrix over the first page form, passed it under a roller and pushed it into a steam table. In four minutes he released the press, drew the form out, pasted a few strips of cardboard in the hollow places in the back of the hard-baked papier-mâché matrix, and sent the type form back to the news editor. The matrix was then slipped in the circular casting box of an automatic plate-making machine and in a few minutes it had served as a mold for the casting of half a dozen curved stereotype plates. Shaved and trimmed and cooled as they passed out of the plate machine, the plates were carried to the press room and bolted upon the proper rolls of several rotary presses. The plates for the other pages were already in place and a pressman was setting the latest news into the "fudge" roll. The news consisted of a handful of linotype slugs which read, "World Series Score 2 to 0 at

THE COPYREADER'S PART 17

End of Sixth Inning," and carried the score by innings up to the last moment. When the last fudge bolt was twisted tight, the signal was given and the rotaries started grinding out copies of the "Afternoon Edition" at the rate of many hundreds per minute. On the front page of each was the interview with the mayor. Inside of a short time, final score of the game had come in over the telegraph wire in the press room, a linotype machine standing beside one of the presses had set it up in new slugs, the presses were then stopped long enough for a pressman to change the slugs in the fudge roll so as to include the final score of the game. The mayor's interview occupied the same place as before.

In the meanwhile, more complete news of the hotel fire had come to the office and a two-column story was in type. The news editor remade the front-page form so as to include it. The fudge space was omitted, but even then there was not enough space and he was forced to cut down some of the other stories. Among others, the mayor's interview was cut to three hundred words and by the time the presses were printing the next edition it was a very much less prominent story than when the reporter wrote it.

By the time the presses had printed enough copies to make up the "Home Edition" for the newsboys, the news editor had remade the paper for the "Mail Edition." Page by page, he had opened up the forms of the four or five news pages and inserted national news for local news and changed their content. When he reached the front page he decided that the mayor's interview was not of interest to people outside the city. Rather than throw it out entirely, he picked up its lead from the first-page form and slipped it into the miscellany column headed "City Items" on the fifth page. In the papers that reached the out-of-town subscribers the reporter's original eight-hundred-word interview had dwindled to seventy-five words, but not a line of it had been reset.

Into this finished newspaper, every employee in the plant had added his share. The business department had obtained and put into copy many columns of advertising, both classified and display. The circulation department had prepared for the marketing of the edition, through paid subscriptions and street sales. The mechanical force had set up and paged many thousand of linotype slugs and individual pieces of type, besides stereotyping and printing thousands of copies. The editorial department had supplied from 60,000 to 100,000 words of new reading matter, all duly classified. The editorial writers had contributed two or three columns of editorials; the department editors and special writers had turned out a column or a page each. The reporters and correspondents had prepared two or three times as much reading matter as was needed, and the copyreaders had boiled this down, composed headlines for it, and reduced it to the uniform style of the newspaper. The work done by the newspaper plant for this one edition was greater than that required to write and print several books—and the plant had accomplished it in less than twenty-four hours. By the time the presses were at work on the last edition, every desk and bench throughout the plant was cleared for action and work had begun on the issue to follow less than twenty-four hours later.

III. THE DESK MAN'S PART

The copy editor's part in the work is an important part, even though it is a modest one and without fame. A reader comes to know the newspaper's writers from their signed articles, their visits as newsgatherers, and their opinions on the editorial page. But he is seldom aware that such a person as the copy editor exists. He does not know that it is the copyreader who reduces all this written matter, coming from the pens and the typewriters of many scribes, to the uniform style and quality which characterizes the newspaper itself. He does not know that it is the copy editor who is the watch dog that wards off errors and libelous statements, besides writing the headlines that catch the reader's eye and sum up the news so that he can read the entire paper in a few moments.

The work done by the copy editor requires a broader training and a larger store of knowledge than almost any other post in the newspaper office. Certainly it requires much more than that demanded of the reporter or correspondent. To edit copy swiftly and accurately, the desk man must have a thorough understanding of English grammar and diction, must know news value more thoroughly than the average reporter does, and must be acquainted with the intricacies of the libel law. He must know his own city inside and out, must know the affairs of the nation, and must be on more than speaking terms with all the great questions and thoughts of the day. He must know type and printing processes as thoroughly as his printers. Headline writing in itself is an art that can be developed only by much training and knowledge of typography. The mere summarizing of an idea whose expression has taken several hundred words is task enough, but to make that summary fit a typographical scheme mapped out in unit letters and spaces is much more difficult.

The young desk man should remember that the duties of his position require above all that he be a critic of the first water and also that he be enough of a writer to recast instantly the feeble attempts of other writers. But half the difficulties of his work will be met by a proper knowledge of its requirements. Only study will point out these requirements, for no city editor has time to put his assistants through a course of instruction. In this study he will find that a good textbook is the work of other copy editors, as shown in the newspapers they edit. This textbook is merely a summary of observations of the methods of work of many copy editors.

Constructive Journalism

In the midst of all the technical details, the newspaper desk man must not lose sight of the fact that there is an element in his work far more important than mere mechanical skill and expertness. It is power and leadership—the opportunity to wield a potent influence, for good or bad, upon thousands of readers and subsequently upon the community and the nation. For his is not a skilled trade, but a profession with ideals and ethics and aspirations. The newspaper man who is not aware of this quality in his work is behind the times.

What has the desk man to do with "constructive journalism"? Is it not rather the concern of the owner and editor-in-chief? The answer is that it matters not what

THE COPYREADER'S PART

lofty, or lowly, ideals the editor may have nor what tone he wishes to achieve, he is powerless to carry them out unless his desk men and reporters understand them and coöperate with him. In the newspaper, details count for more than the total. It is the individual headline, the individual adjective, the individual inaccuracy, the individual error of grammar, that gives a newspaper a good or bad reputation. These are in the hands of the desk man. He must know the big movements in modern journalism, to help keep his paper abreast of them.

He must not overlook his responsibility to the English language. If the newspaper is the only reading matter that comes to the hands of thousands of readers, its influence on the mother tongue is greater than that of the schools, the church, and all other printed matter. Setting the standards of daily speech, teaching the language to the young and to the immigrant, the American newspaper—through its reporters and copyreaders—may destroy the mother tongue or preserve it in all its richness and beauty.

Exercises

1. Begin systematic study of well-known newspapers. Analyze a different newspaper each week, paying particular attention to the class topic of the week, and embody the results in a 500-word weekly report. Prepare headline schedule of each paper.

2. Carry on critical study of the desk work evidenced in all available newspapers. Find examples of all practices discussed in this book.

3. A good "copyreader's eye" may be developed by reëditing front pages of local newspapers, marking every error. This should be done again and again on different papers.

4. Make a diagram to visualize the typical newspaper staff.

5. Trace a story through a local newspaper office.

6. Note local practices that differ from those presented in this chapter.

7. Study the local newspaper—learn the names of owners from published statement; note extent of office organization and names of persons in various positions; note advertising and subscription rates; visit mechanical departments.

8. *Analysis of a Newspaper.*—Each student should bring the same issue of the same newspaper and together analyze it, story by story, to see what it is made of and how it is made:

Things to be noted in each story are: 1. Original tip and assignment. 2. Sources of information. 3. How reporter worked. 4. If dateline story, what agency brought it. 5. Structure, emphasis, method of writing. 6. Evidences of copyreading. 7. Kind of headline and relation to story. 8. Evaluation of news of the story. 9. Emphasis given by make-up. 10. Kind of reader interested. 11. Degree of interest to any and all readers. 12. Whether story is as effective as possible.

Other things that may be noted in newspapers (measure column inches with footrule): 1. Number and kinds of subjects on front page. 2. Whatever policy evidenced in news. 3. Relation to political party. 4. Kinds of news emphasized. 5. What is its definition of news? 6. Proportion of local and outside news. 7. Competition in local field. 8. Amount of material supplied by each person or department mentioned in above chapter. 9. Press associations and others news gathering agencies employed. 10. Amount of special correspondent material. 11. Use of standard local news runs and sources. 12. What stories on special assignment. 13. Evidence of use of "datebook." 14. Follow and rewrite stories. 15. Reprint matter and miscellany. 16. Forecast follows on stories used. 17. Development of local ends. 18. Is routine news classified?

19. Use of illustrations and their source. 20. Use or misuse of banner headline. 21. Typographical style—compared with class style sheet or Appendix II. 22. System of subheads and

THE COPYREADER'S PART

division heads. 23. Headline schedule—form, structure, typography of headlines. 24. Relation of display to possible sensationalism. 25. Use of by-lines, local and telegraph.

26. Display advertisements—local *v.* foreign—number, size, kinds of business. 27. Size and technique of classified ad section—special promotion devices. 28. Circulation and promotion devices.

29. Syndicate matter—kind, source, credit lines. 30. Smaller regular features—source. 31. Comic strips—source, position. 32. Cartoons—source, position, subject. 33. Humor column—source. 34. Other non-news matter—source and kind.

35. Make-up and content of editorial page. 36. Analyze editorials—local or non-local subjects, timely, expository or argumentative. 37. Rest of editorial page.

38. Departments—character, editors, source of material. 39. Sport department—size, local *v.* telegraph, syndicate, press association, number of sports, amateur *v.* professional, relation to betting, style. 40. Social news and personals. 41. Woman's page—subjects, material, source. 42. Markets.

CHAPTER II

COPYREADING

In all publication work—be it newspaper, magazine, or book—there is always an intermediate step between the written manuscript and the composed type, known as copyreading, or editing. Since man first began to multiply his written ideas, there has always been a third person between the writer and the printer to "edit" the manuscript. His office is that of corrector, auditor, or checker. In the magazine or book publishing office he is known as an editor. In the newspaper office he goes by the more commonplace title of copyreader, since the newspaper "editor" is ordinarily occupied with other things beside the editing of copy. To avoid confusion in our discussion of his duties, we shall call this intermediate person simply the copyreader and his work copyreading.

The work of the copyreader consists in preparing manuscript for the printer. He works with other men's penned or typewritten manuscript and his only tool is a large soft lead pencil. He rarely does any writing himself but he often develops sufficient individuality in his alteration of manuscript to be cordially disliked by some reporters. However true may be their accusations against him, he is a very necessary member of every newspaper staff, and the tone of our publications would suffer without his work. To rectify errors of fact, spelling, grammar, punctuation, typographical style, and sentence structure, to tone down the bubbling exuberance of some reporters, to brighten up the dead matter-of-factness of others, and to write the necessary interpretation in others constitute his task, and the extent to which he brings his own individuality into the task is entirely a matter of his personality. If an error or a libelous statement "gets past" him to appear on the printed page of many thousands of newspapers, it is not usually the original writer of the article who receives the blame, but the copyreader, who should have "caught" the error when he edited the copy.

In the large American newspaper office, the copyreader works directly under the charge of the city editor who directs the newspaper's staff of reporters. He is the "desk man" who is always in the office and far away from the glamour of newspaper reportorial work. He is, in fact, the assistant of the city editor and his office grew out of the overcrowding of that dignitary's duties. In smaller, poorer offices, where the income of the paper puts narrow limits on the size of the staff, this assistant to the city editor is lacking and his work is done by the city editor. When a copyreader is added to the staff, he simply takes over a portion of the city editor's work—that of editing copy and writing headlines. The city editor still has charge of the reporters and directs the writing of stories.

Morning newspapers of larger size usually have two or more separate "copy desks"—the city desk, handling local copy; the telegraph desk, handling news from outside the city; and perhaps a sport desk. Some metropolitan newspapers have separate cable desks, and a few have desks for business and market news. Because of the greater speed required in their many editions, afternoon newspapers are quite generally adopting the "universal," or "combination," desk to handle news of all kinds. Smaller newspapers usually have but one copy desk. In current vernacular, the head copyreader is "the slot man" because he sits "in the slot" inside the semicircular table at which the copyreaders work. The desk men around him are "rim men" for they work "on the rim" of the table. Lately there has been a growing specialization among "rim men," whereby each handles one or more particular kinds of copy—*e.g.* local politics, labor news, "social unrest," etc.

When a reporter comes in from his run or assignment with the facts of a news story, he reports to the city editor and receives directions as to the length of the story he is to write, its character, and the feature that is to be emphasized in it. As soon as he has completed the story, he takes the copy directly to the city editor. If he has no copyreaders, the city editor must himself prepare the story for the printer. But if he has desk men to assist him, he glances through the story to note its content and then passes it over to one of his copyreaders for editing and headline. He usually accompanies the copy with a few brief verbal directions, to guide the copyreader and to indicate the kind of headline desired.

What a copyreader does to each story that passes through his hands may be summarized thus:

1. Corrects errors of fact or expression.
2. Enforces the rules of "office style."
3. Trims or expands story to prescribed length.
4. Guards again libelous matter.

5. Polishes or improves English of the story.
6. Eliminates expressions of opinion.
7. Coördinates story with other news of day.
8. Puts on necessary marks to guide printer.
9. Writes headline, subheads, captions, etc.
10. "Slugs" story for record and make-up.

Each copyreader has his own way of accomplishing all these quickly and thoroughly. He may do it in one reading, in two, or even in three. At any rate, whatever his own shortcut, he reads it through carefully to correct all the errors in it and makes all the alterations on the manuscript. He may perhaps rewrite the lead or he may cut off several paragraphs. Here and there he inserts a word or two to clarify the meaning or crosses out half a sentence to eliminate repetition and wordiness. When he has finished editing it, the story is in final form, with guide-lines and type directions, ready for the printer. Then in the blank half-page above the beginning of the story, he writes a suitable headline of the size designated by the city editor—but the writing of the headline is another task which will be considered in a separate chapter. Before he calls the copy boy to send the manuscript to the composing room, he makes a record of the subject of the story, its length, the name of the reporter who wrote it, the size of headline written on the story, and the exact time it was sent to the composing room. The record may look something like this: "Smith—Council Meeting—800—No. 8—10:45." His task would be easy if he had only one or two stories to edit and plenty of time in which to edit them, but usually the stories are coming to him in a continuous stream, as fast as he can handle them, and along toward press time he may edit several stories at once, page by page, as they come from the reporters' typewriters. One moment he is editing page 3 of a fire story, the next he is dashing through page 5 of the account of a political convention, a minute later he is writing a new lead for an interview with one of the candidates nominated, and then as the last page of the fire reaches his hands he writes the headline to be carried above it. He must pass the pages on as rapidly as possible so as to keep all of the linotype machines working at full capacity. He must therefore hold the content of several stories in his mind at once, keep them separate, and edit each one as accurately and painstakingly as if he were a schoolmaster leisurely marking a bundle of student themes.

Although the copyreader's work combines the writing of headlines with the editing of copy and not infrequently a bit of proofreading, we are concerned at present only with his work of editing or copyreading.

I. Revision—Not Rewriting

The first thing about his work that the young copyreader must understand thoroughly is that he has been employed, not as a writer, but as a corrector of other men's writing. His job is to revise and reconstruct, not to rewrite. And before he has held his desk position long he will come to realize that the ability to revise is quite different from the ability to write and that it requires the cultivation of very different methods of thinking. The young copyreader's first impulse, when he is given a badly written story to edit, is to throw the reporter's copy into the waste basket and rewrite the story. Very often, of course, that is the easiest and quickest way to make the story printable. But as a general practice such copyreading methods involve too much duplication of work for a busy newspaper office. If the reporter who was employed to write the story is not able to do so, he has no place in the office and should be reported to the city editor for discharge. More often, however, the fault lies with the copyreader, for only a small amount of the copy that comes to him is so bad that it must be rewritten. The feeling that the story must be rewritten is usually the result of the copyreader's unconscious inability to subordinate his own manner of expression to that of another—to see good in the writing of others although its qualities may not accord with his own ideals of writing.

A young copyreader must first of all remember that his office is merely that of corrector and reviser. If he does not have it at the outset, he must develop the ability to correct and revise another's writing, without destroying in it evidences of the original writer's personality. As he grows older in the work he will learn that there are few stories that he cannot whip into shape without rewriting, and that the impulse to rewrite is merely an evidence of inexperience.

II. The Copyreading Signs

The established copyreading signs—the tools of the desk man's trade—are few and simple and should be thought of as time-saving signals to indicate changes to be made in the copy. Their development has been a gradual evolution and is not universal. Their usefulness depends upon the printer's understanding of them, and therefore some offices in which the copyreaders and printers have worked together for a long time have a more fully developed system of copyreading signs than offices in which the employees are more transient. In general, the group of signs listed below will be understood by all printers, except in the smallest country offices, and the copyreader may use them with perfect confidence. The one thing to remember about them is that they were developed by daily use and used accordingly.

Unlike the signs used in proofreading, these symbols used by the editor of copy are not placed in the margin, but in the body of the written matter. The reason for this difference is simple. When a printer is revising proof, he does not read the content of the proof but glances down through it to note the corrections; it is therefore necessary to indicate corrections in the margin so that he will surely see them. In setting up material that has been edited, however, the printer must read each word and line and needs no signal in the margin to draw his attention to a correction. The placing of copyreading corrections in the margin muddles the copy and leads to confusion. In other words, *never "proofread" copy*. All corrections and marks should be placed above the line to which they refer so that the compositor will see them before he reaches the words involved. Inserted material should be written between the lines or on a separate sheet, marked "insert," never in vertical lines along the margin; since marginal insertions make it difficult for the copy cutter to divide the copy into takes. In editing copy, furthermore, the copyreader should use a soft black pencil and should make heavy black signs that will show distinctly in the feeble light that illuminates the copyholder of a linotype machine.

Copyreading Signs

Circles around figures or abbreviations indicate that they are to be spelled out.

Circles around words or numbers spelled out indicate that they are to be abbreviated or expressed in figures.

One line under a letter or word indicates that it is to be set in Italics. (In some offices single underscoring, or a wavy line below, indicates bold-face type.)

Two lines under a letter or word indicate that it is to be set in small capital letters.

Three lines under a letter or a word indicate that it is to be set in capital letters.

An oblique line, from right to left, through a capital letter, indicates that it should be a small letter.

Letters are brought together by a half circle below.

Letters are separated by oblique lines from left to right.

A cross, or a period in a circle, is used for a period.

Quotation marks, either double or single, are often set off with half circles to indicate whether they are beginning or end marks.

The beginning of each paragraph is indicated by a paragraph mark or an angle. The paragraph mark is always used to mark a new paragraph, not intended by the author.

NEWSPAPER EDITING

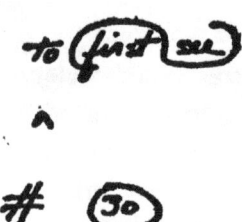

Elements to be transposed are encircled in a long figure 8.

A caret indicates the spot where material is to be inserted.

The end of a story is indicated by the end mark (#) or the number 30 in circle.

The "run-in" or "bridge" line is used to connect two consecutive elements separated by material that has been crossed out.

The use of these signs may be illustrated by the following piece of newspaper copy edited and marked for the printer:

III. What Errors to Look for

Although armed with all the copyreading signs and the ability to use them, the copyreader will find his efficiency greatly increased if he analyzes and studies the errors to look for in the copy that passes through his hands. There are certain errors that are likely to appear in any copy and a classification of them may assist him in catching them all. Knowing what errors to look for is easily half his work.

Reporters' mistakes in general may be classified in the following six general groups:

A. *Errors of Expresssion*
  1. Grammatical errors
  2. Errors in spelling
  3. Errors in punctuation

B. *Typographical Style*
  1. Capitals
  2. Figures
  3. Punctuation
  4. Quotation marks
  5. Addresses and titles

C. *Inaccuracies*
  1. Misstatement of fact
  2. Misrepresentation of fact through omission of qualifying facts
  3. Inaccuracy in names (in spelling, initials, or identification)
  4. Carelessness in handling and copying figures
  5. Mistakes in dates

D. *News Values*
  1. Inadequate lead
  2. Failure to begin with the feature

3. Inadequate summary of long story
4. Failure to follow up the feature
5. Failure to prepare for cutting in make-up
6. Lack of paragraph unity
7. Comment and opinion

E. *Diction and Style*
 1. Use of long sentences and complicated grammar
 2. Use of unemphatic sentence beginnings
 3. Failure to use short, compact paragraphs
 4. Use of unemphatic paragraph beginnings
 5. Wordiness
 6. Use of general rather than concrete, definite nouns
 7. Failure to use bright, vivid verbs
 8. Lack of dignity of expression, especially in the use of nicknames, undignified reference, and slang

F. *Libelous Statements*

A. Errors of Expression

1. *Grammatical Errors.*—Among the grammatical errors that occur in reporters' copy, certain ones appear with sufficient frequency to be watched for constantly. They are:

1. The lack of agreement between subject and verb, especially when the two are widely separated, when the subject consists of one or more singular nouns, or when the predicate noun is of a different number:

A different outlay of funds and assets were ordered.
None of the employees were on duty.
The man with the gun and his accomplice was convicted.
The backbone of a newspaper are the news stories.
There has been in every city examples of such conditions.
Color and brushwork is the basis of his technique.

COPYREADING

Each family must decide for themselves.
Neither the driver nor his passenger were hurt.

2. The use of dangling participles which have no definite grammatical relation to the remainder of the sentence and therefore are indefinite and lacking in emphasis:

The policeman stood his ground, the robbers fleeing.
The train having gone, the reporter hired a taxicab.
They were married in secret, Justice Smith officiating.
Any man under 30 is eligible, thus opening a large field.
Pay checks are left at the bank, thereby facilitating payment.
Wisconsin easily defeated Michigan, the score being 12 to 6.

3. The separation of relative clauses from antecedents so that the reference is not clear:

He saw the ladder against the wall that the robber had used.
It was the pleasant secretary of the chief whom I met.

4. The use of a sentence (unquoted) as the subject of *is* or *was:*

The bank is on firm footing is the statement made by——

5. The use of a conjunction between a relative clause and the principal clause:

He bought the red auto, but which had no self-starter.
He saw the man from the station and whom the sheriff wanted.

6. The use of a subordinate when or where clause at the end of a sentence to express later action—usually the most important action in the sentence:

We were walking down Main street when suddenly a man fell.
He moved to Dakota where he later became wealthy.

7. The relation of pronouns to their antecedents:

A crowd of we boys went fishing.
When we met him, he said that he had not seen him.
When a child sees something they want, their parents must come with them to buy.
Every student will select their own course.

As the servant's quarters were on the third floor, they were not aware of the fire.

It was "Filipino Night," and the program was given by them.

8. The position of adverbs in relation to the words they modify:

To indefinitely postpone the action is his proposal.
He said he only wanted to get his pay.
He repeated the summons again gruffly.

9. The tense of infinitive after a past tense verb:

It was unnecessary for you to have been there.
He hoped to have come with me.

10. The omission of auxiliaries:

One trainman was killed and three injured in a wreck—

11. The omission of the infinitive sign:

He began to advertise, dress up his windows, and in general spruce up his business.

12. The use of a relative clause without a noun or pronoun antecedent:

The revising of the tariff cannot be done effectively by Congress, which is often overlooked.
Jones is said to be against the road program, which is a wrong impression.
The government formally took over the work, which insured immediate action.

Seven hints for better grammar are the following:

1. Remember that clear, logical writing is the reflection of clear, logical thinking, and that doubtful grammar usually evidences cloudy ideas.

2. Develop the habit of thinking out sentences before writing or editing them.

3. Watch for bad grammar in all you read and practice correcting it—to develop the instinct for good usage.

4. Learn the art of transposition. If a sentence is not

smooth, correct, and clear, juggle its parts around into the proper places, instead of trying to patch it up with commas.

5. Remember that English is the most elastic language in the world and that there is scarcely an idea that cannot be expressed in several different grammatical ways. Try several instead of being content with the first that occurs to you.

6. Notice that "a sentence badly started" is the most fruitful source of bad grammar. Instead of trying to patch it up, begin it again in some other way.

7. When in doubt about the correctness of an expression or a construction, instead of laboring with it and arguing about it, try some other form that you know is correct. The present participle, for instance, is a cause of much difficulty; avoid it, therefore, unless you are sure of its correctness.

2. *Errors in Spelling.*—There is, of course, an infinite number of misspellings that may creep into reporters' copy and there are few rules to help the copyreader in catching them; his only resource is a dictionary, a good memory, and a vigilant eye. But there are some varieties of misspellings that are more common than others; for instance:

(*a*) The misuse of doubled letters, especially before a suffix. In most cases a knowledge of the derivation of the words will assist here: *repeated, omitted, referred, occurring.*

(*b*) The failure to drop the final silent *e* before a suffix: *judgment, statement.*

(*c*) The forming of plurals of nouns ending in *y* or *ey*: *chimneys, families.*

(*d*) The combination in one word of certain pairs of words: *all right* (*alright*), *percent* (always two words).

As the servant's quarters were on the third floor, they were not aware of the fire.

It was "Filipino Night," and the program was given by them.

8. The position of adverbs in relation to the words they modify:

To indefinitely postpone the action is his proposal.
He said he only wanted to get his pay.
He repeated the summons again gruffly.

9. The tense of infinitive after a past tense verb:

It was unnecessary for you to have been there.
He hoped to have come with me.

10. The omission of auxiliaries:

One trainman was killed and three injured in a wreck—

11. The omission of the infinitive sign:

He began to advertise, dress up his windows, and in general spruce up his business.

12. The use of a relative clause without a noun or pronoun antecedent:

The revising of the tariff cannot be done effectively by Congress, which is often overlooked.
Jones is said to be against the road program, which is a wrong impression.
The government formally took over the work, which insured immediate action.

Seven hints for better grammar are the following:

1. Remember that clear, logical writing is the reflection of clear, logical thinking, and that doubtful grammar usually evidences cloudy ideas.

2. Develop the habit of thinking out sentences before writing or editing them.

3. Watch for bad grammar in all you read and practice correcting it—to develop the instinct for good usage.

4. Learn the art of transposition. If a sentence is not

smooth, correct, and clear, juggle its parts around into the proper places, instead of trying to patch it up with commas.

5. Remember that English is the most elastic language in the world and that there is scarcely an idea that cannot be expressed in several different grammatical ways. Try several instead of being content with the first that occurs to you.

6. Notice that "a sentence badly started" is the most fruitful source of bad grammar. Instead of trying to patch it up, begin it again in some other way.

7. When in doubt about the correctness of an expression or a construction, instead of laboring with it and arguing about it, try some other form that you know is correct. The present participle, for instance, is a cause of much difficulty; avoid it, therefore, unless you are sure of its correctness.

2. *Errors in Spelling.*—There is, of course, an infinite number of misspellings that may creep into reporters' copy and there are few rules to help the copyreader in catching them; his only resource is a dictionary, a good memory, and a vigilant eye. But there are some varieties of misspellings that are more common than others; for instance:

(a) The misuse of doubled letters, especially before a suffix. In most cases a knowledge of the derivation of the words will assist here: *repeated, omitted, referred, occurring.*

(b) The failure to drop the final silent *e* before a suffix: *judgment, statement.*

(c) The forming of plurals of nouns ending in *y* or *ey*: *chimneys, families.*

(d) The combination in one word of certain pairs of words: *all right (alright), percent* (always two words).

(e) The splitting of certain words into two words: *something, sometime, anybody.*

(f) The misuse of *ance for ence: occurrence, countenance.*

(g) Misuse of digraph *ei* and *ie: receive* and *believe.* A good way to remember these is to note that if *l* precedes the digraph, *i* follows *l;* if *c* precedes, *e* follows the *c,* as in *Alice.*

(h) The confusion of two words of different spelling and meaning, but the same pronunciation: *correspondent, corespondent.*

3. *Errors in Punctuation.*—To many young writers, punctuation is a serious problem because to them it is a mere matter of arbitrary rules. But if they will consider punctuation marks as tools that have been developed by the necessity to indicate the breaks in written speech, as pauses and inflection mark them in spoken speech, they will be able to formulate very logical rules for their guidance. The chief fault that the copyreader will discover in reporters' copy is excessive punctuation, and he can adopt the maxim of eliminating every punctuation mark for which there is not some definite, logical reason. Even if he carries this to an extreme degree, he will do less damage than the writer who uses too much punctuation —too few points cause less confusion and easier reading than too many. Every point also takes up almost an em of space.

The following rules of punctuation will, in general, cover most cases that arise in newspaper writing, since the simple sentence structure demanded in the newspaper office makes unnecessary many of the rules followed in literary writing.

COPYREADING

Use the comma:
1. To separate the clauses of a compound sentence only when the subject changes.
2. To separate the clauses of a complex sentence only when the dependent clause precedes the principal clause.
3. To separate the succeeding members of a list—whether the members be nouns, coördinate adjectives or adverbs, parallel clauses, parallel phrases, or any other parts of speech. The comma is needed between the last two members of the list, whether or not there is a conjunction, because the purpose of the comma is to indicate the extent of each member rather than the omission of a possible conjunction.
4. In pairs—in the places where our forefathers might have used parenthesis marks—to set off explanatory material which has no grammatical place in the sentence. This includes substantives in direct address, appositives, absolute phrases, geographical names explaining preceding names, non-restrictive phrases and clauses, and all other parenthetical matter.
5. (N. B. There is no need of commas in newspaper writing to indicate pauses or to avoid misunderstanding—outside the above cases. The fact that a comma seems necessary is sufficient proof that there is something wrong with the sentence. Good newspaper grammar is so simple, direct, and straightforward that no artificial explanation, in the the way of commas sown broadcast, is needed.)

Use the semicolon:
1. To separate groups of individual members and modifiers in a list following a colon.
2. To separate the clauses of a compound sentence when

they are not separated by a conjunction. It is understood that only "and," "but," and "or" can qualify as conjunctions in such a case.
3. (N. B. There is no reason in newspaper writing to add to the above rule that the semicolon is often needed with a conjunction simply because the several clauses are so complicated or so bespattered with commas that the line of division is not clear. This defense is sufficient evidence that the grammar is bad. Such a sentence should be broken into two or simplified. More punctuation marks add complication.)

Use the colon:
1. To precede a list or a quotation which begins with a new paragraph.

Use the dash:
1. To mark an intentional break in grammar.
2. To emphasize the element which follows it.

Use the hyphen:
1. In compound numbers and fractions; in compound adjectives; in titles composed of two or more words; after one-syllable prefixes when (*a*) the last vowel of the prefix precedes the same vowel, and (*b*) the prefix is attached to a proper noun.
2. (N. B. The modern tendency is toward less hyphenation and the putting together of words into an unhyphenated word. In general, compound *nouns* are less often hyphenated than compound *adjectives*).

The commonest punctuation errors of which reporters are found guilty are the following:
1. The omission of the second in a pair of commas (see Rule 4).

2. The omission of the comma before the conjunction in a list (see Rule 3).
3. The use of unnecessary commas.
4. The use of a comma instead of a semicolon when a conjunctive adverb separates two independent clauses (see Rule 2).
5. The use of semicolons in places where commas will do the work.
6. The use of colons in place of commas and semicolons.
7. Excessive use of the dash to remedy loose construction.

With reference to other punctuation marks not discussed above, the copyreader will find it necessary to keep watch for the following errors:

8. The omission of apostrophes in the possessive case and in contractions.
9. The omission of periods after abbreviations.
10. The confusion of single and double quotation marks.
11. The misuse of quotation marks in continuous quotations of several paragraphs.
12. The omission of the quotation mark at the end.

To aid himself in eliminating the many and varied errors of expression that often mark the printed page of newspapers and magazines, the copyreader will find that he can use to advantage a large dictionary and a good handbook on English grammar, punctuation, and spelling. He must think of grammar and punctuation as a logical thing developed for practical use. He will often find, moreover, that the quickest and easiest way to settle a mooted point of grammar or punctuation is to recast the sentence into some other form. There are so many possibilities and varieties of expression in the English language that there is little reason to allow a questionable expression to pass or even to approach the borderline of argument. If the sentence in one form strains grammatical rules, he need not stop to puzzle over the intricacies of it, but may quickly recast it into some simpler form.

B. Typographical Style

Inasmuch as there are many matters of capitalization, punctuation, use of figures, etc., that are not absolutely definite and may vary in even the best English usage, every reputable newspaper office has its own office rules to cover many of these matters. Sometimes these office rules, known as "typographical style," are unwritten and rather intangible, but often they are embodied in compact form in a pocket booklet, or on a card, called a "Style Sheet" or "Style Book." The mandates of the style sheet are often arbitrary and sometimes rather queer, but they have one defense that makes them necessary and desirable—"uniformity in typographical style is necessary throughout the publication." For the sake of uniformity in its columns, then, every newspaper demands that its writers and editors follow its rules of typographical style. However arbitrary some of them may seem to the copyreader, he must follow them to the letter. Furthermore, the copyreader is the one who must enforce the rules. With a constantly changing staff of reporters and a shifting group of journeyman printers in the linotype room, uniformity of typographical style would soon go by the board were it not for the man who edits the copy. While every one else in the office is trying his best to violate them all, it devolves upon the desk man to check up every capital letter and every figure to see that it conforms to office style—simply to insure uniformity. He must come to think of an error in style as seriously as an error in grammar, spelling, or punctuation. The result will be a "clean" uniform sheet that critics will call "well-edited." However trivial a capital letter or a misspelled word may seem to the young copyreader, he must remember that it is difficult for the reading public to credit the accuracy of large statements in a newspaper that is bespattered with minor inaccuracies. The presence of trivial errors and lack of uniformity spell to the newspaper reader lax office methods and he questions its general truth-telling accordingly.

Usages of typographical style vary in different sections of the country; while the newspapers in several adjoining states use "down" style (few capital letters), another entire section follows "up" style (many capitals). Some general tendencies are:

1. In capitalization, most newspapers agree in capitalizing the following: proper nouns; months; days of week; principal words in title of books, plays, lectures, etc.; religious denominations; nouns and pronouns of Deity; sections of country and city; races and nationalities.

    They disagree in the following: titles following names; Negro; the final common noun in names of associations, companies, societies, and other organizations; the final common noun in geographical names; political party names; names of national, state, county, and city buildings, officers, boards, etc.; points of compass; common religious terms;

school and college studies, classes, and degrees; seasons of year; a.m. and p.m.

(N. B. The standard rule for names of books, addresses, etc., which are set in capitals and small letters, is: Capitalize all words except conjunctions, articles, and prepositions of less than four letters —capitalize first word always—*e. g.* "A Man Without a Country"; "The Lady or the Tiger."

2. In use of figures, most newspapers spell out small numbers and use figures for large numbers, but disagree on the dividing line between "small" and "large." Some divide at 10; others at 100. The division is the basic rule; other figure rules are merely exceptions to it. Commas are used to set off groups of digits in all numbers except *serial* numbers—that is, in numbers that say "how many" but not in numbers that are designations. *e.g.*, 10,587 people, but License No. 13784.

3. Quotation rules are practically standard in all American newspapers.

4. In abbreviation, newspapers disagree, especially in titles, names of states after cities, months, and such words as street, railway, company, etc. Each style sheet, however, leans definitely toward much or little abbreviation.

5. In dates, datelines, and addresses, there is much disagreement.

6. In titles, while certain usages are standard, general objectionable "drifts" are to be noted, especially in smaller newspapers:

(a) In spite of laxness in some newspapers, the best edited still require strict usage in religious and denominational titles, including "the Rev."

(b) Although some newspapers are careless in using women's names, the best papers require that

Miss or *Mrs.* be used with *every* woman's name—even in police news.

(c) According to standard usage, *Mr.* is not used before a full name (*John H. Jones*) but is used before the surname (*Mr. Jones*) if the man deserves it. Partly because *Mr.* is omitted in telegraph copy, to save expense, carelessly edited papers are becoming lax in its usage, but the best papers follow the standard custom.

(d) Striking carelessness in the misuse and omission of titles of governmental officers is seen in some papers. The president, governor, mayor, and others are spoken of as *Coolidge, Blaine, Kittleson,* without even *Mr.* This practice is bad because it fosters disrespect of government among less intelligent and foreign-born readers.

Common Errors in Style.—It is impossible to classify all errors in style that occur in reporters' copy beyond the extent that they are classified in the average style sheet. They are usually concerned with (1) the use or misuse of capital letters; (2) the use of figures; (3) the overuse of abbreviations; (4) the form of street address; (5) the handling of titles; (6) the mooted questions of punctuation; (7) the use of quotation marks. Although rules of grammar and punctuation are often debatable, the copyreader has in typographical style a set of hard and fast regulations that he can enforce absolutely. He should know his newspaper's style sheet from beginning to end, besides understanding its general intent and being able to read between the lines of printed rules. If the general intent of the style sheet is "down" (that is, it advocates the use of small letters instead of capitals when there is any option) he should follow out the intent by adopting the maxim: "When in doubt, use a small letter." Styles in newspaper make-up are changing constantly, and no two newspapers have exactly the same ideas of beauty in the printed page, but the copyreader must be as ready to change his style as his coat and to feel as much at home in the new one. (A typical newspaper style sheet is included in this volume, Appendix II, for classroom use in the development of accuracy in details.)

Three Hints for Mastery of Style Sheet:
1. Note the general tendency of the style sheet in the various matters discussed: *i.e.*, whether *up* or *down* in capitalization; whether dividing figures at 10 or 100; whether toward much or little abbreviation. Interpret the rules accordingly.
2. In reading the style sheet, check the rules that are *new* or *unfamiliar* to you. Learn them only.
3. Note the *examples* after the rules; they usually express more than the rules themselves.

C. Inaccuracies

Although the commonest criticism of the American press is that it is inaccurate, a careful study will indicate that newspapers are in general remarkably accurate, considering the speed and difficulty under which they gather and record news. Unfortunately, however, every error, no matter how trivial, is displayed for public inspection. Not only are they essentially accurate in the larger aspects of their work, but it is to be noted that no other business has developed so elaborate a system or spends so much money to insure accuracy as does the American newspaper. The copyreader is an essential part of this elaborate system; the chief reason for his existence is to insure accuracy. The newspaper profession knows that the greatest fault of the average reporter is inaccuracy, and the copy desk is provided to counteract this fault. The copyreader must realize that his chief duty is to wage continual war on inaccuracy, big and little, careless and intentional, if his newspaper is to escape the blanket accusation of criminal inaccuracy that many critics make against American newspapers in general. But the task is a difficult one. Inaccuracy in newspaper writing crops out in so many and devious ways that it is practically impossible to classify all the possibilities. To eliminate all the inaccuracies that appear in the copy on his desk, the copyreader would need to be practically omniscient. The material which he is called upon to edit includes in its scope every phase of human activity and every branch of human knowledge. To accomplish his task, he would need to be a specialist in every art and science. Even so, his memory would fail him occasionally, or his watchfulness, and some few glaring misstatements would pass him.

But there are some approaches to the task within reach of any copyreader of average intelligence, if he makes a conscious effort to equip himself for the work and is determined to uproot as many inaccuracies as possible. Although newspaper copy puts no limits on its range of subject matter, most of it is concerned with material that any alert man can keep in hand if he makes the effort. (1) To do his work with fair efficiency, the copyreader should be thoroughly acquainted, above all, with the city in which his paper is published. He should know its geography, its industries, its history, its politics, its people, and its interests, as thoroughly as the clergyman knows his flock. Fifty per cent of the copy he edits will be taken care of by this knowledge. (2) The affairs of the nation must be familiar to him—its history, its present and past politics, its finance and economics, its prominent people. (3) So far as possible, the history, politics, business, people, and geography of other countries should be at his finger tips. (4) He should have a general knowledge of every subject of general information at the present time, whether art or science, material or spiritual. Familiarity with the technical language of these subjects increases his efficiency. All of this means that he must devote much of his time to reading—he must read newspapers, magazines, books, pamphlets, everything that comes to hand, for the purpose of extending his acquaintance with the world's affairs. And he cannot rely on former reading—the interests of the newspaper change not by years or decades, but by days and minutes, and he must keep up with the changes. But better than all the knowledge that he can crowd into his brain is a systematic acquaintance with all sources of information. If the copyreader is not acquainted with the subject in hand, he should at least know where to find the information he needs.

The inaccuracies that appear in reporters' copy may be classified loosely in the following groups:

1. *Misstatement of Fact.*—This includes both the basic facts of his story and the minor facts that make up its background. Nothing but a broad fund of knowledge and common sense will enable the copyreader to check up all the facts that appear on his desk. But he can do much by putting them all to the test of reasonableness. A fact or a statement that seems to him unreasonable or absurd should never pass unchallenged, even if

the challenge involves a confession of his own ignorance. No statement at all is better than a misstatement. Whatever appears absurd to him will appear absurd to the paper's readers, and his challenge may result in an inserted explanation that will make evident the fact's reliability.

Analysis of reporters' work will indicate that misstatements of fact result from these tendencies:

1. Lack of sufficient knowledge of the news field and of conditions and events behind the story.
2. Lack of sufficient judgment to distinguish information from misinformation.
3. Lack of sufficient questioning in interviews to get a clear understanding of the facts.
4. "Jumping at conclusions" instead of searching for facts.
5. Unconscious twisting of facts because of "stock" prejudices and notions.
6. Failure to run down all possible clues.
7. Reliance upon only one version of the story.
8. Failure to apply test of reasonableness to facts.
9. Failure to realize that, while many persons are trying to hide their doings from the public, others try to mislead the reporter to obtain publicity, to push pet schemes, or to make thrusts at enemies or rivals.
10. Lack of understanding of what constitutes "evidence."
11. Failure to question reliability and fitness of witnesses.
12. Effort to heighten interest and to make a "bigger story."

2. *Misrepresentation of Facts through Omission of Qualifying Facts.*—The omission of necessary qualifications will often make a true statement appear as inaccurate as a false one. This appears most frequently in

the quotation or explanation of men's statements and opinions. The reporter gives the public their broad general statements and neglects to add the modifications, limitations, and reservations, or he reports their negations without the affirmations that accompanied them. Very often the careless omission of a qualifying phrase or even an adjective will make the major statement ridiculous, and it is this very fact that enables the copyreader to catch the inaccuracy. The best test that he can apply is that every fact must meet the demands of his own common sense.

It is well for the copyreader "to put himself in the other fellow's shoes"—to consider the feelings of the quoted speaker when he reads the printed story. Would the copyreader care to take the story in person to have it approved? If not, is it really a fair, accurate, and decent report? Misquotation in interviews or speech reports is a vice of American newspapers which makes a host of enemies. Rare is the public speaker who is not a cynic about the press. Inaccurate quotation may be due to the reporter's reliance on his memory or, more likely, to his ignorance of the subject under discussion. Whatever it is, the copyreader's job is to check the evil.

3. *Inaccuracy in Names.*—Not only in attaching the right names to the right actors in a story are reporters careless, but also in handling a name when it is the right one. The copyreader must check the spelling of the name, the initials or first names, the address or other identification that accompanies it. The fault of "getting names wrong" brings more ridicule than any of the other inaccuracies of which the newspaper is guilty. It is impossible for the copyreader to prevent all inaccuracies in

names, because the compositor may add a few after the copy leaves his hands, but he should be sure that every name is correct when he reads the copy. In many cases, especially in local stories, he can trust to his own knowledge and memory, but he must not depend too much upon them. He must have at hand a city directory, a telephone directory, a copy of "Who's Who," and other directories of names. It will take him but a moment to run through the pages of the directory and verify every name that appears in the copy he reads—and the moment will be well spent. Errors in the use of names are not limited to names of persons. The copyreader must verify all geographical names, all names of clubs, societies, and organizations, all names of business firms and commercial or political bodies. Many a libel suit has resulted from confusing the name of a bankrupt house with its more prosperous neighbor of similar name—as many as have resulted from reporting before the bar of justice the reputable citizen whose initials are only slightly different from those of the vagabond who was arrested. Many of the principal persons involved and many an honest citizen have been enraged by the appearance of his identical name and initials in connection with an activity which he does not countenance. Since newspaper reporters cannot be trusted to "get names straight," the duty of verifying them falls upon the copyreader—and he must consider it a solemn duty, since a man's name is a sacred thing.

4. *Carelessness in Handling and Copying Figures.*— How often the public has been amazed by a variation of four deaths in two reports of an accident, and how often newspaper critics have scoffed at the fact that in three reports of a fire loss the figures may vary by $50,000.

The newspapers answer that the mistake is due to difficulty in getting the facts. Often, however, it is due to a reporter's failure to grasp the significance of the figures and a copyreader's failure to check them. Working at his desk in an office, the copyreader often has difficulty in verifying the figures that a reporter has brought in, but he can be sure at least that there are no contradictions in the figures contained in the story and that the figures stand the test of his common sense.

Four checks to catch errors in figures are:

1. Check all figures in the story by adding, subtracting, multiplying, or applying other arithmetic.
2. Ask yourself whether the figures seem reasonable.
3. Require reporter to check the figures with his notes or to turn in his notes, to catch errors in copying.
4. Ask reporter to write out numbers in his story, regardless of office style; it is better for the copyreader to "ring" the numbers than to pass incorrect figures.

5. *Mistakes in Dates.*—Dates cause less trouble than other exact facts, but they are often wrong in spite of this. It is the duty of the copyreader to check every date that he reads and be sure that it is right—arithmetically and otherwise.

Safeguards against Inaccuracy.—In the battle against inaccuracy, the copyreader may employ these aids:

1. Knowledge of the local news field—city and county—its geography, industries, history, politics, people, interests; a systematic survey of maps, directories, local histories, and other sources will be of value.
2. Knowledge of the affairs of the nation—history, politics, finance, personalities, through reading of current books and magazine digests that tie together

the loose ends that appear in the newspapers. A college education is essential but it must be kept up to date.
3. A specialty—one field in which he is an authority.
4. A broad range developed by poking his head into every field of human knowledge—science, art, philosophy—to counteract present tendency toward specialization. This is an age of specialists in reporting and editing, but the specialty must not get all the attention.
5. Faithful news reading; some offices forbid the reading of competing papers, but they are fortunately rare, for every copyreader must know more of the news than comes over his desk. He must read all local papers and his "trade journal" must be the journal of opinion that ties up the scraps of news and interprets them.
6. Systematic library reading, by selecting each week several big news topics and spending an evening in the public library reading up on them.
7. Mastery of names through systematic grouping of them; the preparing of lists of local officials, city aldermen, state and national officers, cabinet members, supreme court justices, ambassadors, business men, etc., will make the names stick.
8. Familiarity with sources of information and, above all, with that great source—the encyclopedia.

The books of reference that the copyreader may use in checking up reporters' inaccuracies are numerous and varied. They include: the latest city directory; the latest local telephone directory; telephone and city directories of all near-by towns and cities; *Who's Who in America; Who's Who in England; Wer Ist's* in Germany; *Qui*

Etes-vous in France; the *World, Tribune, Daily News,* or other newspaper *almanac;* the *Times Digest* of the year; a standard encyclopedia; latest copy of state laws and statutes, etc. The copyreader should also make a habit of treasuring all lists of names and printed directories that come to his hand. Even then he will often find that he must fall back on the newspaper's "morgue" and general library.

D. News Values

Because the basis of newspaper writing is news value, the copyreader must be an arbiter of the form of the news stories that pass through his hands. In the large, rich office he will find that the reporters know news values and the news-story form as well as he and he will seldom have to revise a story except to change its emphasis. In smaller offices where the staff is largely composed of "cubs," he will find that he must bear the brunt of teaching the new reporters the form in which to write their stories. For, with the exception of the feature story and the occasional narrative story, news stories follow rather generally a conventional form—a form which consists of a summary lead and a crowding of interest toward the beginning. If he has not learned this form through experience as a reporter, he must learn it through a study of newspaper stories. For the news-story form is as much an inherent part of American newspaper making as the bulletin headline.

There is no space in this book to go into the definition or evaluation of news, or to discuss the various appeals and interests in the public mind that make news values. It should be noted, however, that it is difficult to write a definition of news that will be universally true for any period of time because: (1) news valuation is relative—"one story against another"; (2) news values and topics are constantly changing; (3) standards of news vary in different sections of the country; (4) the definition of news is set by the size of the community and of the newspaper; and (5) local community and newspaper policy change news values. A common fault in news evaluation is the "follow-leader" habit, the tendency to do "what the other fellow does," regardless of the public interest—to consider a story "big news" because other newspapers play it up. A good axiom would be to watch "the opposition paper" less and to study the public more. News is what the public is interested in, regardless of the difficulty of getting this or that story or of the actions of rival newspapers.

In editing stories into the proper "news story form," the copyreader may list the requirements as:

1. A "summary lead," or introductory paragraph, presents the gist of the news story in brief, bulletin form, with answers to the reader's questions, *who? when? where?* etc.
2. The "news feature," or most interesting fact or angle of the story, is "played up" in the lead, usually in the first line.
3. An "inverted pyramid" in the rest of the story places the more interesting facts early and the less interesting at the end.
4. Short, unified, "block" paragraphs are used, each making a particular point and usually beginning with a "high light" of interest.
5. An impersonal point of view presents the facts without the writer's opinion.

Without going into a detailed discussion of the news-story form, it is possible to point out some of the common faults that appear in "cub" reporters' stories and certain tests of the structure. The copyreader must remember, however, that they are all to be subordinated to the general idea of presenting the story's most interesting content at the very outset and summarizing the entire story in the lead, or first paragraph. The common faults are:

1. *Inadequate Lead.*—The lead fails to give the gist of the story and to summarize all the elements that follow. Perhaps it fails to answer all the reader's questions about this summary, viz., *when, where, who, how,* and *why.* The summary may not give both sides of the question or may mention only one phase of a story that contains many phases. For instance, the lead may give the impression that the story is a report of one man's speech although the story is really a report of a meeting including a number of speeches. It is quite evident that such a lead gives undue prominence to the one speaker and may lose readers who are not interested in this man or his words. The lead, in other words, should include or suggest every phase of the story—the story in its entirety—to give a rounded impression and to attract as many readers as possible. This summary may require one paragraph or half a column, but it must be complete before the running narrative begins.

Seven tests of the adequacy of the lead are:

1. Is it sufficiently complete and clear in itself to be cut off from the rest of the story and to be published alone among the "News Briefs"? If not, put in the details needed to make it clear.

2. Does it answer the questions, *who, when, where, why,* and *what,* which arise in the reader's mind?
3. Does it mention all phases; is it an adequate "table of contents" of the story?
4. Is it conclusive; does it finish the action reported or merely introduce it?
5. Does it give the source or authority for the news, fixing responsibility and making the story authentic; or is it just an anonymous and hearsay statement?
6. Does it give the "keynote word" on which the news value hinges?
7. Does it indicate clearly whether this is a "first day" or a "second day" follow story?

2. *Failure to Begin with the Feature.*—The lead should always begin with the most interesting fact in the story—the *feature,* as it is called. Never should it begin with general explanation, the time, the place, or any subordinate element, unless that element is more interesting than everything else in the story. The copyreader must learn the advertising value of the first printed line. The white space above the first line causes it to stand out with as much prominence as if the first six or seven words were heavier, blacker type. This important position should be devoted to six or seven words that are interesting enough to hold the eye that is drawn to them by their prominent position and to carry the reader down into the story. Partly because they do not realize the importance of the beginning of the news story and partly because it is psychologically difficult to begin a narrative with the climax, young reporters are inclined to waste the beginning in useless words. Or, understanding the significance of the beginning, they may strain too hard and make the beginning unnatural. Their inclination may be

to go outside the story for a beginning—to drag in a witticism or a parallelism or an unwarranted superlative. Such a beginning is just as much a waste of space as the other, for it is the facts of the story that the reader wants and not a feeble attempt at cleverness. If a story is worth printing at all, there is some fact *in it* that deserves the first line, and it is better to seek out this significant *part* of the story than to ramble around the world in search of a clever saying that will *lead up* to the story. In general, the ideal lead is simply a summary of the story beginning with the most significant element in that summary.

In editing leads, the copyreader should refuse to pass any story which buries any fact more interesting than the facts in the lead or any story which has phases not summarized in the lead. If all the facts are there, the rest of the problem is a mere matter of grammar. Practice will enable him to see the most effective way to put these facts together grammatically, by rearrangement or breaking up of sentences.

Four tests of the adequacy of the feature are:

1. If the first six words are the "show window" of the story, does it contain something to attract hurrying readers?
2. Is any other fact, item, or angle that is buried in the body of the story more likely to catch the reader's interest?
3. Is the content of the first line an essential part of the story or something dragged in from outside?
4. Can the top deck of the headline be built out of the first line?

In some offices, "That" is taboo as the first word of a lead. In others, direct quotation beginning is under the ban. Neither of these beginnings is objectionable, of course, unless it is overused. Stereotyped lead forms should be avoided; the copyreader should try to give each lead an individual touch. Above all, a lead should not be allowed to begin with a statement of time, unless that is the feature of the story. It is seldom that superlatives in leads are warranted; copyreaders should question them, as well as all statements that sound exaggerated.

3. *Inadequate Summary of Long Story.*—This fault is a part of the preceding fault. Many reporters stubbornly refuse to recognize that the lead is sometimes more than the first paragraph. Their stories begin with an interesting feature and contain a summary of facts related to that feature but fail to suggest the rest of the story. The fault appears most often in a long story—the report of a series of speeches, for instance. The writer neglects to list the speakers in the lead and hence in make-up some of the speakers, who are mentioned only at the end of the story, are cut out of the report entirely. The copyreader must insert a summary paragraph ahead of the running narrative, to gather up the loose ends that the lead has neglected.

4. *Failure to Follow Up the Feature.*—This occurs most often in stories that begin with some striking circumstance. The reporter uses this fact, the most interesting in the story, for his beginning, and then forgets to mention it again. The reader feels that he has been cheated out of something, since the feature played up in the first line is more or less an advertisement of what he is to find in the story. Often this feature, which is neglected in the narrative, is the only thing in the story that has news value, that is worth printing. For instance, a

reporter writes a 300-word story on a fire whose only interest is a strikingly unusual cause—say, a cat and a candle. To attract attention to the story, the reporter begins with the cause and then forgets to explain how the cat and the candle accomplished their costly work. The reader, whose only idea in reading the story is to find out what the cat and the candle did, is decidedly disappointed. The story has advertised something that it doesn't have in stock. The writer should have devoted the major part of the story to the feature, or at least one paragraph.

5. *Failure to Prepare for "Cutting" in Make-up.*—The exigencies of make-up in many offices require that every story be written in such a way as to allow for cutting after it leaves the copy desk. Some offices require this because it makes possible the gradual cutting down of stories through successive editions, without rewriting or resetting. But many young reporters do not grasp the idea at once. Usually the fault lies in an inadequate summary in the lead and failure to crowd interesting facts toward the beginning of the story. The copyreader must remedy it by adding to the lead and by rearranging the rest of the story.

Three tests of "inverted pyramid" outline are:

1. Can you cut off the last paragraph—or cut anywhere?
2. Is a climax developed toward the end of the story?
3. Is some statement of importance "tacked on" the end—something forgotten earlier in the story?

6. *Lack of Paragraph Unity.*—Each paragraph, except the first, should be a separate unit by itself that may be omitted without seriously injuring the story or breaking up the coherence. Each paragraph must be perfect

COPYREADING

in unity—that is, it must deal with one phase of the story and be absolutely complete in itself. Then an alteration of the story to match later news is possible without resetting. But many reporters, failing to outline their stories carefully, build them up of straggling, mixed-up paragraphs. The copyreader must reparagraph.

Test paragraph unity thus: If the paragraphs are as unified as they should be—"separate blocks"—it is possible to shift them about, to cut and paste them in a new order without rewriting.

7. *Comment and Opinion.*—There are few newspapers which permit their reporters to pass judgment on the facts discussed. The editors prefer to gather all the judgment and comment into the editorial columns. But the young reporter has an almost irresistible impulse to give his readers an inkling of his opinion on the facts. He fills his stories full of inconspicuous comments that color the story, and the copyreader must edit them out. Sometimes the comments are so subtle that it is difficult to find them—only the general tone is noticeable. They usually creep in through qualifying and comparative adjectives and adverbs; sometimes a verb is responsible; again the use or omission of a title will give the tone. Superlative expressions are probably the most common offenders, for reporters seldom realize that a superlative is in itself a comment. The copyreader must watch closely for "feeling" in the stories he edits and must eliminate *the particular words* that give the feeling.

Four tests of comment and opinion are:

1. Can the reader discover whether the writer approves or disapproves of any person, fact, or action in the story?

2. Is any "color" introduced through adjectives, adverbs, too vivid verbs, or too glowing nouns?
3. Does reporter tell what he *thinks,* or what he *knows?*
4. Is the story written for newspaper men or for outsiders—is its point of view to beat the rival paper or reporter, or to inform the public?

E. Style and Diction

Many of the other faults that the copyreader must look for in copy may be grouped under this general head. They are not so conspicuous as the errors listed above but they are nevertheless flaws and must be corrected. Some of them are:

1. *Use of Long Sentences and Complicated Grammar.*—Since an essential requirement of the modern newspaper is that it be easy to read, its diction must be clear and swift. The rapid reader of to-day in glancing through the news will not take time to decipher involved sentences, to dig through complicated grammar, or to wade into a sentence so complicated that its writer must go back and pick up his subject again on the second breath. The grammar must be clear and straightforward; there must be no turning back or reversal of idea; even a change from active to passive voice is often confusing. The only style that will satisfy this is one made of comparatively short, simple sentences. The length is not so important as the simplicity; a sixty-word sentence is often easier to grasp than a four-word sentence. But the average young reporter, trained as he has been in the flowery, oratorical style taught in the usual school composition class, delights in tangling his ideas into an impenetrable mass of complicated grammar. Until he learns that, however valuable the oratorical style may be in other

writing, it has no place in the newspaper, the copyreader must untangle his grammar and make it readable. Usually the easiest way to simplify it is to break the sentences into several shorter, more unified sentences.

2. *Use of Unemphatic Sentence Beginnings.*—Since the emphatic sentence beginning which rapid reading demands is directly contradictory to the sentence emphasis which the young reporter is often taught in school composition, the copyreader finds that a large part of his editing consists in breaking down climactic periods and overturning oratorical efforts. Before he has been "on the desk" long he will find himself unconsciously throwing explanatory material back into the sentence and dragging emphatic phrases to the beginning. He may think that he is doing it to put "punch" into the story, but really he is making it easy to read. The reporter, before he took a place on the staff, was taught to write the kind of style that is most effective when read aloud, and he must learn that the same thing is not effective when read silently and rapidly. While he is learning that in journalistic writing he must put his best foot forward in each sentence, as well as in paragraph and story, his copyreader will find the earmarks of the oratorical style throughout his work. The most evident of them are the many sentences beginning with "He said—" and "They are of the opinion that—"; the sentences that are halted by "however" and "nevertheless" on the front doorstep. One sweep of the pencil carries these obstructions back into the sentence out of the way and when the trained copyreader has finished, the sentence begins with its most interesting content in the first few words. Periodic sentences, generally speaking, are out of place in news-

paper writing. Under no circumstances should a newspaper sentence begin with explanatory matter.

3. *Failure to Use Short, Compact Paragraphs.*—Coming to the office with a thorough training in the writing of 200-word literary themes, the young reporter forgets that he is now writing for a column only two inches wide—for lines of only six or seven words. He forgets that the narrowness of the columns makes his paragraphs look twice as long and that there is nothing so uninviting to a newspaper reader as a long paragraph. The copyreader must therefore become very adept in scattering paragraph marks through the reporter's copy. An easy guide that the copyreader may follow is that one typewritten line makes almost exactly two lines of type; since twelve lines is a heavy paragraph in a newspaper, six lines of typewritten copy should be almost the limit of length. Gradually he will learn how to estimate longhand copy to produce printed paragraphs of the proper length. In the same connection, he will notice the reporter's tendency toward burying his quotation marks in the midst of his paragraphs and combining summary and indirect quotation in the same paragraph. Realizing the value of a quotation mark to catch the reader's eye, the copyreader will put paragraph signs in front of most of the quotation marks he finds thus buried.

4. *Use of Unemphatic Paragraph Beginnings.*—Just as the first line of the story is emphasized by the white space above it, the first line of every paragraph is set off by the white space of the indention and the short line above it. Each paragraph beginning is therefore a spot which the reader's eye is likely to strike, and the copyreader must see to it that the first line says something of

interest. In other words, the emphasis of each paragraph, just as in the entire story, must be thrown toward the beginning so that the content may be grasped quickly by the reader.

5. *Wordiness.*—Conciseness is one of the most important characteristics of newspaper writing, because every day the paper gathers more news than it has space to print. Conciseness, almost to the point of baldness, is demanded of its writers. No word should appear in a story unless it has a definite reason for existence. But conciseness is a very hard thing to learn because it is built of close, compact thinking. The copyreader must wage continual war on wordiness. He must question the value of every word, phrase, and clause; he must constantly try to substitute one word for several words; he must continually tighten up the loose sentences his reporters write. Sometimes the wordiness results from needless repetition; again it can be blamed on a small vocabulary. One of its chief evidences is in the splitting of an idea into two sentences—half the space can be saved, without sacrificing content, by condensing the two into one. This condensing process is called "boiling." It consists in pruning the language down to the thought. It is not necessary to eliminate any thoughts or facts in condensing; the mode of expression may simply be boiled down, so that two ideas may be expressed in the space of one. The process is justifiable in the newspaper office because to the newspaper writer English is a means rather than an end—he cares more for the thought than for its expression. And the meaty, close-packed style that results from the copyreader's boiling is characteristically journalistic. It has a greater specific gravity.

6. *Use of General, Rather than Concrete, Definite Nouns.*—This is a subject that is worth a volume in itself because it involves the life of newspaper writing. The question of vocabulary would seem to be rather a concern of the reporter than of the copyreader, but the copyreader must make up for the reporter's shortcomings. He must accept the excellencies which the reporter possesses and add to them his own. He must coöperate with the reporter in keeping newspaper writing from becoming a dead, dry rehearsal of facts, and certain things he may well bear in mind as he scans for actual mistakes. Brightness and interest in writing depend upon exact, definite words. Whenever he sees a broad, general, meaningless word he must cast about for a concrete expression of it. If the reporter says, "many persons rushed to his aid," the copyreader can make the sentence more interesting by substituting the exact number. He will also make the sentence more credible, for we are more likely to believe definite statements than hazy ones. The more he sets forth the exact details of the story, the more likely we will be to see the picture in its entirety and to be interested in it.

The search for the vivid picture word has, however, in recent years led many newspaper writers into word coinage. Newspapers have been full of such expressions as "hammer slayer," "love bandit," "hatchet killer," "bobbed hair bandit," "poison pen," "death candy," "moron," "death car," "half-wit slayer," "death area," "water steal," "booze sleuths," and countless others. This colorful vocabulary has largely resulted from the borrowing of headline words for use in the story itself, and, while limited space in the headline may justify such word coinage, it is doubtful whether any equally good excuse can be found for their use elsewhere. To some extent they have been used to tie together "first" and "second-day" stories so that references will be quickly grasped—to make a "serial story" of a continuing event. Follow stories on court trials have thus been hitched together briefly. But, in general, these words tend to sensationalize every trivial event, to fill the newspaper with "stock" pictures instead of real pictures of the news, and to starve out good English. In the long run they will do great damage to newspaper writing and to the vocabulary of newspaper men. There is no occasion to stamp them out as a class, but each should be questioned.

7. *Failure to Use Bright, Vivid Verbs.*—Interest demands more vivid expression. How many verbs there are in English to express a man's manner of walking, and yet how many reporters are satisfied with "he crossed the street"! How many ways there are of recording vocal expression, and yet how much "he said" is overworked! For almost every action in the world, English has a verb and the more of them a story contains the more interesting it will be. The copyreader must not be satisfied with the old stand-bys; he must usher out some of the little used nouns and verbs. He will then find less occasion for the use of slang.

One of the greatest faults of young reporters is overuse of the stiff many-syllabled words of Greek or Latin origin—partly because they sound "big" and learned. If the copyreader will substitute shorter, more vivid Anglo-Saxon words, he will improve the story. Many handbooks for newspaper men contain lists of overused Latin derivatives and their Anglo-Saxon synonyms (see Bibliography, Appendix III). Other good sources are the dictionary and the King James Bible which is almost 97 per cent Anglo-Saxon.

The question of active and passive voice is important. Action expressed entirely in passive verbs gives the feeling of walking backward—the receiver is continually preceding the giver; the result is ahead of action. To right about face and proceed face forward gives the style swiftness, directness, and interest. A careful study of reporter's copy will disclose the fact that more than half his verbs are passive, and hence the copyreader, to eliminate this fault, must question the presence of every passive verb he sees.

Trite expression should be avoided. Not all the old stand-bys of newspaper writing are trite. Some of them are simply good words worn threadbare. But many are simply would-be clever expressions worn to the bone. No good English word in its proper usage is trite or tiresome; you say "noon" every day of your life without tiring of it or realizing its presence. The trite word is the word that is taken out of its proper place and given a new meaning. It tickles the reader the first time it is used, but the third time it is stale. The first reporter who said, "They staged a good fight," had invented a clever expression, but we are tired of it now because "staged" is out of its proper meaning and no longer clever. The same applies to many of the tiresome newspaper expressions that the reporter dashes into his copy. He uses them because he does not take time to think and the copyreader can brighten his story by crossing out the trite words and substituting good English words.

Trite words are chiefly to blame for the disparaging

term, "journalese." The straining for synonyms, the habitual use of nicknames for states, teams, cities, and persons, the seeming abhorrence of calling things by their right names, the sickly counterfeiting of humor through clumsy allusion, the painful effort to ornament statements that should be simple and straightforward—that is "journalese." It may be seen at its worst in the sport writing of smaller newspapers. It has been dubbed "rubber stamp" writing because it consists entirely of other persons' ideas. If newspaper writing is to be crisp, interesting, original, the stock words and phrases must go.

Word Diet.—An effective remedy is a "word diet"— a systematic barring, one after another, of the commonest trite words from all copy in the office. To bar "sleuth" for one week would benefit humanity. Another remedy is a definite effort to enlarge vocabulary through study of the dictionary and of good literature. To add ten new words a week would benefit any writer's or editor's style.

8. *Lack of Dignity of Expression.*—The accusation that the newspaper is having a bad influence upon American speech is partly due to the lack of dignity in the columns of many papers. Through haste and carelessness, rather than through viciousness, many newspaper workers forget the great educational influence that their words spread broadcast and shirk their duty as educators of a large share of the population. If they but remember that one coarse expression which they pass to the composing room may be picked up and gleefully repeated by thousands of readers, young and old, they will hesitate before they take the responsibility of lowering American life by so much as this one coarse expression. The bustle and rush of their work makes them unmindful of its in-

fluence. Sometimes they feel that they must "get down" to the level of their readers. But some of the most successful American newspapers are successful because they have stood steadfast in their high place and brought their readers up to their own level. The educational influence of the newspaper makes it imperative that a newspaper, while gauging the level of its readers, should strike slightly above their heads in its expression and so educate them up slowly to a higher plane. Every copyreader, therefore, should think twice before he allows to pass any of the undignified expressions that his reporters pick up on the street. For in every case he will find words just as bright and vivid in the dictionary. This applies especially to the use of slang and other perversions of the mother tongue. It also applies to the numerous nicknames and undignified references that reporters delight in sprinkling through their copy. To refer to a man by other than his proper name is to be rude and familiar, and the action reflects not upon the man but upon the newspaper.

There is no good reason why American youth should be brought up on underworld slang, police court vulgarities, the jargon of sport training quarters, the dialects of the slums. A sprinkling of such terms may be used by a skillful writer to lend a bit of life to his story. But in most cases, their use evidences nothing more than the zeal of a very young and very green reporter to "show off" his amazing knowledge of life. To him reporting is still thrilling and exciting; it has not yet become a serious business. Copyreaders must curb his tiresome smartness.

Lack of respect for law, government, and constituted officials is a growing problem in this country. In some cases, it is blamed upon the failure of newer elements in American society to grasp the true American attitude toward constituted authority, duly elected after partisan strife. But no small part of the blame may be laid at the door of the newspapers which, in recent years, have shown increasing carelessness in the use of governmental names and titles, a subtle disrespect or ridicule of law and its enforcement, a carrying over of political partisanship into every mention of government authorities. The effect of this upon the immigrant and the ignorant is obvious—if Americans do not speak of law and officials with respect, evidently they have no respect. Copyreaders can do a good work by enforcing the use of full name of officials, proper titles, "Mr." in the customary usage, and the elimination of party antagonism in stories of government—a discrimination between partisan politics and constituted authority.

Common courtesy must not be overlooked. Some newspapers have the rule, "This newspaper expects a reporter to be a gentleman." Why then should not the reporter write courteous and gentlemanly references to persons in the news? Yet the average newspaper is full of petty discourtesy, expressions that no decent reporter would use to a man's face. The cause is carelessness of reporters and copyreaders, and a misguided effort to save space. "Mr." has its proper place in American life and should be used accordingly.

A new responsibility to the English language has come with swelling circulations. A few years ago, when a newspaper was read by perhaps 2,000 educated men, there was no such responsibility. Now that the newspaper is almost the only reading matter of the masses, the newspaper man becomes the teacher and the arbiter of language. In some cases, he is writing an English primer from which the immigrant learns our language.

F. Libelous Statements

The copyreader is the watchdog who must keep libelous statements out of the news columns; at any rate, he usually receives the blame when his newspaper suffers libel action because of statements he allowed to pass. The position is an uncomfortable one, for the exact nature of libel is an indefinite thing, depending as much upon circumstances and the verdict of the jury as upon law, and no newspaper can fulfill its office as a dispenser of news without now and then laying itself open to libel action. It is practically impossible to print all the news, at the time when it should be printed, without running into danger of hurting some one's good name to a damageable extent; but for one libelous statement that results in legal action and recovery, ten as serious go by unnoticed. Hence the desk man learns to judge individual cases by instinct, balancing the news value of stories against their libel content and deciding each case on its own merits.

A libelous statement is an untruth that hurts someone's private, professional, or business reputation. The old basis, "the greater the truth, the greater the libel," no longer holds good; now only an untrue statement is libelous. But all untrue statements are not libelous; they must hurt some one to be libelous. Just what constitutes damage to one's character is the question concerned. In general, any statement that holds an individual up to public contempt, ridicule, scorn, or shame, if untrue, is libelous—to accuse him of a loathsome disease or to sug-

COPYREADING

gest lack of morality or integrity in his business or private life. In the case of a professional man, anything that suggests lack of skill or knowledge or charges incompetency is libelous, but the statement must "touch him" in his professional capacity. The same applies to business concerns and enterprises. Public officials, while open to criticism in their public capacity, cannot be attacked as private citizens or accused of moral or mental unfitness for office. Criticism must be concerned with their official acts. But any of these accusations or implications is harmless of libel if the newspaper can prove it true. When it is untrue, and the victim wishes to retaliate, he can do so by bringing suit and recovering such damages as the jury thinks are equivalent to the injury he has suffered. The case is not decided on the basis of the newspaper's intent or innocence of malice, but on the basis of the injury suffered by the victim. This is true except when the statements may be such as to lead to a "breach of the peace" and the evident motive results in criminal proceedings against the publisher.

Besides truth, however, the newspaper has another defense in its injurious statements about individuals— "privilege." Certain statements, even though untrue, are protected from libel action because they are *privileged*— because the information came from a privileged source. This privilege covers all information obtained from the proceedings of judicial, legislative, and other public or semi-public bodies whose doings are of public interest. If the newspaper publishes damaging facts derived from such proceedings and publishes them fairly and accurately, it is protected from libel action even though the facts are untrue. But there are dangers even in this. In the fraud. They have been collecting money on a "fake" song publishing scheme.

It is said that Harper fled Chicago a year ago after he had forged a number of checks. Bailey is thought to be a notorious swindler wanted in the South.

What Newspapers Cannot Print.—In connection with libel, it is well to note that certain things cannot be printed in any case. These are forbidden by federal law:

1. Treasonable and seditious matter as defined in the United States Penal Code.
2. Fraudulent weather forecasts or warnings credited to governmental sources.
3. Reproductions of certificates of citizenship.
4. Reproductions of any kind of paper money.
5. Obscene, lewd, lascivious text, pictures, or advertisements.
6. Pictures, text, or advertising concerning lotteries, gift enterprises, or offering of prizes dependent upon lot or chance, including references to raffles or card parties which involve admission charges or prizes.
7. Matter that aids or abets mail frauds.
8. Reproductions of postage stamps, post cards, stamped envelopes, money orders, etc.

Beyond these federal restrictions and the state libel laws, the American press is entirely free of censorship or legal prohibitions. Public opinion constitutes its one great curb.

IV. The Requisites of Good Copyreading

1. **The Ability to See Errors**

The knack of seeing errors is one of the first things that a young copyreader must cultivate. And it is a difficult thing to acquire. The ordinary reader does not see half the mistakes in the things he reads. Even a second reading will not bring all the errors to his attention. It is because he has a tendency to seize the thought without noticing the means of expression; he reads by sentences and clauses rather than by words, grasping a line at a time and skimming through the elements that make up the expression. The copyreader must, however, concentrate on the means of expression and take into his mind, not only the thought, but the individual words. This ability to see errors comes only with practice and can be developed to the point of being an unconscious habit. The beginner can cultivate it best by going back to the elemental actions that constitute the process. He must first break himself of the habit of scanning what he reads; he must train himself to read word by word, developing the faculty of seeing and noting every letter and every punctuation point. At first, it may be necessary for him to read line by line with a card, as the proofreader does, to force his mind to concentrate on the details. Not only while he is actually reading copy should he watch for errors, but he should force himself to watch the details in everything he reads, until the process becomes a habit. Not until he has become so observing that a misspelled word and a misplaced comma stand out like a blot, is he a good copyreader.

2. Neatness

A good copyreader takes pride in leaving the copy he has edited as presentable as it was before. His office is to prepare it for the printer, as well as to correct it, and he should increase rather than impair its legibility. For legibility and neatness, he uses a large, soft pencil whose mark may be readily seen in the dim light over the linotype's copyholder. When he puts in a run-in line to guide the printer's eye, he makes it definite and straight. When he crosses out words, he eradicates them thoroughly and draws a bridge around the gap to emphasize the fact that the word is gone. Whenever there is any doubt about consecutive positions, he connects the doubtful words with run-in lines. He is especially careful to do this when his cutting has left a word stranded at the beginning or end of a line. With his firm, black lines he blazes a trail through the corrections, for he knows that the printer is trained to follow the connecting lines. He also uses as few marks as possible and takes pains to write legibly whenever he inserts words. Inserted material he writes above the line—in fact, all marks are placed above the line, so that the compositor will see them in time, and no additions are written vertically in the margin because this complicates the task of cutting copy into takes. Where the revision requires so many corrections that they become confused, he rewrites the sentence or paragraph on a separate sheet of paper and pastes it into place. He prepares each piece of copy as if it were to be handled by the most stupid printer on earth and as if it were to be a record of his neatness in editing.

Young copyreaders often feel that it is useless to correct every obviously misspelled word, to straighten out every transposition of letters, to check every capital and figure, to insert every necessary punctuation mark, to put in each paragraph mark. They leave these details to the compositors. Experienced copyreaders do not; they leave nothing undone in their work for they realize that they are "the official correctors." Thoroughness is the whole job; mere "paragraph marking" is not copyreading. It is often said that every newspaper is hunting for at least one good desk man—one copyreader who can do the job right. There are plenty of "copy butchers" and "paragraph markers" but good copyreaders are always scarce.

3. Swiftness

There is no place in the busy newspaper office for the man who must putter and ponder. But at the same time the good copyreader realizes that haste makes waste on the copy desk as elsewhere. Instead of plunging into the copy and deluging it with corrections, he stops long enough to decide the easiest and quickest way to make the desired change. The fewer the marks, the better the editing. When he sees a fault, he analyzes it clearly and chooses the simplest remedy before he touches his pencil to the paper. He is sure then that his correction has accomplished its work and has not added confusion. In the end, he gets through the work faster than the man who blunders blindly ahead, altering the beginning of a sentence before he has read the end, and "butchering" the first line of a paragraph before he has found out how essential it is to the rest, or crossing out an adverb before he notices that the next sentence requires its presence. Every correction that the copyreader makes must have a reason, and the blunderer is never as efficient as the man who works rapidly but keeps his head.

4. Mere Cutting

Some copyreaders seem to have a feeling that their work is not complete unless they have crossed out so many sentences and slashed off so many paragraphs. Such copyreaders are rightly dubbed "copy butchers" by their reporters. Indiscriminate copy cutting is bad because it deprives the story of its coherence and continuity. If condensation is necessary, it should be accomplished by boiling—by eliminating useless words without throwing out facts and ideas. A story that is ruthlessly cut is usually worse than it was before, because it has lost many of the facts that make it worth while, and what remains is just as wordy and scatterbrained as before.

There is at present much hue and cry about "news suppression." A study of individual stories, however, will indicate that, for one case of "policy suppression," resulting from office mandate, there are dozens of cases resulting merely from careless slashing. Stories must be trimmed down to meet space requirements, but the good copyreader knows that this can be done without eliminating essential facts or ideas—the trimmed story may be just as complete and truthful as before. In some offices the reporters come to learn that a careless desk man always slashes the last paragraph or two of every story, whatever its content, and clever writers put on a "slash paragraph" to satisfy the copyreader's habit. The ridiculousness of such trimming is obvious.

5. Boiling

Intelligent boiling must be practiced. It is concerned with words and phrases rather than with sentences and paragraphs. Condensing, skillfully done, leaves the story better because it has stripped much of the useless fat from the meat of the thought. It consists in substituting one word for several, in putting related sentences together, in compressing the original thought into smaller space with-

COPYREADING

out allowing any of the thought to escape. Nine out of ten of the stories that come to the copyreader's hands will be improved by careful condensation. Good writers practice it on their own work to counteract their tendency toward wordiness. They find it a better way to cut length than to slash out entire paragraphs of ideas and facts.

Effective trimming and boiling, through the elimination of useless verbiage, is illustrated by the following. The words in *italics* may be eliminated with slight changes in context:

Prospects for *a busy and successful year along* minor sports *lines* at the university during this season *of 1924* are *looming larger and* larger every day and claiming *an increasingly* greater *amount of* attention as *the* spring *fever season begins to* crowd aside cold weather sports.

The results so far *in all the different phases of sport at the university have been such as to* equal the expectations of the *most optimistic* supporters. The *splendid* victory of the track team on Saturday night, over *the* Purdue*ites, gives* promising *indications of* future conference victories *this spring*. Captain Bob Jones' *performance* in the two-mile, *a race in which he* hung up a new Wisconsin indoor track record for 10 minutes, 2/5 seconds, *certainly shows that when distance events are on the bill of fare one Robert Jones Esq. has a mighty big appetite.*

A fitting team mate for Captain Jones is Dow Smith, *the brilliant little* distance man, *who* won the mile *so handily from* Purdue*'s aspirants* in time which compares *favorably* with other conferences *indoor* records. Philip Brown, *the much heralded* interscholastic star, *is another man to be reckoned with in coming track contests. He* was the greatest individual point winner Saturday night. In the middle distance event *another star was also uncovered in the person of* Ray Williams *who* ran the quarter like a veteran.

* * * * *

With a *loud,* deafening roar that *violently* aroused hundreds *from their beds of slumber,* the *monster* gas holder *occupying the southwest corner of* South Blount and Main streets, *at the gasplant of* the Madison Gas and Electric company, collapsed very *suddenly* at 6:30 this morning.

The cause of the collapse was *at first clothed in deep mystery, before the officials of the company had time to investigate.* However, it was definitely ascertained during the morning when Mr. John W. Jackson, *the* secretary *of the company, being interviewed by the Daily News,* stated *that the immense* quantities of snow on the roof of the holder *were primarily responsible.*

6. Expanding

To lengthen stories is just as necessary in copyreading as condensing them and should be done as intelligently. Some writers expand stories by reiterating and repeating ideas already covered. This kind of expansion has no place in the newspaper office. No story should fill more space than is required to present its facts clearly and concisely. There is only one way to expand intelligently and that is to add additional facts. The copyreader, working at his desk far away from the source of a story, is often at a loss for additional facts. He will find, however, that most stories suggest far more facts than they elaborate sufficiently to insure clearness. He may expand stories by the simple process of writing in the facts that are suggested. But he must expand systematically so as not to destroy the story's balance. The easiest way to decide what phases are in need of elaboration is, he will find, to look at the story from the point of view of the reader and to determine what parts of the story are the most interesting or most in accord with the interest built up by the lead. Usually he will find that the facts in the lead are the best ones to elaborate. But this elaboration does not mean the invention of imaginary facts to fit the case; it means the writing in of real facts that the reporter has suggested but has failed to make clear.

Sometimes this is a matter of "editing the story for the reader," rather than for newspaper men. To a reporter who has been trailing the story all day, it is "old stuff"; to the reader every angle of it is new. The copyreader who has seen a full account of the news in a morning paper from another city may forget that most of his local readers have not seen it, and that there is every reason to print every detail of it in his afternoon newspaper.

Often the "fattening out" of a story, to make it complete, adequate, and interesting, requires recourse to the morgue, to "Who's Who," or to what the copyreader knows. This is most often true in foreign or other telegraph dispatches; it is also true in official news, such as announcements of appointments. Legitimate copyreading supplies missing initials, identifications, and other needed details. The following story, and possible insertions (in italics), will illustrate:

ORIGINAL STORY

The extension of Capitol avenue, as recommended in the new zoning ordinance, will be favorably reported on Friday night by the special realty committee appointed by the mayor to investigate the project. To open the street, the city must spend $125,000, according to John Smith, chairman, but will make a profit of at least $25,000 on excess land. Adjoining lots should be classified "light industrial," according to Smith.

EXPANDED STORY

The extension of Capitol avenue, *from Fifth street to Second street,* as recommended in the *major street plan adopted last*

October as a part of the new zoning ordinance, will be favorably reported on Friday night by the special *appraisal* committee.

The committee of ten real estate men, which was appointed by Mayor *H. R. Miller last February, completed its survey last week.* John *H.* Smith, *former alderman and* chairman *of the committee, declared today that the committee will urge immediate action.*

To open the street, the city must spend $125,000 *to purchase a strip 300 feet wide adjoining the new avenue. Through increased values and sale of* excess land *on each side, the* city will make a profit of at least $25,000, *Mr.* Smith said.

Adjoining lots should be *changed from the present "C" residential to* light industrial, *to permit the building of retail stores on the avenue,* according to *Mr.* Smith.

ORIGINAL STORY

Governor John H. Groves today announced the appointment of Harry Hall, Boonton, as regent of the state university from the sixth district. (Expand item by looking up Mr. Hall in a book of reference, telling who he is, telling whom he succeeds, giving the length of his term, recalling other recent appointments of regents, and noting when other terms expire, etc.)

7. Estimating Space

In the trimming and expanding of stories, the space to be occupied may be estimated on the following basis: One full line of standard pica typewritten copy fills two lines of 8-point type in the ordinary newspaper column. Thus eight lines of copy fill 16 print lines.

In some offices, stories are measured in "sticks." A stick is 2 inches of type or one-tenth of a column. For 8-point type, about eight lines of copy make a stick. For 7-point type, between nine and ten lines of copy fill a stick.

Other offices measure stories by the column-inch. Under such orders, the copyreader estimates: four lines of copy make an inch of 8-point type; nearly five lines fill an inch of 7-point; six lines fill an inch of 6-point; three lines fill an inch of 10-point; and two lines fill an inch of 12-point.

In a few offices, reporters are required to set their typewriter margins to write line-for-line with printed space; such a practice alters the estimates.

V. Practice That Will Assist the Copyreader

The beginner may develop his proficiency at copyreading by undertaking the task as systematically as the pianist learns the technic of his art. There are finger exercises in copyreading as well as in instrumentation. (1) The first is to watch for errors, grammatical, typographical, and logical, in everything he reads—to edit mentally everything that comes to his hands. In this way he will sharpen his copyreading eyesight. (2) Another is to begin reading copy word for word, perhaps moving the lips to assist the mind in concentrating. If necessary, he may force concentration by following the copy line by line with a card. (3) As there are so many things to look for in copyreading (listed A, B, C, D, E, and F under III above), it is often good practice to begin the study by looking for one kind of error at a time. The first reading may be devoted to catching errors of expression; the second, typographical style; the third, accuracy, and so on. This method will insure thorough work until the copyreader has learned to watch for all of them at once. (4) Since it is impossible to do much with the news value of a story until one has grasped its entire content and a complete reading is necessary to learn the content, a young copyreader can often improve his work by consciously breaking the task into two readings. During the first, while he is grasping the story's content, he will correct all the small errors, *e.g.*, A, B, and C. He is then ready to go over it again to change the arrangement, *e.g.*, D, E, and F. Careful preliminary practice, like the pianist's finger exercises, will in time enable him to gather in the story at a glance and correct it page by page as it comes to him.

Many experienced copyreaders use the three-reading method, thus: (1) Glance through story to get its sense without correcting anything. (2) Read thoroughly and correct every detail as well as trim or expand. (3) Check over to see that story is coherent and corrections are right, as well as to gather ideas for headlines. Subheads are inserted during this reading. Type directions, guide lines, and other markings go in last.

VI. Preparing Copy for the Printer

In addition to correcting the manuscript and numbering the pages, the copyreader must also mark it with printer's directions and label it for reference. All of these marks must be placed directly on the manuscript, in the margin, at the head of the first page, or at the end. The usual custom is to inclose them in circles so that the printer will not set them up.

1. Type Directions

Type directions are placed at the head of the first page, usually at the left. They indicate the type, length of line, and character of display. Ordinarily it is not necessary to specify the type for the headline further than to indicate the style of head—No. 5 for instance—since the printer knows from his schedule what type is desired. In newspaper work, the copyreader is not greatly concerned with the style of type since only a slight variation is possible. He may mark it 8-point or 7-point, as the case may be, although the office practice will usually make that unnecessary. If he desires display, he may mark it "bold face" or "leaded," or "indent 1 em," or "1 em hanging indention." In some cases he may mark it "double measure," meaning lines stretching across two columns. More exact type specification, necessary in other kinds of work, will be discussed in another chapter.

2. Guide Lines

Guide lines are signs or labels by which the copyreader indicates the content of a piece of copy and the position it should have in make-up. Their purpose is to facilitate make-up and to keep track of the many pieces of copy that he sends to the composing room. The term guide line, or catch line, includes a number of different kinds of labels with different purposes. One kind of guide line indicates the position of the story as a whole; another designates the position of various parts of the story. But whatever its purpose, the guide line is usually set up by the printer and placed at its head, so that the same label appears in all the proofs until the paper has been made up. The make-up man removes the guide slugs when he places the stories in the form.

Every story is given a name or short designation as soon as it reaches the copyreader's hands. The name may be "Smith Murder," or "Council Meeting," or "Wreck No. 1," or "Wreck No. 2"—some short name that indicates its content. If the story is sent in one piece with headline attached, the name serves as a handy designation. If the story is sent to the composing room in sections the name becomes an identification of the various parts.

For example, if the city council is holding a prolonged session and the staff of the morning paper is receiving the story in sections and rushing it to the linotype machines, it may be labeled thus: The first piece sent down carries the catch line, "Council Meeting" at the head and "More to come" at the end. A turned slug at the end of a galley is the printer's "More to come." As the various parts are written and edited, they are labeled "First Add Council," "Second Add Council," and so on. If other items are to follow the story under the same headline, they are designated "First Follow Council," "Second Follow Council," and so on. When the lead is ready it is marked "Lead Council." The head that goes down a few moments later is marked, "Head Council." If after all is ready, the reporter brings word that the council had at the last moment delayed adjournment long enough to transact a piece of business more important than all the rest, the copyreader must prepare corrections. First he sends down a piece of copy marked "Insert Council After Lead." Perhaps there are inserts "A" and "B" or more. Then "New Lead Council." After that "New Head Council." Perhaps then he is forced to send instructions to "Kill Fourth Add Council"—meaning to throw away part of the original story. With a series of guide lines such as these a copyreader is able to label each piece of copy with brief instructions to the printer. It will be noted that each invariably contains the original name of the story. In some offices these catch lines that designate the various parts of a single story are not set in type and do not go beyond the man who puts the story together in a galley. Very small stories are not ordinarily "slugged," as the small headline is set on the same machine and serves as sufficient identification.

Another use of guide lines is to indicate the department of the paper to which a piece of copy, item, or story, belongs. One story is labeled, "Society," another "Sports," another "Market." The catch lines are set in type at the head of the story; in some cases, in fact, the office has a series of department slugs already cast in larger type for this use. When a story appears in the proof with such a designation it is said to be "slugged."

The one guide line that the copyreader never omits on any story is some mark at the end to tell whether or not the story is complete. If it is complete, as it stands, he always places an "end mark" below the last line. The mark may be a double cross, "#," or the telegrapher's end mark, "30," or simply "End." If the story is not complete, he writes "More to come," "More," or some definite information like "List to Follow." Unless there is some such designation at the end of the copy, the printer cannot be sure whether to close up and set aside the story or to hold it open for additions.

In the writing of catch lines, care must be taken to use expressions that will not offend readers or cause a laugh if the slugs slip into print. "Add Society" may cause no damage, but "Kill widow" or "Capitol bunk" may be misunderstood. Some "slug" jokers carry the game too far.

It must be remembered that the discussion of catch line

usages given above is only general and typical. Practically every office has its own system, and the systems change constantly. Even the guide lines used in press association telegraph copy change almost year by year under new filing editors.

In large offices, stories are "slugged" by the city or telegraph editor before they reach the copyreader. In small offices, the copyreader "slugs" the story, often using the first line of the headline as a catch line.

3. By-Lines

The designation of stories that are to carry "by-lines," or signatures of the writers, is usually determined by the city editor. But it is well for the copyreader to note the tendencies in their use. The extensive "signing" of stories came into use just a few years ago, partly to counteract the disappearance of "personal journalism" and the growth of "anonymous journalism." Among the first signatures were those of famous correspondents who were permitted to inject some of their opinions of the facts they reported. The press associations began "to sign" their best writers. The local staffs followed with by-lines for the sport editor, the society editor, other department editors, and finally for local reporters. At first it was the "star" who received a by-line, and probably the name meant something to the reader. Now the by-line has become largely a matter of office discipline—a reward for greater accuracy, better newsgathering, or clever writing—and the "cub" is as likely to have a by-line as the star. Hence the practice is rapidly becoming meaningless and confusing to the public and is not likely to continue in its present form.

COPYREADING 91

4. Other Copyreading Terms

Although every city and every newspaper office has its own copy desk terminology and slang, some expressions are quite universal. The terminology of printing and of headlines will be found in other chapters, but a few terms may be given here which refer primarily to the handling of copy. All illustrations are called *art*. The point where a story turns to another column or page is *the break*. Clippings from other newspapers or the morgue are *clips* or *exchanges*. Miscellaneous filler matter, mainly *reprint* from other papers, good at any time, is *grapevine, miscellany,* or *bogus news*. Short stories that may be put in anywhere are *fillers*. A diagram of a page is a *dummy*. A story that rival papers do not get is *exclusive*—a *beat,* a *scoop*. A brief wire bulletin is a *flash*. Matter is marked *follow copy* if unusual spelling, punctuation, or style is to be reproduced. When marked-out material is to be retained, it is marked *stet*. Matter set half-column wide is *half-stick*. *Hold for release* means to set up but not to print until further orders or at the time specified in *release date*. Discarded copy is *hooked, spiked,* or *killed*. A story that must be printed under any circumstances is *must* copy. Material that is set up for future use is *time* copy. Matter that is already set up and is to be added to a new story is *pick up*. Body type set irregularly around a cut or other display is *run around*. Stories that are sent to the composing room in *takes* or stories that follow an event chronologically are *running stories*. The stories available for the day are *on the schedule*. Any headlines, boxes, or other matter used day after day and not reset is *standing*. Any tabulation is a *table*. An article that runs from the bottom of page 1 to the top of column 1, page 2, is the *turn story*. Matter that has few errors is *clean copy*. When copy has all gone to the compositors, it is *all in hand;* when it is all in type, it is *all up*. The making up of pages is done *on the stone*. Young copyreaders must not confuse *follow*, or second-day, stories with *Folo* used as a catch line.

Exercises

1. The technique of learning to copyread:
    - (*a*) Learn the symbols and how to use them.
    - (*b*) Analyze kinds of errors and commonest forms of them.
    - (*c*) Exercise in searching for errors without correcting them.
    - (*d*) Read different pieces of copy, searching in each for one kind of error.
    - (*e*) Read a piece of copy again and again, searching each time for one kind of error—see A. B. C. D. E. in chapter.
    - (*f*) Practice 3-reading method.
    - (*g*) Finally develop 2-reading method.
2. Materials for class exercises:
    - (*a*) At first, for comparative work, it is well for entire class to work on same story, mimeographed. Stories may be "made to order" to provide enough errors, or special kind of errors, through rewriting of newspaper stories. Some may be prepared to emphasize each type of error. Many of these duplicate exercises will give rudimentary drill.
    - (*b*) Ready-made copyreading exercises, in duplicate, may be purchased—see Bibliography, Appendix III.

COPYREADING

(*c*) Read copy on carbon duplicates of stories written by students in reporting class or on student newspaper.

(*d*) Local offices of press associations will often supply carbon copies of reports for a few days.

(*e*) Many syndicates will supply their services for use in copyreading classes.

(*f*) When students become proficient, they may edit copy of student newspaper, or "sit in" on copy desks of local newspapers. Rudimentary drill should precede this.

3. Best results are accomplished when small groups (five to ten) work around the "rim" of a table with the teacher in "the slot," dealing out the copy, correcting it at once, and handing it back for further editing. This will develop speed, proficiency, and, if the session is two hours long, "staying power." Later students may take turns in the slot.

4. Follow a style sheet strictly. A good way to master it is to take it up one section at a time. (1) Capitals. (2) Figures, etc. Note *Three Hints*.

5. Class may draw up punctuation rules for class use—"office rules"—deciding on them by vote.

6. All doubtful matters may be decided by class vote to establish "office policy."

7. Draw up a list of trite expressions and adopt a "Word Diet," barring one after another.

8. Draw up list of long Latin and Greek derivatives often found in copy—with their Anglo-Saxon synonyms.

9. Draw up a list of roundabout, "word-wasting" expressions and their short-cut synonyms.

10. Draw up a list of words most frequently misspelled. Students may conduct "spelling contests" by trying to find all the misspelled words in very bad pieces of copy.

11. Compile a list of all available local directories and reference books and note their contents.

12. Practice putting in subheads.

13. Practice making up daily schedule of stories and preparing copyreader's record, working on news in yesterday's newspaper.

14. Prepare proper guide line and slugs for all stories in one issue of a newspaper.

15. Supplement study of kinds of errors with references to other textbooks—see Bibliography, Appendix III.

16. Form a Bureau of Accuracy and carry out a check of every name and fact in local newspaper—using all reference books.

17. Read further on libel (see Bibliography). Look up state statutes on libel. Search for libelous matter in newspapers—applying queries suggested.

18. Elaborate short dispatches, by writing another paragraph or two of "background."

19. Practice trimming stories to various specified lengths.

20. Read newspapers constantly and criticize their copyreading.

21. Reëditing is good practice. After one student has read copy, another may criticize his work.

22. Analyze news value, by studying relative interest of various stories on front page of a newspaper.

CHAPTER III

HEADLINE WRITING

FEW newspaper readers realize that the modern American headline, as it appears in every daily and weekly newspaper in the land, is a native American invention and almost an exclusive characteristic of our newspapers—that it is barely sixty years old—that it is one of the most difficult and exacting kinds of writing that fall to the lot of the newspaper worker. It is one of the things that make the American newspaper up-to-the-minute, interesting, and easy to read. Like the summary lead of the news-story, the verbatim interview, and many other inventions of the newspaper men of this country, it was developed to meet the needs of our busy, wide-awake life and, for all the faults of which it is guilty in unskilled hands, it makes our newspapers what they are—"newspapers" rather than "journals." That it is typically American is shown by the fact that it was adopted throughout the United States almost on the morning after its invention, and even today, sixty years later, is very slightly used in other countries outside the western hemisphere.

When the American citizen gleans the news out of twelve or sixteen newspaper pages of fine print and acquaints himself with all the world has done overnight, in the short time given to his morning coffee or his ride to the office, he is doing something that only an American can do. He is extracting the gist of 60,000 to 80,000 words of reading matter in the time required to read half a column. To be sure, he is getting only the gist of the news, but the elaboration is there also and is in such shape as to be found without much hunting through material that does not interest him. That is because his newspaper was written especially for him by men who realized how short a time he can devote to learning the world's events. It is because, before the paper was left on his doorstep, a newspaper desk man had painstakingly extracted the gist of all this news and put it in the most readily available shape.

Some critics, among them newspaper men, are now pointing out that the overdevelopment of the "bulletin headline" is causing the American people to become a nation of "headline readers." That is, the typical reader is said to be acquiring a habit of scanning the headlines and reading none of the material below them. How true this impression may be and what effect it may have on the future development of the headline is beyond the scope of this book. But it is in order to point out the growing emphasis of the headline and its effect upon American thinking. The "slant" blazoned by the headline is unconsciously taken up by the reader, regardless of the wording of the story, so that it colors his understanding of the entire news event. The tremendous coinage of short, vivid headline words is affecting all American speech and writing. Because of the space limitations of the headline, the display type can give but a scrap of the news, and the reader who is content to read only these scraps lives on a diet of very small bits of the news.

Furthermore, if ten persons write headlines for the same story, probably no two of them will present exactly the same angle. Should "office policy" enter in, the particular angle may have somewhat the effect of an editorial. From that point of view, the problem is many-sided and complicated. Since this volume is devoted primarily to the technique of headline writing, it must leave for other books the adequate discussion of ethics. But certainly no person should undertake the writing of headlines without having a thorough realization of the vast amount of public service and ethical consideration that is bound up in the work.

When the statement is made that the American headline is a characteristically American device, the statement refers, not to the form of the headline, but to its content. The idea of placing a title or heading in larger, blacker type over every article is as old as printing. The practice, also, of dividing this heading into a series of decks, or layers, is not new. But the idea of saying something—of making a definite, concrete statement in the heading—is the American invention.

Early Headings

Back in the early nineteenth century, when newspapers were weekly budgets of opinion-molding editorials, rather than recorders of events, editors placed at the tops of their columns such headings as "Local Intelligence," "European Events," "Marine News." But the heading was a mere *label* of the kind of news contained in the column and the same label might be, and was, used day after day regardless of the significance of the facts that it announced. Even later when editors tried to make their daily newspapers more interesting by expanding the single title into a series of display lines extending halfway down the column—the impressive headline was merely an elaboration of the first title or a series of subtitles appropriate to the variety of news reported below. To the American newspaper man of today it seems incredible that these trade ancestors of his could use so much type and say so little. It was as if they had purposely tried to put as many different labels on their bottle as possible, without revealing its contents.

The New Idea in Headings

Not until the days of the American Civil War did newspaper editors conceive of the idea of substituting for this meaningless *label* a headline with something to say. They discovered it then because the war was their first big "news story" and, in handling it, they were forced to develop the methods that are inherited by us of the present day. It was only within the previous twenty or thirty years that newspaper men had come to understand that *news*, rather than editorials, was what the American people wanted, and until their first big story came in the Sixties they had been entirely concerned with learning the vast number of things that constituted the news and how to report them accurately and speedily. Before the war they were so interested in gathering facts that they cared little about the form in which they were presented, and their readers were glad enough to get the news without questioning the time required to extract its kernel from the verbose, roundabout, boastful articles of the newsgatherers. But when day by day the news of the great war came into the cities, the editors began to realize that their readers were not satisfied to plow through lengthy dissertations on the difficulties encountered by the brave correspondent, finding at length his glowing account of the battle and its result. They wanted the result first and the explanation afterward. As the editors began to realize this, they turned the correspondents' stories around and put the result first—developing thereby what we now call the *news-story summary lead*. And to the same end, they threw out the label head which announced day by day "The Great War," or "News from the Front," and used its space to present the answer to the readers' great question—"Vicksburg is Taken"—"20,000 Killed on the Potomac." The first editor who substituted such a war bulletin for the standing label was the inventor of the American headline.

One Effect of War on Newspapers

What the Civil War taught American newspaper men in headline writing was to *bulletin the news* in headline and lead. More recent wars have taught them other things. The Spanish-American War added to this the idea of using the same headlines as *advertisements* of the contents of their papers. It was during and just before the war of '98 that headlines grew in size and blackness and spread beyond the column rules until sometimes they stretched entirely across the front page. The sensational newspapers, to be sure, had been developing the advertising possibilities of their headlines, but it was the Spanish War that brought the "spread" and "banner" into common use. The World War brought many other changes, including the daily use of the banner by newspapers that had never used it before. For many years, newspapers will be assimilating the new ideas learned during the period from 1914 to 1918.

I. What the Modern Headline Tries to Do

The modern American newspaper headline has two distinct purposes: to bulletin the news and to advertise the news.

A News Bulletin

The modern headline bulletins the news by presenting in display form the content of the story printed below it. It selects the gist and the most salient facts in the story and displays them in concise, readable form for the benefit of the rapid reader. It is a complete statement that would be clear in itself without the explanations that follow. Its many-deck form emphasizes the most interesting phase of the story in the first deck and presents, deck by deck, the subordinate facts that qualify it. If the headline is well written, the rapid reader need not read the story to know its content.

A News Advertisement

The advertising value of the modern headline is a corollary of its bulletin nature. If the news bulletin is sufficiently interesting in wording and prominent in form, it catches the reader's eye and interests him in reading the story. This applies both when the reader is browsing through his paper and when he is looking over the newsstand to buy a paper. The banner head, which is merely a news bulletin in large type across the page, serves the same purpose in America as the "news contents bills" which the London newsboys display in selling their papers. It catches the eye and interests a possible buyer in what the paper has to sell. Its sales value is evidenced by the fact that it was first used by afternoon papers which depend largely on street sales for their circulation. It is doubtful now whether it is of value except on street editions.

Is It Sensational?

In considering the advertising value of the large, black headline, it is necessary to point out the fact that large headlines are not in themselves an indication of sensationalism. The quality of sensationalism in American newspapers is not at all dependent upon make-up. A paper that is most conservative in its make-up may be extremely sensational in its appeal and "yellow" in its treatment of the news. Another paper with a screaming front page may, on the other hand, be decidedly conservative and fair in its news. It is merely trying to sell its editions. "Yellowness" is a matter of content and appeal, rather than of display and make-up.

II. How the Headline Fulfills Its Purpose

To constitute a bulletin and an advertisement of the news, the modern headline must possess several distinct characteristics:

1. A Summary

It must summarize the story which it heads and present the gist of the content. It should display the facts of the story in skeleton form.

2. The Newsy Feature

It must present in the first deck the feature of the story—the fact that gives the story its news value. As all the emphasis is in the top deck, this should be the most interesting. Since the news value of the story often hinges upon certain ideas already in every reader's mind, the first deck should make a direct appeal to these ideas. Whenever the story's entire interest is embodied in one word or one phrase, as is often the case, that word or phrase should be in the first deck.

3. A Verb in Each Deck

The first deck, and as far as possible every other deck, should contain a verb. As a bulletin of events, the headline must contain action, and only a verb or some part of a verb can express action.

4. Definite Statements

The headline should contain definite concrete information. General statements have no place in it. It is a bulletin of a specific story and could not be used over any other story.

5. Easy to Grasp

Each part of the headline should be easy to read. Unless the reader can grasp it and understand it clearly at a glance, it is of little value as a bulletin.

6. Complete in Itself

The headline should be perfectly complete and clear in itself. It should contain the necessary qualification and explanation without needing the story to explain it. The puzzling, mysterious title to be explained by its story has its place in other kinds of writing, but not in newspaper writing. No newspaper reader can be expected to go back and solve the meaning of the headline after he has read the story.

III. The Form of the Headline

The form of the headline has become more or less established in American newspapers. Much latitude is seen in the size and character of type and the combination of parts, but the character of the parts offers little possibility of novelty. Every headline is made up of a series of layers, or "decks," extending horizontally across one or more columns and separated by short rules. According to present practice, a headline may be made up of one, two, three, four, or even more decks. The headline of more than four decks is rare although formerly headlines often had as many as twenty decks. Each headline is built on a specified plan usually indicated in the office by a *headline schedule,* in proof or printed form, designating each kind of headline by number or letter. The schedule shows the models to be used for different purposes, as well as their form and typography. As the printers have the same schedule, the copyreader indicates by the key *number* or *letter* the model for which his copy is intended. In writing a headline of any given form, the desk man must take into consideration, not only the number of parts and the length of each part, as specified in the schedule, but also the number of letters and spaces in each line since the size of type designated regulates the number of letters in the line.

Kinds of Decks

The briefer lines in larger type are known as *display* decks. The longer, less prominent decks placed below are *banks*. The four common varieties of decks are: (1) the cross-line; (2) the drop-line; (3) the pyramid; and (4) the hanging indention.

1. *The Cross-Line.*—The cross-line is, as its name signifies, simply a single line stretching across the space allotted to the headline. In the one-column head, the cross-line may be "flush," so as to fill the entire space from column rule to column rule, or it may be short and "centered" in the space between the rules. For example:

PACKER SUED BY ARKANSAS

HE KILLED THREE MEN

2. *The Drop-Line.*—The drop-line is a cross-line that has been separated into two or more parts in succeeding lines. This headline is also dubbed *stepped* line, *step*-line, *break*-line, *lap*-line, or *split*-line, in various offices. Its first line begins flush with the left-hand column rule and extends to within two or three units of the other rule leaving white space at the end:

**BURIED ALIVE 6 HOURS
    IN WELL, MAN SURVIVES**

This two-line heading is an example of the commonest form of drop-line deck, called the two-part drop-line. As this and the following illustration shows, in the two-part drop-line the second line is indented two or three units at the left but extends to the right-hand rule:

**AMERICAN TO WIN
BRITISH GOLF CUP**

In the three-part drop-line, the middle line is of the same length as the others but centered. All three lines are correspondingly shorter than in the two-part drop-line, for example:

**HOME RULE ACT
IS IN SHAPE FOR
QUICK PASSAGE**

The four-part drop-line (and the rare drop-line of more parts) is built on a similar scheme and the lines are correspondingly shorter:

**COURT RAISES
PHONE RATES
10 PER CENT
WITHIN CITY**

3. *The Pyramid Deck.*—The pyramid, commonly used as a subordinate deck, may have any number of lines from two to five. It is distinguished by the fact that each of its lines is shorter than the preceding line, and each is centered in the middle of the column. The last line sometimes contains only one word. It has the appearance of an inverted pyramid and appears most often in three-line and four-line form. The following are typical examples:

> **High Ocean Rates the Only Present
> Emergency**

> **New Milwaukee Sanatorium Has
> Capacity for 250 Patients**

> **Legislature Will Be Asked to Enlarge Appropriation Made
> for Work in 1925**

> **Judges McMurdy and Sadler
> Assert Law Would Curb
> Powers to Restrict
> Licenses**

4. *The Hanging Indention.*—This is a series of two or more lines, in which the first fills the entire space between the column rules and the succeeding lines are indented at the left but flush with the rule at the right. The last line, indented like the others, usually does not fill the full space, although some newspapers require that the

last line of a hanging indention reach the right-hand rule also:

> Mayor Now Disposed to Shift Park Department to Refectory Building in Franklin Park

> Children's Museum to Stay—Mayor Disposed to Shift Park Department to Refectory Building in Franklin Park

> Members of Ministerial Union Adopt Resolution Opposing His Appearance Here as a Revivalist and Calling His Methods Irreverent

> NATIONAL GUARD AND RED CROSS HANDLE RESCUE WORK; GOVERNOR HASTENS HOME TO RAISE BIG RELIEF FUND

As variations of these four standard deck forms, original new varieties appear constantly and are used to some extent. One is the flush drop-line, consisting of a series of lines that entirely fill the space between the column rules:

HARESFOOT TROUPE LEAVES ON ANNUAL ROAD TRIP MONDAY

A more recent development is the pyramid top deck used by the Hearst newspapers and a few others:

PILGRIMS QUIT BURNING SHIP IN RED SEA

Combination of Decks

With the four common kinds of decks as a basis, newspaper men have devised various combinations of the various decks with the idea of combining symmetry with display. In so doing they have established certain precedents that are seldom violated. The cross-line and drop-line are the forms ordinarily used in display lines. The cross-line is commonly used for any deck, although most frequently as the first or third deck. The drop-line usually appears as first deck, in two-, three-, or four-part form, and frequently as third deck, in two-part form. The pyramid and hanging indention are ordinarily subordinate decks, or banks. They appear as intermediate decks—second and fourth—between display cross-lines or drop-lines. Both forms may be used in the same headline, customarily with the pyramid above, although usually the two intermediate decks are of the same kind.

Headlines are most commonly built in two, three, or more decks. The present tendency is toward a smaller number of decks; the single-deck headline is common

HEADLINE WRITING

and two-deckers are more and more popular. Headlines may be conveniently classified as *major* heads, for important stories placed at the top of the column, and *subordinate* heads, for less significant stories lower down.

The major headline usually consists of three or four decks set in the largest headline type used in the paper. If it is a four-deck head, its first deck is usually a two- or three-part drop-line, its third deck is a cross-line or a two-part drop-line, and its intermediate decks are pyramids or hanging indentions. If it is a three-deck headline, the only variation is the omission of the last bank.

The subordinate headline rarely has more than two decks. The first is usually a two-part drop-line or a cross-line. The second is always a pyramid or a hanging indention. The most frequent combinations are a drop-line and a pyramid, or a cross-line and a hanging indention.

Type Used in Headlines

In the matter of type for their headlines, newspapers follow precedents as in other respects. Until recently, the top deck was almost always set in capitals, but many papers are now using capitals and small letters in many if not all of their headlines. Subordinate "bank" decks—pyramids and hanging indentions—are either in capitals or in small letters with important words capitalized.

The style of type in the top deck is quite uniformly an extra-condensed bold-face letter, and for many years one of the many kinds of extra-condensed Gothic was most popular. In recent years, however, many newspapers have abandoned the Gothic to experiment with more rounded, decorative faces. Caslon, Cheltenham, Bodoni, and similar faces are now as commonly seen as the Gothic. The change in headline type, as well as the use of capitals and lower case letters (U. and L.C.), results from a recent interest in the readability of headlines and the desire for more pleasing typography—a subject that was little thought of a generation ago. Certain metropolitan newspapers have employed typographical experts to design their complete headline schedules. A few have had special type designed. It is not uncommon for a newspaper to use the same family of type in various sizes, in all headlines. From the large cities, the idea is spreading to smaller newspapers and becoming nation-wide. It is far from the idea of using as many different types as possible, which maintained a few years ago. The average editorial staff is now intensely interested in typography, and the next few years are likely to see an increasing number of innovations.

Headline type varies in size from 10-point to 36-, 48-, and even 72-point type in the first deck. The average in major heads is about 36-point, while in subordinate heads a smaller type is ordinarily employed. In other decks than the first, the usual size is 8-, 10-, or 12-point, although it may run larger in the three-deck cross-line.

IV. How the Headline Is Built

To fulfill its mission as a bulletin and an advertisement of the news, the headline has acquired a more or less stereotyped form which dictates the content and character of each deck's message. Part of this results from the relative display of the various decks and part of it from the demand in the mind of the reader which has been built up by headline practice. The experienced headline writer knows the requirements by instinct, for he has learned it from many mistakes and blunders. But the beginner, to develop the instinct, must resort to the outlining of material necessary in the building of a successful headline. If he does this conscientiously while he is learning, he will form habits that will later enable him to do the work by instinct—and do it well.

We say that a headline is "built" and not "written," because each deck is put together separately and because the headline builder undertakes each deck as a separate problem and may write any deck first. If he has planned the separate parts carefully, the finished portions will fit together into a complete whole.

The first thing to be noticed in the building of the headline is the manner in which it is to be read. This largely determines the contents of its various parts. The headline is designed, in the first place, to suit the tastes of two very different kinds of readers. (1) One is a rapid reader who scans rather than reads and takes into his mind only the words that his eye chances to fall upon. It is to interest him that the headline writer alternates brief display decks with more extensive decks in smaller type —just as the newspaper writer crowds his most interesting words into the first lines of paragraphs. Each is striving to catch the hurrying eye and hold it. (2) The other reader is a more leisurely one who, once he has started to read a story, reads it from the top deck of its headline to its last word. Both kinds of readers are included in every newspaper's circulation and both must be pleased. The headline must therefore be clear and interesting to the man who reads only part of it, as well as to the man who reads it all.

Since it is easy enough to write for the man who reads it all, headline writers are more concerned with making an appeal to the rapid reader. This appeal is accomplished mainly by making some decks more attractive than others. And to be attractive to the rapid reader, the decks must be brief. In the four-deck headline, this appeal is made in the first and third decks. We can be reasonably sure that the first deck will be read, if any is, and by setting the third in type that makes it stand out beyond the second and fourth, we can count on having that read also. If the rapid reader peruses more than the first and third decks, it is likely to be after he has read the display decks. In the headline below, for example, we are quite sure that the first deck and the cross-line will be read:

MAY LET WOMEN BE MUM ON AGE

—14½ Units
—14 Units

County Judge Scully Seeking Loophole in Law on Matter

—9 Words

WOULD BOOM REGISTRY

—19½ Units

Says He Will Remove First Ward Officials Living Outside of Precincts

—11 Words

For the sake of illustration we may take the four-deck headline as typical of other forms and use the above form as our model. In laying out the content of these four decks, we shall work on the supposition that the order of importance of the decks is first, third, second, fourth. To insure the proper emphasis we shall build them in that order. In the first deck we shall aim to summarize the entire story with the most significant feature in the first line. Then we shall choose the next most interesting fact, preferably a striking one, for the cross-line. The other two decks we shall devote to explanation of the display decks.

We can best understand the process of headline building by the study of a concrete example. For this purpose let us take this story which appeared in a city daily:

> Every known obstacle in the way of a start in building the new Union station is believed to have been removed.
>
> At yesterday's meeting of the city council an ordinance was unanimously passed, giving the Baltimore & Ohio Railroad the right to build a new coach and freight yard in the vicinity of Fifteenth and Lincoln streets. This will move the railroad's property out of the zone of development of the Union station and leave a clear field for the $65,000,000 project.
>
> The work on the new station must be started by March 23. March 15 is the time limit for beginning work on the Baltimore & Ohio's new yard.
>
> The council also passed an order in favor of the Pennsylvania Railroad, giving it the right to erect a temporary freight shed so that the work of wrecking the sheds along Canal street can be started.

The first step in building a headline for this story is to select the facts that should be presented in it. They are in general as follows:

The new Union station *may* now be built.
All known obstacles are out of the way.
This was accomplished by the city council's action yesterday.
The B. & O. Railroad was given the right to build a new coach and freight yard at Fifteenth and Lincoln streets to leave room for the station—must begin by March 15.
It is a $65,000,000 project.
The work must be under way by March 23.
The Pennsylvania Railroad is permitted to build temporary freight sheds to clear Canal street.

The significance of these facts was of course immediately clear to any newspaper desk man in the city. The project of building a new Union station had been hanging fire for many years and many obstacles had already been disposed of. The council's action in this case did not mean that it would be built or that the railroads would take advantage of its action. The story meant simply that the council had granted these privileges to remove what seemed to be the last obstacle and declared that the railroads must comply before the date specified to secure the privileges. To the headline writer, the story indicated that the outlook was promising, although he realized that the railroads might reject the proposal. His problem was to point out this significance without overstating the case.

With the above schedule of facts as possible material for the headline, the next step is to arrange the facts in four groups to correspond with the four decks. The first group must contain the most significant fact, and for the third group, the facts should accord with the

HEADLINE WRITING 115

prominent position and the shortness of the cross-line. The outline might be as follows:

1. The new Union station now seems assured.
2. Action of city council removes last obstacles in way of $65,000,000 project by granting privileges to railroads—one privilege is to allow the B. & O. to move yards to Franklin and Fifteenth streets.
3. The work must begin by March 23.
4. Pennsylvania Railroad allowed to build temporary sheds to clear Canal street.

All that remains now is to express these groups of facts in words and phrases that will fit the required space. The first deck, we find, has two lines of 15 units each. Here are several possibilities that suggest themselves at once:

**MAY BEGIN UNION
STATION IN MARCH**

**TO BREAK GROUND
FOR UNION DEPOT**

**MAY START WORK
ON UNION STATION**

All of these are weak in that the first lines contain little of importance, and each is guilty of overstating the facts. The first is especially bad because it splits "Union Station." Let us try in our next attempts to keep within the facts:

LAST OBSTACLE TO UNION DEPOT GONE

FIELD CLEAR FOR NEW UNION DEPOT

RIGHT OF WAY OPEN FOR UNION STATION

TRACK IS CLEARED FOR UNION DEPOT

These are closer to the facts, but in each the first line is insignificant. Some of them are too "fat" and some have other faults. Evidently, we may improve on them by reversing the idea and beginning with the subject, and our next efforts are an approach to a satisfactory first deck:

NEW UNION DEPOT MAY BE BUILT NOW

UNION DEPOT HAS CLEAR FIELD NOW

NEW UNION DEPOT HAS CLEAR FIELD

The last two are better, but "field" is not exactly the right word, although the reporter used it in his story. Substitute a synonym, thus:

NEW UNION DEPOT HAS CLEAR TRACK

This is more effective because "track" has a railroad flavor. It indicates the possibility without assuming too much. The use of the word "depot" instead of "station" would probably be permitted in such a case by most newspapers.

Deciding that the above is satisfactory as first deck, we are ready to attack the cross-line and try to express the idea we have decided it is to carry in the 20 units allowed.

|WORK MUST BEGIN MARCH 23|

This first attempt is good but the line is five units too long.

|WORK BEGINS MARCH 23|

It fits the space but is not entirely true.

|MARCH 23 IS TIME LIMIT|

Space requirements are met but the line is not entirely clear. Noting that the issue on which we are working is for February 19, we may try a different way of expressing the time:

|ONE MONTH TIME LIMIT|
|MUST BEGIN IN A MONTH|

Not so good because the first is not clear and the suppressed subject in the second may cause difficulty. Perhaps the third is the best.

We next juggle with the content of the second deck which is to contain about nine average words. As we expressed it in the outline, "Action of City Council Removes Last Obstacle in Way of $65,000,000 Project by Permitting B. & O. to Build New Freight Yards," it is twice too long. Try cutting the first expression, "Council Removes Last Obstacle in $65,000,000 Project by Permitting B. & O. to Build New Freight Yards." Still too long. "Council Removes Last Obstacle in $65,000,000 Project by Permitting B. & O. to Move Yards." This is shorter, but it is evident that we must sacrifice some of the content. "Council Removes Last Obstacle by Allowing B. & O. to Move Yards." This is possible but it involves hyphenating "obstacle." More juggling gives us this:

| City Council Opens Way
| by Allowing B. & O.
| To Move Yards

The fourth deck undergoes similar manipulation to condense its content to ten words. "Pennsylvania Road Permitted to Build Temporary Sheds to Clear Canal Street," "Pennsylvania Road May Build Temporary Sheds to Clear Canal Street," "Pennsy Road May Build Temporary Sheds to Clear Canal Street." Our efforts to fit the space and avoid awkward breaks at the ends of the lines evolve this:

| Pennsylvania Road May Build
| Temporary Sheds to Clear
| Canal Street

Selecting the best of the attempts for the various decks, we put the headline together as follows:

NEW UNION DEPOT HAS CLEAR TRACK

City Council Opens Way by Allowing B. & O. To Move Yards

ONE MONTH TIME LIMIT

Pennsylvania Road May Build Temporary Sheds to Clear Canal Street

Another headline writer might have arranged the material thus:

1. The way is now clear for the new Union station.
2. City council opens way for $65,000,000 project but railroads must comply by March 23.
3. The last known obstacles are now removed.
4. B. & O. permitted to build new yard and Pennsylvania Railroad given right to build temporary sheds to clear Canal street.

Working on this basis he might have evolved the following headline:

UNION DEPOT HAS CLEAR TRACK NOW

Council Opens Way for $65,000,000 Terminal Long Promised

LAST OBSTACLES REMOVED

B. & O. and Pennsylvania Roads May Move Yards and Freight Sheds

The experienced headline writer would hardly work out the material so minutely, but the process illustrates the way in which the headline takes form in his mind. The student should group his facts and formulate a written outline of the various decks, as illustrated above, while he is learning to arrange his material.

V. Mechanics of the Headline

The building of this headline has brought out many of the mechanical details involved in headline writing but they may be summed up to advantage in a series of mechanical requirements which have grown up gradually with the development of the headline. This list can never be complete for any time after the day on which it is compiled, since every time a headline writer meets a new difficulty and solves it in a new and acceptable manner he has added another item. In general, however, the precedents are well established and recognized in all offices.

The mechanics to be taken up are the following:

1. *Length of lines*
    (a) Counting the letters
    (b) Latitude allowed
    (c) Form of copy
2. *Headline based on lead*
    (a) Headline versus story
3. *Interrelation of decks*
    (a) Interrelation of content
    (b) Interlocking of grammar
4. *Verbs in headlines*
    (a) Verb merely understood
    (b) Infinitives and participles
    (c) Tense of verbs
    (d) Adverbs of time
    (e) Active verbs
    (f) Imperative headlines
    (g) "In" as a verb
5. *Choice of words*
    (a) Five hints concerning diction
    (b) Repetition of important words
    (c) Articles
    (d) Contractions and colloquialisms
    (e) Slang
    (f) Unconventional synonyms
    (g) Reformed and simplified spelling
    (h) Rhyme and alliteration
    (i) Allegorical headlines
    (j) Headline jargon

HEADLINE WRITING

6. *Typographical style in headlines*
   - (*a*) Punctuation
   - (*b*) Abbreviation
   - (*c*) Quotation marks
   - (*d*) Figures
   - (*e*) Division of words
   - (*f*) Capitalization in banks
7. *Emphasis in headlines*
   - (*a*) Meaningless generalities
   - (*b*) Exactness and definiteness
   - (*c*) Label and wooden heads
   - (*d*) Person's name as feature
   - (*e*) Telegraph and correspondence heads
   - (*f*) Anonymous headlines
   - (*g*) Ambiguity
8. *"Color" in headlines*
   - (*a*) Humorous headlines
   - (*b*) Questions

1. Length of Lines

It seems almost unnecessary to repeat that the first consideration in headline writing is to suit the copy to the space allotted to it, but the problem of line length is the first stumbling block that the beginner meets. Because of necessity for symmetry, the words must exactly—not almost—fill the space. More headlines are faulty in line-length than in almost any other essential, and, because of this, it is almost necessary to lay down the rule, "When in doubt, consider symmetry first and content afterward." For, no matter how nicely a given series of words may express the idea, it cannot be used if it is too long or too short for the allotted space. "Type is not made of rubber," as the printers say. If a line will hold only

19 units of type of a certain size, 19½ is as impossible as 40, for it will bulge the column rule. Too short a line, in the same way, destroys the symmetry, and an attempt to space out between the letters is an acknowledgment of failure. Unless the headline writer takes this carefully into consideration he will cause endless trouble in the composing room and will spoil the appearance of his newspaper.

Counting the Letters.—Before attempting to write copy for any headline, the writer must ascertain the number of units which each line will hold and mark them opposite the lines on the headline model. In counting the units, he must figure each letter and each space (between the words) as a unit. This applies to all letters except M and W, which count as one and one-half units each—and I and the figure 1, which count as one-half unit each. All punctuation marks, except the dash and the double quotation mark, count as one-half unit each—the latter count as full units. A growing practice is to count spaces in all-cap decks as one-half unit.

The process of "counting in" a headline deck may be illustrated thus:

JONES WILL HEAD —14 units

LABOR DAY BODY —13 units

LEADER IS HURT, BUT —16½ units

U. S. AIRMEN GO ON —15 units

A slightly different set of units must be used in counting display headlines set in capitals and small letters (u. and l.c.), and the system varies with the type used because of the difference of letters and figures in various faces. In general, if the lower case letter is taken as one unit, the usual capital will be about one and one-half units. Also, since more variable spacing between words may be used, the space is reckoned as a unit. Perhaps the best general rule is: "Count *every* letter and space as *one* unit each—then temper with judgment."

Latitude Allowed.—After the number of units allowed in the line is ascertained, the writer can then figure out exactly how much latitude he may take. In the drop-line, he may allow himself a margin of one unit each way. That is, if the normal line contains 16 units, he may consider 15 or 17 possible; but he should not go below 15 or above 17, for 18 or 19 will probably fill the entire line from rule to rule. In a cross-line, he should figure the maximum of the line, from rule to rule, and keep within that. Less care is required in the building of the pyramid and hanging indention, for a certain amount of space may be taken up between words. In these decks, it is sufficient to count the words, but one must consider the varying lengths of words. The best rule is to estimate the number of *two-syllable* words—or the number of words of six or seven letters each. Also the skillful headline writer takes care to estimate the length of the words so as to avoid breaking a word at the end of the line, and in case of a hanging indention whose last line is full he must be even more careful.

Form of Copy.—To fulfill space requirements it is best to write the head, line for line, in exactly the same form as it is to appear in type and to count the units in each line. In fact, most offices require copyreaders to write the headline copy deck-for-deck, line-for-line, word-for-word, as it is to be set up. Also, the copyreader indicates the form of each deck with the following conventional markings:

For the cross-line:

]RAIN HALTS ROAD WORK[

For the drop-line:

\ BIG RADIO SHOW OPENS \
\ AT EAST SIDE LIBRARY \

For the inverted pyramid:

\ Brings Suit to Cancel Leases /
\ Signed Last Fall—Tenants /
\ Refuse to Move /

For the hanging indention:

Badger Batmen Outhit Gophers |
] But Runs Are Missing—Hill |
| Pitches Seven Innings |

No headline should be considered finished unless the number of units in its major lines exactly matches the number allowed by the schedule. The bad appearance of headlines that are too short or too long is illustrated by these:

**WELL KNOWN WESTERNER
KILLED BY TRAIN**

**ABERCROMBIE MAKES FINAL
FIGHT FOR CONTROL OF CARDS**

Legibility of copy is very important. Many a puzzling headline gets into print because the compositor cannot decipher the copyreader's longhand scrawl. If it were convenient to do so, it is likely that newspapers would require typewritten headline copy; it is advisable to typewrite when possible. In all cases, unless the copyreader writes a very legible hand, he should *print out* proper names and all doubtful words. Many offices require this to be done.

What happens when the copyreader's scrawl is misread is illustrated by this headline taken from a small newspaper:

**START REVOLUTION
OF PROPERTY LOAN**

The headline meant to say, "Start Revaluation of Property Soon." It illustrates some letters most likely to be confused in longhand—*i.e.*, small *o* and *a*, capital *S* and *L*, small *u*. This headline, "Man, Burned Alive, Breathes Through Pipe," resulted from misreading of the word "Buried."

2. Headline Based on Lead

The mechanics of newspaper make-up establish the necessity of basing the content of the headline on the content of the story's lead. All facts and ideas in the head must be taken from the lead, and no facts should appear in the headline that are not included in the lead. This axiom is made necessary by the fact that there is no surety that any article will retain its original length in print. The make-up man usually has the right to cut down any story to suit the space at his command, and the breaking of unexpected news just before press time may require that he cut down any story—even to the lead. The editorial department prepares for this emergency by crowding the important facts in every story into its lead so that the killing of any number of paragraphs at the end will not destroy the story's clearness. The headline writer prepares for the emergency by confining himself to the lead, the only part of the story that he is sure will appear. If the lead does not contain the facts that he feels must go into his headline, he must rewrite the lead so as to include the necessary additions. If the headline writer violates this rule, the reader is likely to have his attention drawn to a story by an interesting statement in a headline and then find that the story itself contains no explanation of the statement. He does not know that the original story contained further explanation that was cut off in the make-up, but he jumps to the conclusion that the headline writer has read something into the story on his own account. Even if the statement appears in the last paragraph, the reader is annoyed by having to read so far to find it. The evil is especially noticeable when the entire headline is based on some minor detail mentioned casually near the end of the story. In this discussion, *lead* means not necessarily just the first paragraph—it means the entire introductory summary that "leads off" the story. It may be half a column long.

Headline versus Story.—The relation of the headline to the story should be after this fashion: The headline contains the gist of the story in skeleton form; the lead elaborates this skeleton in an adequate summary of the principal contents of the story; the running story elaborates the various items mentioned in the lead.

The first deck of the headline should be built on the "big feature" of the story, the news angle that makes the story worth printing. It must present the "action" of the story; if there is no action, the most interesting fact or item. If it is a "follow" or "second-day" story, the first deck should indicate that fact by repeating some key word, fact, event, or name from the preceding story. The news value of the story usually hinges upon a "key word" or expression—perhaps a name or place. This should be in the first deck. The head writer must ask himself, "Why is the story newsy, worth printing—what word expresses this idea?" That word gives his start.

3. The Interrelation of Decks

In headlines of two or more decks, the interrelation of contents and grammar of the various decks is very important. As was indicated in the sample of headline building, it is ordinarily necessary to make a schedule of the contents of the story and to outline the various decks before writing any of them. That is the mechanical process involved in solving the problem.

Interrelation of Content.—Each deck should, in general, be devoted to presenting a separate idea, and the ideas in any deck should not be repetitions of the ideas of other decks. Each should be an independent statement. In relative importance, the prominent cross-lines and drop-lines should be considered first, but to what extent may the pyramids be mere elaborations of the display lines? Many headlines, like the following, use the pyramid only as an explanation of first line—a reiteration of the first statement in more complete form:

> **VARDAMAN HAS GOOD LEAD**
>
> Former Governor of Mississippi
> Seems Sure of Senatorship

But more common is the headline, like the following, in which the pyramid presents additional facts:

> **POSTAL SAVINGS BANK**
> **OPENS AT CHICAGO**
>
> Two Hundred Depositors Stand in
> Line to Start Accounts With
> the Government

In headlines of more than two decks, when there is interrelation of content, each pyramid is usually related to the display line immediately preceding it.

Interlocking of Grammar.—Grammatical interrelation is often present where there is no interrelation of content. The brief, skeleton form of the headline makes necessary the suppression of many necessary parts of speech, and a part of speech may be expressed in one deck and understood in the next. The greatest difficulty is caused by the suppression of the grammatical subject. Whether the succeeding decks be an elaboration of, or an addition to, the idea of the first, space may require that one noun may do duty as subject for the verbs of several decks. The subject may be expressed in the first deck and understood in subsequent decks, thus:

BRYAN WILL EXAMINE INTO HIS AUTHORITIES

Notifies Democratic Leader Underwood That If He Finds Press Report Correct Fur Will Fly

If the predicate is more significant, the subject may be suppressed in the first deck and expressed in a later deck, thus:

|MUST SCRUB CITY HALL FLOOR|

Melrose Boy Ordered by Court to Remove Stain Caused by Spitting Tobacco

Either practice is seen in the best newspapers, but both are full of dangers. Unless great care is taken, some of the verbs reaching backward or forward into other decks for subjects will be in the wrong tense, number, or voice, as in the following case:

|WOMEN OF SOUTH NOT URGING NEGRO BALLOT|

Says States Have Right to Define| Electorate

This is especially true when the subject is a collective noun like "assembly," "class," or "audience." The noun may be used correctly either as singular or as plural but both forms should not be used together, as here:

INVESTIGATE "WET" VICTORY

Texas Senate Passes Resolution to
Inquire Into Late Election

In long heads there is danger in suppressing the subject of a later deck after several subjects have been expressed in previous decks—any one of the previous nouns may be subject of the later verb.

Even when the grammatical subject is expressed in each deck, it is well to keep the attention focused on the principal idea of the headline. Too many subjects, as in the following, result in too great scattering of interest:

**JEWELS SPILLED
ON SIDEWALK BY
DARING ROBBER**

Paving Block is Hurled Through
Gotham Jewelry Store Window
in Broad Daylight

TRAY OF DIAMONDS SEIZED

Women Scream While Detectives
Shadowing Thieves Make
Prompt Capture

One step beyond this is the suggestion that the verb of each deck be in the same voice, so that the tone of the headline may be uniformly active, or uniformly passive. An alternation of active and passive verbs sacrifices continuity.

When the subject is suppressed in the first deck, care must be taken or the result may be like the following:

URGES BUILDING INSPECTOR
Movement Started After One is Killed in Collapse of Structure

Headlines are often seen in which no subject appears at all. This is especially bad when each deck requires a different subject, as in this headline:

TO HEAR MILKMEN'S STORIES
Directs Health Board to Investigate Complaints of Favor

The grammatical interrelation of decks is sometimes carried to the extent of splitting a sentence between two decks, so that both are necessary for clearness. Such a practice is frowned upon by most newspapers since it is usually felt that each deck should be a complete sentence in itself. The following is an example of the "continuous" style:

LAUGHS AT THIEF'S ORDER
Not in Derision, but to Throw Policeman off Scent

This idea of breaking a sentence into a number of parts to develop decks has been carried to its highest terms in the headlines of the Cincinnati *Enquirer*, with a one-word top deck beginning a sentence that runs through the other decks. In most newspapers, such a headline is considered a novelty suitable only to a human interest feature story—the one kind of story requiring original treatment in the headline.

The common feeling among headline writers is that the headline should be considered a compact whole made up of a number of independent parts. So far as possible each deck should be independent in thought and grammar, but the several parts should emphasize and develop one general idea when put together.

4. Verbs in Headlines

It is now a recognized rule in most newspaper offices that every deck must contain a verb. The use of the verb was the real change involved in the step from the label heading of the old school to the bulletin headline of the present day. As soon as it became desirable to express action in the headline, the verb became necessary and, since action is now the chief characteristic, a deck without a verb is rare. Readers have become so accustomed to the verb that they are unconsciously dissatisfied with the headline without a verb, even if it is excellent in other respects. Besides giving action to the heading, the verb through its tense expresses the time of the story. The ineffectiveness of the headline without a verb is shown here:

| **PROHIBITION IN ICELAND** |

Verb Merely Understood.—Often no verb is expressed but the heading is worded in such a way as to indicate the verb that is understood:

> **LIQUOR A MORAL QUESTION**
> **Should Not Be Allowed to Wreck Political Parties, Says Wilson**

Infinitives and Participles often serve as verbs in headlines. The future tense may be expressed by the infinitive because it saves space:

> **TO PENSION SCHOOL TEACHERS**

Tense.—The usual practice is to write all headlines in the present or the future tense. The past tense is rarely used, if at all. Although the story may be concerned with an event which took place in the near past, the present tense in the headline increases the vividness and emphasizes the freshness and timeliness of the news. Incidentally the present tense is easier to write because in most verbs it is shorter and requires no auxiliaries. Hence the headline of speech reports reads "Hopkins Speaks on Soil," not "Hopkins Spoke on Soil." If it is an event to take place in the future, the infinitive saves the space taken by auxiliaries: for example, "Hopkins to Speak on Soil."

In stories announcing deaths, it is customary to use the present tense, thus: "John Smith, Banker, Dies on Shipboard"—or—"A. H. HUSTING, PIONEER, IS DEAD IN MAYVILLE."

Adverbs of Time.—Amusing headlines often result from the attempt to introduce the time into the head—

whether the tense of the verb should be changed accordingly is a mooted point:

BADGERS VANQUISH SUCKER GYM TEAM LAST SATURDAY

Active Verbs.—When conditions of emphasis and space will permit, it is desirable to use active verbs, rather than passive, because of the greater sense of action in the active voice; also because no auxiliaries or prepositions are required. "Flood Sweeps Snake Valley" or "Fire Ruins Hill Home" are more effective than "Snake Valley Swept by Flood," or "Hill Home Ruined by Fire." But whatever the voice of the first deck, it is desirable to use the same in succeeding decks. The question of voice is, however, often determined by the demands of emphasis. When the subject is less significant than the predicate, it is best to put the predicate first, in spite of the passive verb. Thus, "Governor Run Down by Tipsy Chauffeur" is more effective than "Tipsy Chauffeur Runs Down Governor," since the interest is in the word "governor."

Imperative Headlines.—When the subject of the first deck is suppressed and the line begins with the verb, the statement often exhorts the reader or urges him to action. Newspaper men consider this vocative or "imperative" headline objectionable. Its effect is seen here:

| LYNCH NEGRO SLAYER OF AGED MILL OWNER |

"In" as a *Verb*.—Many editors object to the following use of *in* to take the place of a verb:

**|BROTHERS IN FIGHT
OVER JACKSON WILL**

5. Choice of Words

The words used in headlines should be short, concise, and specific. The limits of space absolutely forbid the use of long words, especially in display lines. Also, the heavy, black type of the headline is difficult to read when the words are long and the lines are not broken by frequent white spaces. The words must be concise and exact because the brief space permits of no rambling, and the headline, however short, must be clear at a glance. They must be specific and concrete so as to give an exact picture and create a vivid impression. The headline writer usually thinks twice before he uses a word of more than two syllables. He learns to speak concretely and to cast his thoughts into sharp, vivid words that snap. It may be said, in general, that words of Anglo-Saxon parentage are the most suitable for the headline—both in thought and size. Compare the alternative wordings in the following examples:

WIND SPREADS DEVASTATION

OR

WIND RUINS CORN CROP

PASS TRAFFIC LEGISLATION

OR

PASS NEW ROAD RULES

Five Hints for headline diction are:
1. Avoid one-word lines.
2. Avoid words of more than two syllables in display decks.
3. Use the concrete example, rather than the general idea, in headlines.
4. Use words and phrases that apply to the particular story so specifically that they cannot be used to headline another story.
5. Make a collection of three-letter, four-letter, and five-letter synonyms for headline use. The larger your collection, the better will be your headlines.

Repetition of important words is to be avoided. It is a generally accepted rule that no word shall appear twice in any of the decks of the same headline. The rule does not apply, of course, to articles and auxiliaries, but does apply to all nouns, verbs, adverbs, and adjectives. Hence a broad vocabulary is needed unless much time is to be wasted on the hunting of synonyms. In the same way, the headline writer avoids duplicating the words and expressions used in the first few lines of the lead. Variety has much to do with the interest of his text.

The monotony of repetition is illustrated by the following headline:

| **CARTER'S DEATH AVENGED** |
| **Friends Avenge Citizen's Death with Double Murder** |

The use of synonyms is the easiest of all devices to avoid

repetition and it is one of the commonest characteristics of the headline, as the following example illustrates:

STEAMSHIP CALLS FOR HELP
Ocean Liner, Centralia, Is Driven on California Shoals

Articles.—The value of space in the headline makes necessary in most cases the omission of articles and auxiliaries. There is little room for "a," "an," "the," etc.; the thought appears in skeleton form. Although they are generally omitted, it is not considered bad form to include articles to help out the balance.

Contractions and colloquialisms are treated in different ways by different newspapers. In some offices their use is strictly prohibited; in others much leniency is evident. A contraction is most often permitted when it is in accord with the generally colloquial tone of the story. In such cases it is effective, while with a more serious subject it would be out of place. The colloquialism tends in general to give the headline a homely, whimsical tone and should be used accordingly, for example:

HUSBANDS AREN'T ALL ALIKE
Widow Smith Is Sure of It, for She's Had Four of 'em

Slang also has its place in headline writing in most offices, although headline writers are ordinarily urged to use it moderately. It should never, of course, be used in the heading of a serious story for it gives a careless, undignified feeling that the reader unconsciously carries with him as he reads the story. Slang in headline writing may be treated on the same basis as in news writing. It should never be used when the idea may be expressed as vividly and as briefly in good English. The chief objection to slang is that it is constantly changing and is not understood by all the readers of the paper. When there is the slightest doubt on this score, the necessity of clearness should bar it absolutely.

Unconventional Synonyms.—Much the same comment is due to the many handy, unconventional short synonyms that headline writers have invented to suit the needs of their work. Common among them are "probe" and "quiz" for "investigate," "solons" for "legislators," "dope" for "prediction," "clash" for "controversy," "grill" for "cross-examine," "white plague" for "tuberculosis," "haven" for "hospital," "dip" for "pickpocket," "Pennsy" for "Pennsylvania," "grab" for "acquisition," "fake" for "pseudo," "hello girl" for "telephone operator," "finest" for "policemen," etc. Some of these are actual misuses of good English words—such as "suicide" as a verb, "deny" for "refuse to grant," "win" as a noun, etc. These words are short and vivid; they express large ideas in limited space, and on that score many newspapers permit their use. But headline writers generally are admonished to use them with care and to be as loath to coin a new word or misuse an old one in headline writing as in other writing.

Reformed or simplified spelling is not permitted in the headlines of most newspapers any more than in their stories. It will be a boon to the headline writer if it is ever generally adopted, but now few newspapers use it.

Rhyme and alliteration are in disfavor. The jingle of a rhyming drop-line is usually considered objectionable and the stuttering alliteration is frowned upon. Occasionally when the tone of a story demands a humorous, trivial treatment, the headline writer seeks rhyme or alliteration for their effect. But in the average serious story the jingle is bad because it calls attention to itself, at the expense of its content. As in all other newspaper writing, headline words should convey the thought without obtruding themselves. The effect is illustrated by the following:

| JACKSON REPLIES
| PATTERSON LIES |

| TEACHING TEACHERS
| TO TEACH TRADESMEN |

Allegorical Headlines.—Except in feature stories, headlines built on allegory, metaphor, or literary allusion are to be avoided, unless clear to the most ignorant, *e.g.*—MODERN PORTIA BEATS MEN IN LAW SCHOOL—or—REDSKIN BITES DUST IN WATERTOWN SQUARE (Indian monument fell over).

Headline Jargon.—There has been a tendency in recent years toward excessive use of slang and synonyms that is resulting in a "headline jargon" that is as bad for newspaper men as for the public. The jargon is at its worst, of course, on the sport page, but it is rapidly gaining strength in news pages. It is much seen in "serial" stories of large import, such as noted trials, and there it usually colors and exaggerates the facts. The total import of the jargon is that all society is a seething turmoil; doubtless this is the feeling of the ignorant reader. For instance, when the mayor and city attorney disagree over a small legal matter, the headlines shout "fight," "clash," "split," and the ignorant expect bloodshed and arrest. When the Sewing Circle decides to look into the quality of moving pictures, the head writer digs up the old blood-stained "quiz" and "probe." Any newspaper front page, except the best edited, illustrates "headline jargon." Is it necessary to good headline writing? A study of these same front pages will prove that it is not. In some rare cases it results from "office policy." For the rest, it is merely thoughtlessness, laziness, "rubber stamp" work. It is the same story as the careless news writer's habit of seizing the worn-out trite stand-bys that every other careless news writer uses. The same kind of "Word Diet" for the head writer, to weed out these old-timers from this vocabulary, will save him from jargon and give him originality.

6. Typographical Style in Headlines

The ordinary rules of English and newspaper typographical style are followed in general in matters of punctuation, abbreviation, quotation, figures, etc., although some special uses have developed.

Punctuation is used as little as possible. No periods are used at the ends of decks except, in some offices, at the end of pyramids and hanging indentions. The period is seldom seen at the end of display decks. Commas are almost never used in display decks and are avoided as much as possible in other decks. When the use of two independent clauses, not joined by a conjunction, requires a separating punctuation point, the semicolon or the dash is used. The usual custom is to use the semicolon in display decks because it requires little space—thus:

HORSE STARTS AUTO; CAN'T STOP IT; GETS RUN OVER

In pyramids and hanging indentions, the dash is uniformly used, thus:

Stones are Thrown, Shots Fired—One of Wounded Men is Dead

Apostrophes are of course used when necessary; question and exclamation marks appear in their proper places.

Headline writers lately are learning to do many interesting things with punctuation, but it must be admitted that much of the "tricky" punctuation that has come into display decks is merely proof of inability to meet the requirements in a legitimate way. For instance, the use of a comma to show omission of *and* (first example) and the stringing together of nouns without verbs, separated by semicolons (second example) are just lazy shortcuts:

AUTO HITS HYDRANT, INJURES MAN, WIFE

MANY TREES ARE DOWN; STORM; WIND; SLEET

Abbreviation in headlines is usually governed by office rule. Every newspaper, to be sure, permits in its headlines any abbreviations sanctioned by its style sheet—such as "Mr.," "Mrs.," "Dr.," "Co.," etc. How much beyond the style book the matter of abbreviation may be carried depends on the office. Some newspapers permit "U. S.," "Prof.," "U. of W.," initials of railroads, and similar abbreviations; others strictly forbid them. In some cities, such initials and abbreviations as "L" for elevated railroad, "Y. M. C. A.," "S. I. T. & L. Co." for "Southern Iowa Traction and Light Company," "I. R. T." for "Interborough Rapid Transit Company," are permitted. The practice may be carried so far as to allow "S. P. U. G.," for "Society for Prevention of Useless Gifts," "S. P. C. A." for "Society for Prevention of Cruelty to Animals," "I. W. W." for "Independent Workers of the World," "I. R." for "Initiative and Referendum," "J. D. Jr." for the son of the oil magnate, "G. O. P." for "Republican party," etc. It may be said, in general, however, that excessive abbreviation is to be avoided, because it does not look well in type and because the meaning is not always clear. When abbreviations are overdone, as they are in some newspapers, they become an offensive part of "headline jargon." Good headlines can be written without ever using abbreviations; the task is harder, but the headlines are the better for it.

Quotation marks are not used to any great extent in headlines because they take valuable space. The quoting of a single word is seldom necessary since any word usage that is common enough to appear in the headline is too well known to require quoting. The use of quotation marks around slang words is usually a feeble apology.

Occasionally when the headline is a direct quotation of some man's statement, quotation marks are used to set it off. Many newspapers, however, consider quotation marks unnecessary here; a dash is often used instead. Besides taking space, the marks do not look well in type:

> **"STUDY CLUB" AIDS**
> **MANY NEWCOMERS**

> **'YOU ARE ROBBING POOR,'**
> **DECLARES FORUM ORATOR**

Figures are largely used in headlines of many newspapers because they are striking and saving of space, but their use is frequently regulated by office rules. In some cases the headline writer must follow the rules laid down in the style sheet for all news writing. In other cases he may use more figures than these rules permit. The usual practice is to establish a definite dividing line—such as 10 or 100—to use figures for all numbers above the line and to spell out numbers below except in certain specified cases. The commonest custom is to use figures for numbers of two or more digits and spell out one-digit numbers. In the headline, also, it is permissible to begin a sentence or a deck with figures in violation of the copy rule. When a number expressed in figures is longer than the corresponding word—as "1,000,000" or "million"—it is wise to use the word. A common usage is shown here:

> **75 SWEPT INTO RIVER**
> Seven Drowned When Ferry Steamer
> Hits Shoal and Sinks.

Most offices frown upon "padding out" by spelling out numbers for which the style sheet specifies figures.

Division of words is not considered desirable in headlines. Although it is permitted to some extent in pyramids and hanging indentions, it is bad form to break a word at the end of a line in display decks. The bad appearance of hyphenated drop-line is shown here:

| MISS ANNA BARGE ENTER-
| TAINED AT SOCIAL TEA |

In the same way it is bad form to divide an infinitive, a noun and its article or modifiers, a preposition and its object between two lines. The separation of an unimportant word, such as "an," "and," "but," "to," etc., is a violation of the idea of logical division of lines. Thus:

| FARMER IS KICKED TO
| DEATH BY HIS HORSE |

If possible, the words should be divided so that the first line is a separate unit: Not, ACTRESS DENIES HER —SUCCESS WAS ALL LUCK. But, ACTRESS DENIES LUCK—BROUGHT HER SUCCESS.

Capitalization in Banks.—In decks which are set in capitals and small letters, the usual rule is to capitalize all words of more than four letters—all nouns, pronouns, verbs, adjectives, adverbs, interjections, auxiliaries, both parts of a compound verb, and prepositions that are part of a verb (except infinitive sign). A simpler way to remember the rule is:

Capitalize all words except articles, conjunctions, and prepositions of less than four letters.

7. Emphasis in Headlines

The emphatic sentence beginning plays as important a part in headline writing as in other newspaper writing. The first words of every deck are the ones that catch the reader's eye. Headline writers, therefore, make an effort to place the emphasis at the beginning of each deck. This is especially true in two- or three-part drop-lines as top decks. The first line should contain the most striking words in the deck, even if this requires grammatical transposition. In the following examples the second is more effective:

| ENDLESS CHAIN TO COVER |
| STATE FOR TORNADO RELIEF |

| TORNADO AID WORK PUSHED |
| BY CHAIN OF STATE CLUBS |

The last lines, however, must not be neglected. It is decidedly bad practice to pack the gist of the statement in the first line and then to trail out the following lines with useless words to fill the space. The following will illustrate:

| Y. M. C. A. AIDS SPECIAL MEN |
| WITH VERY GOOD RESULTS |

| INDOOR MEET SHOWS WORK |
| OF EXCEPTIONAL INTEREST |

Every word in the headline must count. This display is too valuable to be wasted on words that simply fill space.

Too many young headline writers pad out second and third lines with empty words to reach the required number of units. If the thought selected for the deck, when written in its briefest form, does not fill the space, it should be discarded or amplified with concrete details that add to its significance. Seldom is there a thought so bald that an attempt to give it greater concreteness will not fill the deck and improve it at the same time. The following examples show what might have been done with the padded decks above:

> **Y. M. C. A. AIDS SPECIAL MEN
> IN SECURING NEEDED JOBS**
>
> **INDOOR MEET SCORES TIED
> IN THREE MAJOR EVENTS**

Meaningless generalities have no place in headline writing. If the reporter has failed to reduce the thought to its most concrete form, the headline writer must analyze his expression to discover the exact meaning or significance. The *general* head has little defense. Witness the following generalities and the concrete language that might be used in place of them:

> **DEMOCRATS FAIL TO GRAB
> HARMONY SCHEME BY TAIL**
>
> **DEMOCRATS FAIL TO CLOSE
> WRANGLE ON STATE TICKET**

| ACCIDENT IN MILL
         HAS FATAL RESULTS |

| FIVE MEN KILLED
         IN MILL ACCIDENT |

The *"Label"* or *"Wooden"* Head which merely indicates the *kind* of story and might be used over several stories of the kind—*e. g.,* COURT HAS BUSY DAY—is to be avoided. This "stock" headline—SCHOOL HEAD SPEAKS AT WEST P. T. A. MEET—might be used once a week, but—NEW HIGH SCHOOL IS URGED BY DR. JONES—probably could not.

Exactness and definiteness in headline writing, as in lead writing, requires the use of names and identifications as well as general allusions to the actors, victims, places, etc. This is especially true of the three- and four-deck head which makes possible exact reference. The actor should not be passed over as merely "he" or "she"; somewhere in the several decks the name should appear. In accident and crime stories, the exact place should appear somewhere. The headline, in other words, should not only be a skeleton of the story, but a bulletin—an exact, definite summary that would be clear without future explanation.

A good way to write a headline is to write a ten-word telegram of the news—use the gist of it in the top deck.

Some tests of exactness and concreteness in headlines are:

1. Might the headline be used over any other story of the same general content?

2. Does it answer as many of the five W's (who, when, where, what, why) as are needed for quick grasp of the news?
3. If it is a follow or second-day story, does headline refer to preceding story?
4. Is the "keyword" of the news in the first line?
5. If a person's name is the feature, is it in the top deck? If the name is not reasonably certain to be recognized, does it have proper "news identification"? (N. B. The use of first names of prominent or notorious persons, their nicknames, or supposedly clever allusions to them, may easily be overdone, at the expense of dignity or courtesy.)

Telegraph or Correspondence Headlines should, if possible, carry the name of the city in the top deck. The average reader is much more interested in an accident or crime story in the home city than in one a thousand miles away. When he sees FALLING CORNICE KILLS 3, INJURES 50, his first idea is that it is local and concerns familiar persons or buildings. But when he finds in the story that it happened in another city, he feels duped. The headline should have read, FALLING CORNICE KILLS 3 IN CHICAGO LOOP. It is such small matters that arouse criticism of the press. But, on the other hand, do not say "Here" in a local headline.

In weekly or community newspapers which are developing the use of bulletin headlines over correspondents' letters, the headline is valueless unless it carries the name of the locality concerned. Even when the best news item in the letter is used as a lead and is bulletined in the headline, the news value depends on the place, since the letters are read only by those who are interested in the place concerned. For example, NEW CANNERY TO BE BUILT NEXT YEAR appears to be local news; but MONROE WILL BUILD NEW PEA CANNERY carries the proper "place label."

Anonymous Headlines are those that do not fix authority, responsibility, or source; they announce "Says," "Urges," "Plans," "Advises," "Will," without telling "who." They are to be avoided. For example, SAYS TRAFFIC FINES ARE NOW TOO HEAVY has a different news value when the subject of "says" is a judge, a motorist, a motor club, the mayor, or some one else. Some offices try to avoid this by forbidding the verb-beginning, but the reverse, MOTOR FINES TOO HEAVY, IS CHARGE, is not much better.

Effort to obtain concreteness should not lead the head writer to go beyond the story for facts. No statement should appear in the headline that is not contained in the story.

Ambiguity is closely related to the question of emphasis. Ambiguous words often lead to ludicrous and puzzling headline statements. They can be avoided only by great care in the use of words with two meanings and especially words that may be used either as nouns or verbs and as verbs or adjectives:

| AUSTRIANS CLAIM
| WINS OVER RUSS |

| USED SHELLS FOUND
| AT SCENE OF MURDER |

8. "Color" in Headline Words

Because of the extreme brevity and baldness of headline statements, the writer must think of the meaning that the reader finds between the lines, as well as in the words themselves. He must remember that, since he has room only to suggest a thought, he must word his suggestion in such a way as to direct the reader toward the proper conclusion. He must, in other words, consider the connotation of his words and phrases. In the parlance of the newspaper office, connotation is called "tone" or "color," and the headline which leaves an opening for the reader to "read something into the story" is said to be "colored."

Impartiality is a headline virtue demanded in almost every newspaper office. The headline writer is given no more liberty in the matter of expressing opinions than is the reporter. There are, of course, a few newspapers that deliberately write headlines to prejudice the reader for or against the story, but these newspapers are in the minority. Independent, unbiased newspapers generally insist that their headlines shall do no more than bulletin the news. They forbid any attempt to prejudice the reader or to pass judgment on the facts. If the headline writer has an opinion, he must keep it to himself. He must be as impartial toward the facts he handles as the ideal judge and allow none of his personal feelings to influence his treatment of them.

Perhaps the best test of "color" is this: Can the reader tell from the headline whether the writer approves or disapproves of the news or of any person in it? The necessity of fitting a statement into a definite number of letters and lines forces the use of synonyms that hit "just beside the mark" in connotation. One such word carries a wrong impression into the reader's mind that may undo all the effort for accuracy and exact qualifications of a careful reporter. After one has juggled hopelessly to express an idea in a difficult headline, his sense of accuracy becomes dulled—it is sometimes necessary to ask the man at the next desk to pass on the results of his efforts.

Partiality and color usually creep into headlines indirectly by way of the associations of the words and expressions used. An unobtrusive adjective buried in a long deck may give the thought a twist that will try the case of the story before the reader learns a single fact. A derogatory noun used as a synonym may carry with it a prejudice that precludes open-mindedness. An overvivid verb may qualify its subject to the extent of reading in a final verdict. The following is an example of a headline that is an editorial upon, as well as a bulletin of, the news:

| TWO ROCHESTER BOYS |
| GOT JUST DESERTS |

Humorous Headlines.—The tone of a headline should strictly accord with the tone of its story. If the facts are serious and the story is a straightforward statement, the head should give the same feeling. If, however, the facts are treated lightly or humorously by the reporter, the headline writer may give his bulletin a humorous twist. While summarizing the news, he will also put the reader in the proper state of mind for the humorous article. The following are typical examples of successful humorous headlines:

|EVERYONE ON TRAIN PEEPED|

|HAS SMITH 5 WIFES? 'SURE'|

|JACK DILLON NEARLY
       SINKS GUNBOAT SMITH|

|*Nigh Sixty Year,
but Knows a 'Dip'
When He Sees One*|

Questions are often effectively used in headlines. The headline may ask a direct question of the reader to interest him in the story—this kind of question is seldom effective. Or the content of the headline may be put in question form to indicate that the facts are problematical or supposititious, or to show that they represent a possibility. On occasion this use of the question is effective, but it may easily be overworked. The presence of several question headlines on the same page gives the impression that the content of the entire newspaper is an uncertainty. The following illustrate the two kinds of question headlines:

|WHERE DO COMPLAINTS
    AGAINST POLICE GO?|

|EDUCATION WILL END WAR?|

VI. Faults in Headline Writing

The faults to be avoided in writing headlines are, in general, the violations of the newspaper precedents noted above. There are, however, certain faults that deserve special comment and repetition.

1. Waste of Space

A newspaper headline contains no room for generalities, and yet the wasting of headline space is one of the commonest faults. Unless the headline gives a concrete, definite statement of fact, that is clear in itself without further explanation, it is ordinarily a bad headline. The headline must not only give the nature of the news bulletined, but must include the exact facts that make it news. Many headlines refer to the chief actor in the story as "he" without divulging his identity; they detail the results and circumstances of an event without mentioning the place or time of its occurrence. The fault may be avoided by testing the headline with the questions that it suggests. Does it answer all the essential questions, *e. g.*, when, where, who, how, why? If it does not answer some of them exactly, it is not a good headline.

The best way to overcome this fault is to develop a larger vocabulary, particularly of short words needed in headlines, and to combat "headline jargon." The matter may be treated both negatively and positively: (1) Put yourself on a *word diet*, barring the trite words day by day. (2) Make a business of gathering three-letter, four-letter, five-letter synonyms, for the search will increase your vocabulary. (3) Avoid one-word lines. (4) Avoid words of more than two syllables. (5) Use the concrete example, rather than the general idea. (6) Write a headline that fits no other story except the one in hand.

2. Lack of Symmetry

"Looks" are of great importance; the modern headline is an arrangement of display type designed to improve the physical appearance of the newspaper. Unless its lines are of proper length and balance, it fails—it destroys the appearance of the page. The headline writer who writes lines too long or too short, who fails to count the units and to fit the schedule, is failing in half the requirements.

3. Inaccuracy

This fault takes many forms, some of which have been discussed in earlier pages, and constitutes probably the fundamental consideration of ethics in headline writing. "Inaccuracy" ranges all the way from unintentional errors, thoughtless "color," careless use of words, to intentional overplaying, dishonesty, exaggeration, and "policy" editorializing. It is impossible in this book to discuss adequately the ethics of headline writing, but the subject must be considered by young copyreaders as one of the most important angles of present-day newspaper work. Every time a new means of display is devised to increase the sales value of the headline, the ethical problem is accentuated. Some aspects and causes of inaccuracy are:

(a) *Carelessness and Lack of Knowledge.*—Unintentional inaccuracy may come from one of these: (1) Hazy or insufficient knowledge of the subject of the story; (2) failure to read story carefully; (3) haste in slapping down the first headline that one thinks of; and (4) heedlessness and irresponsibility in regard to the newspaper's

HEADLINE WRITING

relation to the public. Here are some examples taken from newspapers: BOILER BLAST ON SUGAR PLANTATION KILLS NINE (story said "Refinery") —FOUR FAIL TO APPEAR IN COURT (story lists one appearing, three failing)—CHURCH REFUSES AID PLEDGED FOR RELIEF (refused one plan of aid)—INDIANS HELD ON GIRL'S CHARGE (two whites, one Indian)—BUSINESS MEN TALK IN RUM SALE PROBE (testify in court)—DANCE ACT STOPPED BY POLICE CHIEF (movie show, not law).

(*b*) *Too vivid words.*—Attempt to make story bright, to say much in short space, causes apparent misstatement of fact—*e.g.*, 80 POLICE VETERANS FACE OUSTER (story said they retire on pensions)—SORORITY GIRLS ROUTED BY FIRE (chimney fire at 8:45 a. m.)—UNIVERSITY CLASS DROPS ALL OFFICERS BUT PRESIDENT (abolished offices)— CHARGES POLICE SHIRKING DUTY (charges "incompetency").

(*c*) *Omission of qualifications.*—Scraps of ideas, stripped of the careful qualifications which were in the original statement and the reporter's copy, are displayed in heads. This is often seen in reports of addresses and interviews. *e.g.*—FAITH IN CONGRESS IS SPEAKER'S PLEA (he said he had faith)—BONDSMEN TO FORFEIT BAIL FOR MAZARRA (story said if he does not report Monday)—PROM ELECTION IS DEADLOCKED (merely close; recount ordered).

(*d*) *Assumptions Given as Facts.*—A police theory, a lawyer's explanation, a detective's hunch, a reporter's guess, presented as such in the story, appear as facts in the headline, *e.g.*—OKLAHOMA LAWYER DUPED TO DEATH (story said it was police theory)—SLAY YOUTH IN MYSTERY CAR (body found, rest theory)—FUMES OF EXHAUST KILL COUPLE IN CLOSED CAR (physician's theory).

(*e*) *False Quotation.*—Often the headline makes a direct quotation, credited to some one in story, of an expression taken from the reporter's lead summary or of the head writer's size-up of the meaning of a long statement. The headline should not quote anything except the exact words that are quoted in the story, *e.g.*—NOT "BOUGHT OFF," SHE SAYS IN COURT (she didn't use those words in story)—"GERMANY PAYS 6 BILLION BEFORE WE PAY" (quotation of lead summary, not statesman's words).

(*f*) *Exaggeration or "overplaying."*—This results from head writer's overzealous attempt to make the news attractive. *e.g.*—107 FALL IN GERMAN POLICE RIOT (seven killed, 100 wounded)—BLAST IN MINE TRAPS 14 (story said they were unaccounted for, thought to be off duty)—HUNDREDS SHOT IN OUTBREAKS (three killed)—BERLIN BOURSE STORMED (mob tried to).

(*g*) *Personal Equation.*—What the individual copyreader sees in the story makes a great variation in it. These headlines were all written for the same story: WOODS AFIRE ALONG WHOLE WEST SLOPE—FLAMES SWEEP GREAT FORESTS OF SEABOARD—DRY FORESTS FEED FLAMES ON COAST—WEST HAS WORST FOREST FIRES IN YEARS.

(h) *"Policy" Headlines.*—Few newspapers desire their editorial policy, in regard to politics, foreign affairs, finance, labor, strikes, boycotts, race conflicts, or other public questions, to color their headlines. But readers can often find what appear to be "policy" headlines. To some extent, this results from (1) the fact that the headline writer is overconscious of his newspaper's editorial policy, (2) certain "stock" notions and prejudices current in the newspaper profession, (3) familiarity with the majority point of view of the public. A conscious effort is necessary to keep these out. *e.g.*—COAL STRIKE PEACE NEAR (somebody says so in story)—LEAGUE NEAR COLLAPSE, GENEVA VIEW (but not official view) —WAGE SLASH ASKED BY LABOR BOSSES (master builders ask voluntary reduction of wages)— GERMANY TO STOP PAYING (may stop, if).

(i) *Trial by Headline.*—In stories of crime and arrest, the headline must not go beyond the actual status of the case. If the headline insinuates that a man is guilty, just because he is arrested, or if one angle of the testimony is overplayed, public sentiment may be so aroused that a fair trial is impossible. If random facts from unsupported charges made in complaints are played up, the person stands convicted even if the case never gets to court— particularly true in divorce petitions. With the growth of sensationalism, "trial by newspapers" is coming to be a great problem, and most of the evil is in the headlines. *e.g.*—WOMAN QUIZZED ON SHOOTING (story said she volunteered information)—NEGRO CONFESSES UNDER THIRD DEGREE (courts exclude such confessions)—TOOK "OTHER WOMAN" OUT IN FAMILY AUTO (says divorce petition).

(j) *Libelous Headlines.*—Newspapers are often sued for libelous statements in headlines, although there is no libel in the story below. This results from stripping away of qualifications. Omission of the name or use of *alleged* are of little avail. *e.g.*—WOMAN INVOLVED IN PASSING FAKE BILLS (police think so)—MAN ARRESTED FOR THEFT OF CAR (released at once story said).

(k) *Headline Editorials.*—When a headline goes beyond the bare facts in the story and expresses an interpretation of, or comment on, the facts, it is an editorial—and its big type gives it more force than anything on the editorial page. It is often difficult to draw a clear line, but, for one case of such "editorializing" under orders, dozens may be found which result from haste, carelessness, personal prejudice, or the mere forecasting of the results of the event. *e.g.*—RIOTOUS SCENES IN COURT (no riot in story)—MAGNUS TELLS SENATE CHORES THAT NEED DOIN' (farmer senator talks)—BOARD CHANGES COMMITTEE PLAN (abolishes it)—NEGRO TREK NORTH SHOWS 1923 RISE (story gives year's figures but no increase shown).

VII. Special Kinds of Heads

1. The Jump Head

This is a name given to the headline written for the second part of a story that is "broken over" from the front page to an inside page. The jump head introduces the continuation. In some cases the jump head is written by the desk man in advance of make-up; in others it is written by the make-up editor as the emergency of breaking the story arises. The usual jump head expresses the same facts as the original headline in less space and with less display.

The jump head may be the original head set in smaller, more extended type, so that the same words fill the desired space. It may be the same headline, in type and wording, with one or more of the later decks omitted. Sometimes it is merely a repetition of the first deck in its original form. Generally, however, the jump head is the original head rewritten in more compact form. If the top deck of the first headline is a three-part drop-line, the jump head may be a two-part drop-line. A two-part drop-line may be changed into a single cross-line. In some cases the original words are used; in others only part of them appear. The jump head usually makes less attempt to summarize the story; its function is that of *recalling* the original headline. All of these things are regulated by office practice, however, and many headline schedules contain models of the jump heads to be used with various major heads. Here is an example of a headline and its jump head:

HUERTA AND FRIENDS CONFER, DEFYING VIGIL OF SECRET SERVICE

HUERTA AND FRIENDS HOLD CONFERENCES

(Continued from Page One)

2. The Banner, or Streamer, Headline

This is a headline in large type that stretches across the top of an entire page. Banners are used by American newspapers (1) to emphasize the most important news and (2) to assist newsboys in selling papers on the street or the news-stand. The banner sometimes appears as a single cross-line which serves as the top deck of the headline of the principal news story. Some papers carry a series of banners bulletining one or more stories. The top cross-line is, of course, concerned with the most important news and is given greater display than those that follow it. The individual streamers serve as a striking table of contents of the columns below.

In the writing of the banner head, the advertising element predominates since the headline serves the purpose of "the news contents bill" supplied to newsboys by English newspapers to assist them in attracting attention to their wares. Hence the type of the banner must be sufficiently large and clear to be readable at a distance, and its content must be such as to attract the eye and arouse interest or curiosity. With this requirement in mind, the headline writer constructs his banner heads in accordance with the same rules followed in other headlines. He uses a verb and makes the headline a complete statement of fact. He counts his letters and spaces and adjusts the line to the space allowed. When office practice encourages variety in make-up of succeeding editions, the headline writer often decides the wording of the banner without reference to space and then selects a type that will fit the proper space, choosing large or small extended or condensed, type according as the statement is short or long.

Before the World War, the banner headline was almost entirely confined to editions intended for street sale and was thus most commonly used by afternoon papers. Big war news, however, led other papers to adopt the device until it came to be standard on almost every front page. After the war, when big news became scarce, occasion for the banner declined, but the habit persisted. The result was "overplaying" of less important news "to dress up the page." Sales value of stories, rather than real importance, came to be the basis—a street accident or striking crime that the newsboys might shout. The value of such a device for carrier or mail editions is questionable, but the banner has run rampant, not only in the large city press, but in community dailies, country weeklies, and even high school papers. Meanwhile certain prominent newspapers have persistently avoided it, "except when the news warrants."

Among the names now applied to the banner are "streamer," "ribbon," "flag," "line," and other nicknames.

The relation of the banner to the regular column headline of the same story is in general treated in two ways: (1) The banner is considered as a sales bulletin, completely set off by a cut-off rule; the column headline is written without regard to it, and the story is placed anywhere on the page. (2) The banner is looked upon as the top deck of the story's column headline; the story is placed at the top of the column, and the cut-off rule is broken above.

Blanket line is the name most often applied to the page-wide headline that has come into use across the tops of inside news or department pages. It is used for its decorative value—to dress up the page.

3. Spread Heads, or Layouts

The ordinary newspaper headline occupies only one column, and when it grows beyond the column rules it is distinguished by the name "spread," or "layout"; the latter word is borrowed from the art department. The spread was invented by a class of newspapers that try to avoid symmetrical and conventional make-up in displaying the news, and it has since been taken over by the majority of American newspapers. In character and content it differs from the usual one-column headline only in that it spreads over a number of columns. There are no rules for its form; originality is its chief characteristic. Its top deck, which is usually a drop-line of several parts, stretches across the top of the entire layout and may head any number of columns. The pyramids and cross-lines below it may stretch across the entire width of the layout, or cover only part of it. Sometimes several small decks, alike or different, occupy places side by side under the top deck. The story beneath may begin in any column under the spread, or up among the decks.

To write a spread heading, great imagination and knowledge of type are necessary. The attempt is to display the news in a striking way and to give the page an attractive appearance. The editor ordinarily makes a diagram of the top of the page and lays out the space carefully before he begins to write. After deciding upon the nature of the spread and the kind of type for each deck, he estimates the letters and spaces accommodated in each line. With this diagram as his model, he writes contents to fill it exactly. In the spread heading, more than in any other kind of headline, the words must fill the lines evenly.

4. Subheads

Many newspapers break up their stories with small display lines, called subheads, inserted in the columns at specified intervals. Their purpose is to make the paper easier to read. Such display is used as the linotype machine affords—black-face, capitals, or small capitals—and the subheads are usually shorter than a full line. There are no rules governing the frequency of the subheads, but the ordinary practice is to insert a subhead about once in 200 words. In content they correspond to chapter headings, since they summarize the paragraphs that follow or suggest their content in a vivid, interesting way. It is to be noted that a subhead is usually a complete statement, with a verb, and that it attempts to express the idea in an original way. In some cases, the subhead is inserted some distance ahead of the discussion that it suggests so that the reader must go almost to the next subhead before he finds its explanation; by that time the next subhead has caught his eye and his interest is carried further. The subheads are written in by the copy editor as he prepares the copy for the printer. They are seldom used in stories of less than 200 words, and a common rule in newspaper offices is that not less than two subheads shall be used in one story.

5. Divisional or "Folo" Headlines

Some newspapers employ, besides the subheads within stories, another series of display lines to mark larger divisions of the story. They head the individual "takes" or angles developed by different reporters or coming from different parts of the country. Thus they head the parts slugged "Folo." For example, in the report of a widespread storm, the first take is a local story; each later dispatch from another city carries a divisional head. Or in the composite story on the day's automobile deaths or prohibition raids, telegraph dispatches, with "folo heads," follow the local story.

6. Cutlines, Overlines, Captions

These are names used for the titles and explanations that accompany illustrations. The overline is placed above the picture and is usually more of the nature of a label, or title. Many newspapers, however, apply the principles of headline writing to their overlines and make them newsy and interesting. Besides giving the name of the person or thing pictured below, the overline usually points out the picture's relation to the news. The overline is usually set in display type. The caption, which occupies a position beneath the illustration, is usually longer and more of the nature of an explanation of the picture. It describes the person or thing illustrated and points out the significance of the cut. Combined with the overline, it is often so complete that no further story is necessary to explain the picture. Captions and overlines are usually written by the desk men and must fit the more or less irregular space left by the art department in preparing the illustration.

7. News Digests

When a newspaper publishes a news digest or index on the first page, the parts of it are written by the copyreader as he handles individual stories. As he sends the headline to the composing room, he sends along a line for the news index.

8. Other Headline Terms

When the entire headline is set in a frame of column rules, it is a *boxed headline*. Fancy type ornaments used in headline display are *dingbats, bugs,* etc. Dashes used to separate part of stories or headlines are dubbed *dinky dash, jim dash,* etc. In some offices, the column head of the story covered by the banner is called a *drop head*. Newspaper pages are divided in matters of display by the *fold* across the middle. The *name-plate* at the top of page 1, because it is cast in one piece, is often called the *logotype* or the *flag*. Stock headlines used day after day and not reset are *standing heads*. Reporter's by-lines are often called *title lines*. Headlines for tops of columns are *top heads*. Cutlines used beneath pictures are often called *underlines*. The statement of ownership on the editorial page is the *masthead* or *flag*.

Every newspaper office has its own slang for headline usages, and newspaper slang varies in different cities and in different parts of the country.

Exercises

1. Compile headline schedules of representative newspapers, noting number of units and words allowed in each line.
2. Headline exercises may be divided into several steps:

    (a) Comparative work, in which all the students write the same form of headline for the same story. (Material may be obtained by clipping current stories from distant newspapers, mimeographing without headlines, assigning same headline form used in the newspaper, and later comparing students' headlines with newspaper's headline.)

- (*b*) Top deck drill. One after another, practice writing the most typical top decks of representative newspapers, going from the easy, many-unit two-part drops to some of the very difficult types. Here again the students may work on the same form for the same story to compare results.
- (*c*) Multiple decks. Working with the same story, students will first begin "digging out" the outline for two-deck, three-deck, and four-deck headlines. After sufficient practice in outlining, they will write the headlines, all working on the same schedule for same story.
- (*d*) Different schedules. Each student will choose a different newspaper "for employment" and master its headline schedule. Then, working on the same story, students will write headlines according to the schedule selected by each.
- (*e*) Rapid drill on copy desk with teacher or student in the slot, dealing out copy to be edited and headed. Entire desk should use same headline schedule, but students will handle different stories. As each headline is completed, it is criticized and handed back for revision. The material may be current local, press association, or syndicate copy.
- (*f*) Headline writing and editing for student newspaper and "sitting in" on desk of local newspaper.

3. Practice again and again outlining material for multiple-deck headline.

4. Emphasize form and legibility of headline copy.

5. In all headline copy, place total number of units at end of each line. Check them.

6. Search constantly for good and bad headlines in newspapers, as well as for novelties.

7. Prepare classified lists of three-letter, four-letter, and five-letter headline synonyms.

HEADLINE WRITING

8. Prepare lists of words of current "headline jargon" and bar them.

9. Decide by vote what abbreviations shall be permitted.

10. Practice writing various kinds of jump heads.

11. Practice writing subheads and division heads, as well as blanket heads for inside pages.

12. With some stories, prepare lines to go into the News Index.

13. Practice designing spreads, first by searching for good examples and imitating them; then by laying out page and working out original typographical schemes.

14. Practice writing cut-lines for news and feature pictures.

15. With later stories, try writing banner headlines.

16. Good practice in deciding content of top deck may be obtained by writing ten-word telegram of the news.

17. Gather examples of "colored" and inaccurate headlines.

18. Look into old files to see headlines of former years and to note development.

19. Search newspapers for examples of each problem and point discussed in above chapter.

20. Rewrite faulty headlines found in newspapers.

21. Draw up a headline schedule for a particular small community newspaper—daily or weekly.

CHAPTER IV

PROOFREADING

PROOFREADING is the mechanical process of checking the errors that a printer makes in setting type. It is entirely concerned with mechanics and typography; it is not concerned with style or content. Unlike copyreading, it has nothing of the creative in it and implies no license to correct or alter the author's words. The final authority is the writer's copy; the proofreader's office is to make a detailed comparison of this written copy with the printer's mechanical version and to note all deviations from it.

Printer's proof is a hastily made impression of type matter devised to make easier the task of checking up the errors in the typography. It is prepared by the printer as soon as the type is set, and the operation is called *pulling a proof*. The printer places the type matter in a long metal tray, called a *galley*, passes an inked roller over the face of the type, spreads a sheet of paper over the galley, and takes the impression by passing a small roller over the paper or by hammering it into the type with a block of wood. The resulting impression is called a *galley proof*. When the proofreader has noted the errors in the galley proof and the printer has corrected the type accordingly, another proof is taken—a *revised proof* or *revise*. If a reading of the revise shows up many errors, a second revise may be necessary. Still further proofs are required after the type has been taken from the galley and *made up* into page form. These are called *page* and *form* proofs.

Book Proof

In the magazine or book publishing office, the original galley proof and enough revises to insure mechanical perfection are read by the office force. A final galley proof, pulled after the last corrections have been made, is sent to the author for any small alterations in content he may desire. The type is then *paged*, and a proof of each page is read by the office proofreader and the author. If the page forms are to be electrotyped, a proof of the electro pages is read as a final checking up before the plates are placed on the press for printing. Even after the matter has been *made ready* on the press, the first two or three impressions, *form proofs*, are folded and read to see that the pages are in the right positions and printed properly. If the pages have not been electrotyped and the printing is directly from type, a pressman must watch the printed impressions constantly to note any breaking down of type or sinking of type areas resulting in imperfect impression.

Newspaper Proof

In the newspaper office, the first galley proof is corrected by professional proofreaders, or by members of the editorial staff if the paper is small. After the revise, a proof of each galley is sent to the managing editor, so that he may look over the day's edition before press time; another is sent to the news editor or make-up man to be used in making up the pages. After the final revise of the galleys, no further proofs are taken until the type has been placed in the forms of the printed pages. A form proof is then usually pulled for a survey of the make-up and the catching of any mixing of type or articles in the making-up. The only real proofreading done in the newspaper office is concerned with the galley proofs. But every newspaper worker should know how to correct proof quickly and accurately, for only the larger offices afford professional proofreaders. These are members of the mechanical force, rather than the editorial staff; in fact, they are usually members of the typographical union.

The Copyholder

Since proofreading is little more or less than a comparison of proof with copy, the proofreader usually needs an assistant, a copyholder, to follow the original copy. One of them reads aloud—punctuation marks, capitals, paragraphing, type changes, as well as words—while the other, following the copy, notes discrepancies. As the errors are discovered the proofreader marks the proof. This method is necessary to insure the discovery of omissions and additions that would escape notice if the copy were not followed. Quite often the proofreader follows the lines with a card to aid in concentration.

How the Printer Revises

Before one can correct proof intelligently, he must know how the printer handles it in revising the type. The more or less unusual means employed by the proofreader are explained by the fact that the printer does not read through the proof in search of corrections; he simply glances down the margins of the proof and makes the corrections indicated there. He is not likely, therefore, to notice any corrections placed in the body of the proof.

To attract his notice, it is necessary to place all corrections in the margins opposite the lines containing errors and to mark them large enough so that he cannot miss them. When the proofreading sign in the margin has called his attention to the error and indicated its nature, he looks through the line for another mark indicating the exact location of the error. Both marks are necessary to insure accurate correction.

I. THE PROOF MARKS

The proofreading marks used in all offices and known to all printers, except in the smallest country offices, are as follows:

Kind of Type

Cap.	Change to capital letter.
s. c.	Change to small capital letter.
l. c.	Change to lower case, or small letter.
Rom.	Change to Roman type.
Ital.	Change to Italic type.
b.f.	Change to bold-face type.
w.f	Letter marked is from wrong font.
+ ×	Letter marked is broken or imperfect.
9	Letter marked is reversed, or upside-down.

Punctuation

⊙	Insert period.
⁁	Insert comma.
;/	Insert semi-colon.
⊙	Insert colon.

▼	Insert apostrophe.
▼ ▼	Insert quotation marks, single or double.
-/	Insert one-em dash.
ⲭ/	Insert two-em dash.
H	Insert hyphen.

Position

//	Make lines parallel.
=	Make lines straight.
tr.	Transpose order of elements marked.
[	Move to the left.
]	Move to the right.
⌐	Move up.
⌐	Move down.
□	Indent one em.

Spacing

#	Put in space between words.
⌒	Take out space or correct uneven spacing between words.
S	Take out all space and close up.
⌒	Close up but leave some space.
	Insert proper ligature.
⊥	Push down space that prints up.
	Insert space between letters.
|	Straighten lateral margin.

PROOFREADING

Lead.	Insert space between lines.
J Lead.	Reduce space between lines.

Paragraphing

¶	Begin a new paragraph.
No ¶	Do not begin a new paragraph.
Run in	Make elements follow on same line.

Abbreviation

Spell out	Substitute full form of word or number.
Figures	Substitute figures.

Insertion and Omission

^	Caret indicates place where element in margin should be inserted.
/	Oblique line through letter indicates that it is to be changed or removed in accordance with margin mark.
∂ ∂	Take out element indicated.
stet.	Don't make change indicated; let it stand.
(circled)	Allow word to remain as it is.

Uncertainty

Qus.	Is this right or according to copy?
Out. See.	See copy to find what has been omitted in composition.

II. How to Use the Marks

There are many technical questions which arise in the use of the standard proofreading marks and many are settled only by office rules and practice. But the young proofreader will do well to consider them before he attempts to break away from old established customs or to establish new precedents.

1. Position of Marks.

All proof marks should be placed in the margin opposite the error. The printer will not see the correction unless it is so indicated. But the margin signal is not enough. The error must also be indicated in the line so that the printer may know exactly to what word or letter the correction refers.

2. Use All the Marks

The young proofreader often wonders why it is necessary to use so many different marks when, as it seems to him, half a dozen will do the work as well. With an intelligent printer, he reasons, it is scarcely necessary to indicate more than the position of errors and the omission and addition of words. In a large number of cases, to be sure, the error is so obvious that the printer needs only to have his attention called to it. But proofreading, like all other processes involving great accuracy, should be done with the greatest accuracy possible, and a sufficient number of marks to cover all possible cases is necessary. Sometimes the printer is not so intelligent as one might wish; often he is lazy and averse to making any corrections that he can avoid. The proper proof mark, however, settles the matter beyond all dispute. In the case of the intelligent, reliable man, it saves him the time necessary to puzzle out what the proofreader meant. Again, the use of all the marks indicates to the printer that the proofreader knows his business—and that is often a very good impression to create in the composing room. Ex-

PROOFREADING

SEVEN WORKMEN BURIED IN GASOLENE EXPLOSION

Blast and Fires Destroy Experiment Plant—Men in Blazing Clothes Leap from Windows

Pittsfield, Ill., June 25.—Seven men were probaly fataly burned today by an explosion of gasolene in the plorks of the Atlas Experiment Company. All of the fourteen persons on the second floor leaped from the windows blazing like torches.

The explosion came at 3/20 p. m. while most of the workmen were in the Laboratory on the second floor. Without warning a 20 gallon retort burs into flame, and blazing petrol was sees flying about the room.

The cause of the explosion is not known. Experiments on a new process for manufacturing were being made at the time, and is it thought that a retort made at the time became overheated.

"The first hiss of flame was followed by a blast of blazing gasolene," said Charles R. Samuels, foreman of the laboratory, this afternoon. "We boys had no times for firescapes—we jumped!

(Note; this example of corrected proof is the printed version of the newspaper story which was edited on page 28. The first deck of its headline was set by hand; the rest of the story was composed on a Linotype machine.

AN EXAMPLE OF CORRECTED PROOF

perience justifies, all in all, the use of all the proof marks and it is best to begin by learning them all at the outset.

3. Connecting Lines

Very often newspaper proofreaders use a connecting line between the error in the line and the mark in the margin. That is, they draw a line from the error, through the typed matter, to the margin and place the proof mark on the end of it. This method may work out satisfactorily if there are few errors in the proof, but in general it is bad practice. If the proof is very "dirty" or has more than two errors in the same line, the many connecting lines result in great confusion. The standard practice is better in every case.

4. Neatness

Every proofreader should take pride in the neatness of his work. Even if he does not consider neatness an evidence of his skill, he must remember that his careless work may result in serious confusion and delay in the composing room. He should use small proof marks, especially when he is reading closely set small type, and should place them exactly opposite the line which contains the error. If the mark is above or below the line, the printer does not know to what line it belongs. He should also use both margins; that is, he should place the correction in the margin nearest the error. The printer is accustomed to working in from one margin to the center of the line and then going to the other margin to work toward the center again. If a mark is placed in the left-hand margin to indicate an error near the right-hand end of the line, the result is confusion.

PROOFREADING

5. Red Ink

Many proofreaders use red ink because the contrast between the red and the black emphasizes the corrections and because it is easier to make small, legible marks with a fine pen than with a pencil.

6. Oblique Lines

The use of slanting lines beside proof marks is often a cause of confusion and it is well to adopt a uniform practice. A good rule is to use an oblique line, at the right of the letter or word, to indicate that the letter or word is to be inserted. If the oblique line is used only in this case, it will have a definite purpose, besides separating marks. For example: *tr.* means transpose, but *tr/* means insert *tr;* *lead* means more space between lines, but *lead/* means insert the word *lead;* *cap.* means capital letter, but *cap/* means insert the syllable *cap*, etc.

7. Marks in the Line

To mark the location in the line of errors indicated in the margin, a similar uniform practice may be adopted. The caret (∧) should be used to indicate places where words, letters, or punctuation points are to be inserted. The oblique line drawn through the letter or point will indicate that the letter or mark is to be taken out or changed. The use of the two marks for the two purposes is a great aid to the printer in finding the errors to which the marginal corrections refer.

8. Inserted Material

In inserting matter that has been omitted, if the omission consists of more than two or three words, it is best to write the omitted material in the margin near the proper place, put a line around it, run an arrow to the printed line, and indicate the place of insertion with a caret in the line. Material to be inserted should never be written between the lines, and the proofreader should take pains to write it legibly. If more than a line has been omitted or several lines have been mixed up, it is well to bracket the faulty lines and write "See Copy" in the margin.

9. Follow Copy

The proofreader should always follow the author's copy. In every case, the author's copy and the editor's corrections on it are his final authority unless office rules prescribe that he shall follow a certain typographical style and certain rules of spelling in spite of the author's practice. In most cases, however, the editor will adapt the copy to office rules and the proofreader may rely on his editing. In no case should a proofreader attempt to correct proof unless he has the copy for comparison.

III. Some Mechanical Details

Space Justification

In specifying the removal or insertion of letters or words, the proofreader must always bear in mind the mechanical difficulties under which the printer works. The compositor is dealing with one of the most inelastic things in the world—metal type—and one of the most immovable—the column rule. He cannot put into a line one more letter than the line will hold; if he does, the line will bulge the column rule and cause the lines above and below to drop out. He cannot take a word out without putting something in its place; else the line will be too short. When the proofreader calls for corrections that involve the insertion or removal of material in a line, the printer has only one recourse—he must catch up the added or subtracted space by altering the lines immediately above or below the changed line. The only elastic thing in the line is the space between the words and in any given line its limits of elasticity are seldom more than the width of two or three letters. Hence if the proofreader calls for the insertion of an eight-letter word, considerably more than can ordinarily be caught up in one line, the printer must run the last word over into the next line, catch up what he can there, run over into the third, and catch up the rest there. Sometimes one insertion or one removal will require the altering of four or five lines. The experienced proofreader tries, when the character of the copy permits, to minimize this difficulty by taking into consideration the alteration required by a correction. If he is merely substituting new words, he counts the letters and tries to fit them to the space occupied by the old. If he is adding several words, he tries to insert just enough to fill an entire line so that only two lines will be affected.

Linotype Justification

The problem of catching up space occupied by corrections is even more serious in linotype composition than in hand-set type. Here each alteration requires the resetting of the entire line, and each line that is affected by the catching-up process must be entirely reset. From the proofreader's standpoint this is bad, because, in resetting a line to make a correction, the printer may make an error in some other part of the line.

Irregular Spacing

The proofreader sometimes objects to seeing large spaces between words in one line and small spaces in the next and is moved to call for better spacing. Before he makes the marks, however, he should look over the lines carefully to see whether better spacing is possible without much alteration and catching up. Every line of type must "justify"—must come out even—and sometimes the variation in word lengths makes impossible even word-spacing. Sometimes, of course, a printer is careless in this regard and wastes space in justifying; again he may purposely space out material to increase the amount he has set—since he is usually paid on a space rate. In such cases of careless or unnecessarily wide spacing it is well for the proofreader to catch the printer up and require proper justification in his work.

IV. What Errors to Look For

In addition to the errors that may be classed as variations from copy—spelling, punctuation, and content—there are certain mechanical errors that the proofreader must watch for carefully.

1. Alignment

Every line of type should be reasonably straight; that is, the bottoms of the letters should all be on the same straight line. In the case of material set up on a worn-out typesetting machine, perfect alignment is almost impossible, but in the case of hand-set material, almost all imperfect alignment is due to the printer's carelessness and should be corrected.

PROOFREADING

2. Broken or Imperfect Type

This mechanical fault is common in all kinds of set and the strictness which the proofreader uses in correcting it depends upon the character of the work. Very often what appears to be imperfect type is merely imperfect proof, resulting from a hastily taken impression or poor ink. But since the proofreader has no way of knowing what is the real cause—and, if the work is particular—he is wise to mark the doubtful type. His mark on the proof will result, at any rate, in an inspection of the type.

3. Wrong Face

The presence of type of a different size or face in any printed matter is rare in machine work but more or less common in hand-set work. It results from what the printer calls "dirty case," a composing case in which the type has been carelessly distributed. Since the printer works more by feeling than by sight, some letters are more likely to be "wrong face" than others. The chief offenders are *i, o,* and *s.* In some kinds of work it is necessary to watch carefully to see that the small capitals *i* and *o* do not creep in as lower case.

4. Reversed Letters

Upside-down characters are very common in hand-set work, especially when certain fonts are used. Those that cause the chief difficulty are the lower case *o, s, u, n, p, d, c, e.* Sometimes a reversed *n* is used for *u,* reversed *p* for *d,* etc. In every case the error can be noted by the fact that the reversed letter is slightly above the line in most fonts.

5. Other Faults

Other mechanical errors that often get past the sharpest eye are: the insertion of a word that does not materially alter the sense; the repetition of the last word or syllable of one line at the beginning of the next; and the substitution of one word for another of almost the same length and meaning.

V. How to Identify Various Kinds of Composition

It is well for the proofreader to be able to identify the various kinds of composition since certain errors common to one are impossible in another and the character of the composition often affects the corrections. There are three kinds in general use at the present time—linotype, monotype, and hand.

Linotype

Since in linotype composition each line of type is one piece of metal cast integrally, the easiest way to identify it is by the character of its impression on proof or in the press. In the make-up of galley or page, the various slugs often do not stand firmly on the bottom. Hence one line often stands above the others and make a heavier impression; or one end of the line may be up and the other down, with a resulting variation of impression. In some cases also all the slugs may be slightly tilted so that the bottom or top of the type of each line is slightly heavier. This variation of impression *by lines* is a sure indication of the kind of set. If the work is done on a machine whose matrices are slightly worn, another identification is by hair-lines between the letters resulting from the fact that the matrices have not fitted together closely and shreds of type metal have been forced between them. If the metal shreds rise high enough to touch the paper, they print very fine hair-lines that are hardly noticeable except under close scrutiny. Very imperfect alignment is often an identification of linotype composition.

Monotype

Monotype work is more difficult to identify because it is done on a machine that casts each letter separately, so that the result is practically the same as hand work. It can often be identified by the spaces or quads that work up between the words and leave rectangular black impressions on the paper. In hand work, the printer usually uses several small spaces between two words; on the monotype machine, whose line justification is automatic, the spaces are a single piece of metal. This serves as an identification as the single piece is more likely to work up and the black splotch between words is plainly the impression of a single piece of metal. This, combined with the lack of errors common in hand-set and the varying line-impression of linotype work, makes identification possible.

Hand-Set Type

Hand composition is readily identified by the presence of wrong face letters and uneven justification in the same line, since these errors are practically impossible in machine work.

Errors Common to Various Sets

In linotype composition, wrong face is rare, and reversed letters are impossible, but imperfect letters and bad alignment are common, plus the common typographical errors that are possible on the typewriter. In monotype composition, both wrong face and reversed letters are impossible, except after corrections have been made, but the proofreader must watch for "weak" type. If much of the type is imperfect or uneven in impression, this is an indication that the type metal was too hot and the type is honeycombed; if the proofreader allows it to go through, much of it may break down in the press. All errors are possible in hand composition and the proofreader must be on the alert for wrong face and reversed type as well as the other errors noted.

Exercises

1. To obtain the best practice, the entire class should read proof on the same material—a number of proofs of same matter.
2. Good proofreading exercises may be purchased for class use—see Biography, Appendix III.
3. To develop a sharper proofreading eye, students may check and correct each other's work.
4. It is well to use the methods of professional proofreaders, using a pen and all the marks. Connecting lines and other newspaper short-cuts should be barred.
5. Read proof with a card, following line by line.
6. Class may have oral drills to learn proof marks and their use.
7. Practice identifying various kinds of composition in publications.
8. Practice inserting or removing material so as to require as little resetting and rejustifying as possible.

CHAPTER V

NEWSPAPER MAKE-UP

AFTER all the stories for an edition have been written, edited, provided with suitable headlines and set in type, after all the advertising has been written and composed, after all the copy for the editorial columns and other special sections has been "set up," there still remains the task of putting together this mass of material into the form of columns and pages ready for the stereotyper and pressman. This task is called make-up. It involves such a combination of mechanics and editorial problems that it can hardly be said to belong either to the composing room or to the editorial office. In fact, the task is usually performed by a man from each department working together over the same stone or table. The problems involved are so numerous and complicated that it is impossible to point out anything more than general tendencies and common practices.

The importance of make-up, however, cannot be overestimated. Although the reader is less conscious of it, probably, than of other characteristics of the newspaper, he is undoubtedly greatly influenced by the mere "looks" of the paper he reads. If clothes make the man, even more so does mere outward appearance make or unmake the newspaper. Magazine editors spend much time and money on the physical appearance of their publications and ponder a long time over the slightest change, but many newspaper editors do not give the matter a thought. Then the editor wonders why the painstaking work of his editorial room and the strength of his editorial policy do not increase his circulation.

The main considerations in make-up are: (1) to display the news with prominence proportionate to its importance; (2) to make it easy for the reader to find various contents; (3) to make pages attractive in appearance; (4) to advertise news so as to impel the reader to buy the paper. Sometimes one of these aims is uppermost in the editor's mind; again he is concentrating on another. In general, the fourth aim has been so emphasized recently that the first is neglected; the sales idea has led to "overplaying" of somewhat trivial, sensational news.

Evolution of Make-up

Average readers and some newspaper men think of the form and make-up of our daily news periodicals as a standard, cut-and-dried form that some one started years ago and every one since has accepted as the best. They forget that newspaper form and make-up, as we know them, are the result of a long, laborious evolution, a constant trying out and adopting of new ideas. The evolution, furthermore, is not yet completed, for each year brings changes that will last for generations to come. And in this evolution, more progress can be credited to the composing room than to the news office. Every step in the development is more or less directly related to the improvement of mechanical processes. The size and number of pages have changed with the development of printing presses. The character of type has changed with the invention of typesetting machinery. Illustrations have come in with the photographic process of engraving and have been violently affected by the general adoption of stereotyping.

Standardization

The tendency of recent years has been decidedly toward standardization of make-up. Pages, after growing from a pamphlet size to a spread that was dubbed a "blanket-sheet," have settled back into a convenient, pleasing size, so uniform that different papers vary but a few inches in height and width. Headlines have changed from the tiny label to a half-column of cross-lines, and back again to the short-deck form that gives greater display in less space. Column widths have shifted back and forth until the standard twelve and one-half or thirteen ems was reached. Standardized advertising practice and standardized machinery have accomplished this. The number and position of departments have changed until almost every newspaper now carries almost the same sections in the same places. The front page has developed under the growth of street sales from an unimportant cover to most important page in the newspaper, and the back page is still doubtful area. Every element of the present-day newspaper is the result of a slow growth brought about by altered mechanical, business, and editorial possibilities, and until the student of newspaper making realizes this, he is not ready to discuss the problems of make-up. Nothing is *right* in the newspaper simply because it is so; precedents are constantly changing and new ideas in make-up are as significant as new ideas in reporting and editing.

I. How a Newspaper Is Made Up

Before we can study the problems of make-up, we must investigate the mechanical processes involved. Much of the problem is dependent upon mechanical possibilities and the conditions under which the task must be done.

Who Makes Up the Paper

Most newspapers are made up by an experienced printer under the personal guidance of a member of the editorial staff. The latter may be the managing editor, the assistant managing editor, or, if the newspaper is large, a special make-up man called the news editor. Department pages are made up by their editors. Part of the task is preliminary planning, because the act of making-up must be done quickly. Throughout the day, as the various articles are set in type, the news editor receives galley proofs and plans his make-up. He classifies the articles as regards importance, nature, and headlines, and notes the position requirements slugged into the stories by the city or managing editor. He may even make a diagram of the various pages to assist him in visualizing the finished paper. Just before press time he takes the bundle of proofs and his diagram to the composing room and begins the work of making-up. The material is heterogeneously laid out in galleys of type and his problem is to direct the printer in sorting the mass and fitting it into the rectangular steel "chases" that bound the forms, so many columns wide and so many inches high.

The Make-up Man's Problems

The task is complicated by the fact that no two stories are of the same length and usually nothing fits into the space in which it is intended to go. Two stories, for example, whose similar heads call for a balanced position, may vary several inches in length; to place on a line the small headlines below them, the make-up man must quickly decide whether to throw away the last part of one story or to break it over into another column or page. Another article is just long enough to fill all of the column except an inch at the end; the make-up man must find a filler for the space, "lead" out the story with strips of metal between the lines, or cut it down to leave room for a short story below it. The number of mechanical difficulties that arise is infinite. At the same time, while wrestling with the problem of making things fit, the make-up man must remember the display and position demanded by the various pieces of news, for his work will receive careful scrutiny as soon as the first copy is off the press and he may be called to the managing editor's office to explain why he buried such-and-such a story at the bottom of the fifth page, although its importance required a place at the top of the fourth page.

The time element is even more serious. With plenty of time and thought, almost any one could solve the puzzle of making up an edition, but the make-up man must work with one eye on the clock. His task is the last step in the editorial department's work, and it is a serious offense to delay the closing of the forms five minutes, since the time for the last mechanical steps of stereotyping and putting plates on press is figured in seconds.

Dummy Diagram

In most metropolitan offices, the making of a "dummy diagram" is a regular part of the office routine. The

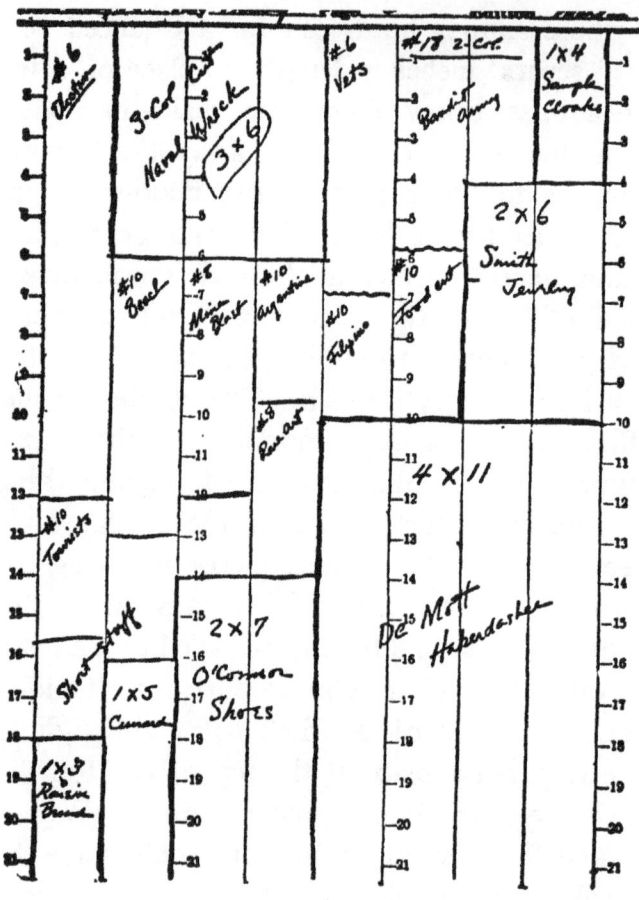

Dummy Diagram

advertising department first submits a dummy of its pages, and the news editor then lays out the news make-up. Certain offices use "the conference system" whereby the managing editor, editor-in-chief, assistant managing editor, and make-up editor listen to "the day's schedules" outlined by the city and telegraph editors and plan the day's paper. It is a practice that may well be copied in smaller offices for it saves time and results in better make-up.

NEWSPAPER MAKE-UP

Preparation for Final Make-up

Every effort is made in the modern newspaper plant to reduce the amount of make-up that must be done during the last few minutes. As many pages as possible are made up and stereotyped long before press time. The editorial page, woman's page, society page, and in general most of the inside pages are made up hours in advance. The advertising is usually set up and placed in the forms long before press time. It is usually necessary to hold open two pages until the last minute, the front page and an inside page to accommodate break-overs crowded out of the front page by late news. Just before press time the inside page is made up and sent to the stereotypers. The front page is, however, left until the last second. The make-up man has it partly made up and knows what to do with the remainder of it, but he cannot lock the form until the editorial office sends down word that the last piece of news is in. Even after he has closed it up, the telegraph operator or a belated reporter may bring in a front page story that involves complete remaking. The last page to leave the composing room is the *starter page*.

Successive Editions

In large offices the process of making up is not done once, but many times, each day. The number of editions put out by the average newspaper may range from two to ten, seldom less than four, and each must be made up anew to accommodate later news and to suit the interest of varying circulation. The "all-day" newspaper is common in the cities, whether it be called an "afternoon" or a "morning" paper. In some cities one may buy after the theater at night the first edition of the following day's paper. The average city morning newspaper closes its first mail edition for distant points between nine and ten o'clock of the evening before. Another mail edition goes to press just before midnight, and a third between one and two A. M. The city edition is not closed until almost four in the morning, and it may consist of two editions, one for distribution by carriers and the other for morning street sale. The afternoon newspaper starts printing its first edition just before nine in the morning. Before eleven it is printing its noon edition. An early mail edition goes to press about noon, and the home edition for the carrier boys is on the press by three. After that it may issue a street edition to catch the reader going home from work, a late sporting edition, or a market edition containing closing quotations. Some newspapers issue ten editions a day, one each hour.

Edition Make-up

Each successive edition means a new task for the make-up man. The news pages must be remade to present later news. The mail editions must carry news of interest to readers outside the city, and the city editions must emphasize local events. The banner heads must be changed with each successive street edition, whether or not later news has come in. Usually certain pages, *i.e.*, the editorial page, woman's page, advertising pages, and feature pages, remain the same throughout all the editions, but the remainder of the paper is changed throughout. As soon as the stereotypers have made a matrix of the front page, even before the plates are on the press, the make-up man has ripped open the form and begun the make-up of the next edition. An edition in-

NEWSPAPER MAKE-UP

volving change only of the front page or an extra remaking between regular editions is a *replate*.

Make-up Language

Some of the expressions used in the printing office indicate the progress of the make-up man's work. When all the copy has been sent to the composing room by the editorial staff, the copy is *all in hand*, and when it is in type ready for make-up it is *all set* or *all up*. Each page *form*, consisting of a steel *chase* which forms the frame for the page of type, is made up on the *stone*, a table with a smooth stone or metal top. After the form is made up, it is *planed* down with a block of wood and a mallet to give it an even surface; any type or slugs that are not standing squarely on their bottoms are said to be *off their feet*. Before the form is *locked up* with wedge-shaped metal *quoins*, it is *justified*—all space is taken up with *leads* between the lines. Unimportant short material used to fill holes in the make-up is called *filler*. The form is then said to be *closed* and is *put away*, or turned over to the stereotypers; if any changes are required after it has been closed, it must be *ripped open*. In some offices, the paper is said to have been *put to bed* when the plates have been bolted on the press ready for printing. The last page to be made up before the *deadline* is the *starter page* because it starts the presses. A new edition making over only the front page is a *replate*. Boxes on either side of the top of the front page, beside the *name-plate*, are *ears*. The blank space left for *stop-press* news, such as sporting results, is the *fudge box*. Matter is *squared up* in adjoining columns under one wide headline. The line that cuts off the bottom of such squared up material, or of any story that is incomplete, is a *cut-off rule*. The *fold* is the important horizontal line dividing the top and bottom of the page.

II. The Real Problems of Make-up

The study of newspaper make-up in its broader sense involves more than the mere mechanical process of transferring type from galleys to form and solving the puzzle of fitting stories into irregular spaces. It involves the entire study of the external, physical appearance of the finished newspaper—the problems of printing design and appeal. Many of the problems involved have no definite solution; many are merely questions of taste; to most of them there are many answers. But the young man who is just entering the newspaper business and the old newspaper man who has spent his life over the copy desk, too busy to think of the printer's work, will find it to his advantage to investigate the answers given to these questions by other newspaper men and the precedents followed in other newspapers. In few of the following discussions will an attempt be made to point out the best practice; the intent is merely to open up the various problems to the interested student. Further study must be carried on with the newspapers themselves. It is hoped that the discussion will arouse interest in the question of why one newspaper achieves a pleasing make-up and why another fails to be physically attractive.

The Front Page

Because the front page is the most important page in the modern newspaper, it must be studied as a separate problem, although many of its questions apply with equal force to other pages. It is obvious that the necessity of uniformity requires that the inside pages conform with the front page, but it is apparent that the front page has many individual problems.

1. *Body type* is the first problem and must be studied with the relation to other type as well as to paper. The selection of body type involves both size and face, with reference to easy legibility and desired appearance. It is obvious that only type can be considered that is available on the linotype machine, since most newspapers use that machine or something like it.

The average newspaper reader would probably declare that all newspapers use the same size of type in the body of their reading matter. Such is not the case. The common practice among city newspapers is to set their reading matter in minion (7-point), with unimportant stories in nonpareil (6-point) and in some cases the editorials and important stories in brevier (8-point). Country and small city papers commonly use brevier throughout. Occasionally a country newspaper is found that uses bourgeoise (9-point) or brevier on a 9-point body. The reason for this is that the city paper desires to crowd as much reading matter as possible into its pages. The country paper, on the other hand, cannot afford to set up so much material, and therefore uses a larger type.

The face of the body type is even less obtrusive, but it has more to do with the appearance of the finished newspaper. It involves the question of tone and contrast. Some newspapers desire great contrast and use a thin-faced body type with a very bold headline type; the contrast causes the headlines to stand out prominently on a background that is almost white at a distance. Other newspapers prefer to give their pages a uniformly gray tone without contrast, for they use moderately black body type with light-faced headline type.

2. *Display in body type* is significant because of its effect on the finished newspaper. Some newspapers set all their reading matter *solid* without emphasizing any individual parts; others try constantly to make the important leads and significant paragraphs stand out from the surrounding matter. The entire question is limited by the possibilities afforded by the linotype machine, since few newspapers will bother to set individual paragraphs by hand for the sake of display. In general only two kinds of display are possible on the linotype machines in use in most offices—the use of larger, blacker type and the utilization of white space. The first involves setting all the reading matter in capitals, small capitals, or boldface type; all of these are possible without changing the machine's magazine, for the average linotype has black face instead of italics. The second involves "leading out," placing strips of metal between the lines, or indenting every line so that the type body is separated from the column rules by white space. It is possible, of course, to set some reading matter in boxes (framed with a line on all four sides inside the column rules), or to use larger type or double measure (lines two columns long), but none of these things can be done without adjusting the machine and adding some handwork.

3. *Headline display* must be considered by itself and in its relation to body type. If contrast is sought, a larger, blacker headline type is used and readability is an important factor. In size, headline type has grown from

the 10-point and 12-point, formerly used, to 24-, 36-, and even 72-point in one-column heads; the average is probably 24- or 36-point in major heads and something smaller in subordinate heads. In general a condensed or extra-condensed type is used, but the face is changing very much. Until recently some form of the Gothic was the commonest headline type, but now a more rounded letter, such as Caslon, Cheltenham, Bodoni, is becoming more popular. At the same time, the all-capital-letter top decks are in many cases being replaced by caps-and-lower-case. One of the most significant movements in newspapers in recent years has been the study of the readability of headline type. Many editors have come to feel that the typical headline schedule is too traditional and in general ineffective; they are breaking it radically. On the other hand, they realize that too much variety of type in headlines is faulty; hence a modern tendency is to use one type family throughout their headline schedule.

The number of decks depends entirely upon the amount of display desired. If originality and variety are desired in the make-up, one of the easiest ways to achieve them is to depart from the standard two- and four-deck forms. The headline of more than four decks is rare because it takes too much space and is probably not read. The use of two varieties of major heads and two of subordinate heads greatly facilitates make-up. The matter of headline display must be decided upon the basis of the newspaper's policy. If the newspaper desires to convey the impression of solid, reliable conservatism, it uses small, inconspicuous headlines; if it desires to appear bright, wide-awake, and enterprising, it uses larger headlines of constantly varying appearance. The most striking tendency of the day is the reduction in the number of decks; there is an increasing number of newspapers that use nothing longer than two decks.

Some modern tendencies may be expressed thus:

1. Do not make headlines so extensive that you develop "headline readers" who do not read the stories.
2. Many typographical experts declare that 18-, 24-, and 30-point type is large enough for any major dropline.
3. Too much display results in confusion and no display at all; the emphasizing of one or two stories is the best way to advertise the news.
4. All stories should have headlines; the use of BULLETIN, LATEST, etc., is useless.
5. Don't set drop-lines of the same form side-by-side, "tombstone fashion"; they destroy each other.
6. Too much variety in headline type is displeasing.
7. The two-deck top head saves space and time and adequately displays the news.
8. Headlines should not be huddled together "above the fold," leaving the bottom of the page without interest.

Banner headlines have undergone a strange evolution. They were invented to assist in street sales. As afternoon newspapers depend more largely on street sales than do morning papers, afternoon papers adopted them rather generally and morning papers did not. The question was decided mainly on the basis of circulation—is it mainly street sale or subscription? That was the status until the outbreak of the World War. Then, because of the bigness of the news, banners were adopted by many morning newspapers, some of which had a decided reputation for conservative make-up. After the war these newspapers, instead of abandoning the banner headline, continued to use it for other news. We then saw them artificially featuring news for the mere purpose of creating a reason for their banner heads. What the outcome will be, time alone will decide. It seems evident, however, that since the streamer's only value is to assist the newsboy, it will gradually be abandoned by those newspapers which do not depend largely on street sales. Whether or not the banner improves the appearance of the paper is a matter of taste. The chief fault of the banner headlines is that it often "overplays the news." About five days out of seven no news warrants the prominence; on these five days, "to dress up the page," a story is overwritten and overplayed. Since the story most suitable for this purpose is usually of the sensational type, the banner emphasizes crime and violent death far above its real importance. Some offices purposely "play" the story with "sales value" regardless of its relative worth. The ultimate result is that it is forcing all newspapers into "street sale competition," and training readers to buy on the street the paper with the loudest scream rather than to subscribe regularly for the worth-while paper.

Spreads and layouts have undergone the same evolution as banner heads. They have been borrowed from the evening papers, which used them for advertising purposes, by the morning newspapers which have little use for them. Many a newspaper that boasted of never using a spread more than once a year now is using them every day. It may be pointed out, further, that the spread has served a valuable purpose in emphasizing the occasional "big" story that the office must handle.

The use of subheads is another questionable point. They undoubtedly make the newspaper more readable, but they also break up its continuity. Many a system of headlines and body type carefully worked out to give the sheet a uniform, pleasing tone has been wrecked by the use of too prominent subheads. Much care must be taken in selecting them. If the editor desires great contrast on his page, he should of course use conspicuous subheads to accord with the conspicuous headlines; black-face type in capitals and lower case will accomplish this. If he desires a uniform tone, his subheads should be set back into the paper; light-face capital or small capital subheads will break up his stories without resulting in great contrast. The frequency of the subheads should be decided on the same basis. In wording and content, the subhead must necessarily accord with the tone of the newspaper. The "snappy," colloquial subhead is decidedly out of place in the thoughtful journal, and the empty, label subhead is as much at variance with the lively sheet. All the various elements of the newspaper must accord with its policy.

4. *Number of Stories.*—Although many readers are not aware of it, newspapers vary greatly in the number and length of the stories carried in a single edition—especially on the front page. Many editors are convinced that their readers prefer to read a little about many different subjects; other editors are equally sure that their readers prefer to know all about a few subjects. It would appear that the first idea would be more in accord with the policy of the light, popular newspaper, and yet there are papers of this class that follow the definite policy of printing a few long stories. Certain it is that no news-

paper has room enough to print all the news and some selection must be made. If many short stories are used, the page contains more headlines and has greater variety; it gives the reader the impression that he is getting a great amount of news for his money. It is impossible, on the other hand, to treat any given story in an adequate, exhaustive way; the reader may get the idea that many things have been hinted at, but few have been fully covered. The result is that the many-story paper appears less thoughtful. It also contains less reading matter because much of the space is devoted to headlines. From the make-up man's point of view, it is much simpler to put together a page of many stories since their relative importance is not so marked and more elasticity is afforded. The policy must be determined definitely; middle ground in the matter is difficult to maintain, since variation of length has so much to do with relative emphasis that it can hardly be trusted to a changing news staff. The character of the news thus handled has little effect on the length of the stories; uniformly long stories may be as guilty of sensationalism as uniformly short stories and vice versa.

5. *The Breaking of Stories from the Front Page to a Later Page.*—There are newspapers that make a practice of completing front-page stories on that page. There are others that uniformly begin many stories on the front page and break them to inside pages. The latter practice gives the varied effect obtained by the use of many short stories, without sacrificing conclusiveness in the handling of the news. There are certain things to be said for each practice. Much breaking over gives much variety and interest to the front page; it crowds more subjects into

that limited space; it gives the newspaper the appearance of carrying more news than it does; it leads the reader into the advertising pages. Break-overs, however, seriously complicate the task of make-up; any change of the front page requires change on an inside page and the making up of succeeding editions involves the remaking of more forms. Many readers, also, find frequent break-overs very annoying. It is certain that a story should not break on a paragraph, and that the breaking-over of just a few lines is decidedly bad.

When all, or nearly all, of the front-page stories are completed on that page without breaking over, the question arises of breaking long stories from column to column. If a story begins in column 2 and is too long to be completed in that column, where shall the rest of it be placed? A few papers prefer to place it at the top of the next column, thus carrying the reading matter continuously from column to column. Others place it at the bottom of the next column, separated by a cut-off rule. The second practice reserves the top of each column for headlines, but it often involves some difficulty for the reader in finding the rest of the story. The former practice is best suited for the reader who peruses his newspaper from beginning to end like a book; the second is best for the reader who scans and reads at random.

6. *Illustrations.*—In former days when wood-cuts were the only illustrations possible, the only question was one of cost. But since the development of the photographic process of engraving and the growth of syndicate cut services, illustrations have been brought within the reach of every newspaper. The question with the individual newspaper is what kind of illustrations, how large and

how many, and in what position. On the front page illustrations of the right kind doubtless aid in the sale of papers. Some newspapers follow the practice of printing one cartoon on the front page each day; others use the space for a single half-tone illustration of some phase of the news; still others use a number of smaller cuts, usually portraits, scattered about the page. When the paper can obtain the services of a good cartoonist, the cartoon is probably the best front-page illustration. But it is much cheaper to hire a photographer or buy photographs from a syndicate; the cost of the engraving is about the same in either case. When no cartoonist is available, the question can usually be reduced to a choice of one large cut or several small ones. The large cut has the advantage in that it can present a more interesting picture than a one-column portrait; on the other hand, it seems to demand a position at the top of the page and occupies the space valuable for featuring important news. The small cuts break up the page, but they can be placed anywhere and occupy relatively unimportant space. The chief difficulty is the position. Unless symmetrically arranged small cuts break up symmetry in typography. If symmetrically arranged, the cuts give the page a stiff, formal appearance. A large cut or layout of small cuts is most difficult to place. In a seven-column paper, the cut must be three, five, or seven columns wide to center in the page; in an eight-column paper it must be two or four columns wide to center. Two-column cuts are too narrow and four are too wide. If the cut occupies the center of the top of the page, it is cut in half when folded on the news-stand and loses its effectiveness. If placed on the right side so as to be on top of the news-stand, it occupies the most valuable space in the newspaper, besides giving an ungainly looking page when the paper is opened. If placed on the left or at the bottom it does not show on the news-stand and therefore loses its value as an attraction for buyers. Some editors can see little advantage in front-page cuts since, unless the stereotyping and press work are excellent, half-tone cuts do not print clearly. The entire problem of front-page illustration is a knotty one and is probably usually solved by the answer of the question, Is the cut worth the valuable space it fills?

7. *Position of Prominence.*—This is not a problem but a fact. On the front page the two outside columns are the most prominent because they are set off by the margins at the side. The top of the last column to the right is the better for two reasons: (1) it is on top as the paper lies flat on the news-stands; (2) its story can be continued in the first column of the second page. The top of the last column to the left is next in prominence because, as the paper is opened, it is the logical beginning of the newspaper. The other columns are almost equal in importance, although those nearer the right are in sight on the news-stand. When a large cut occupies the top of the page, the columns beginning under the cut are emphasized. In judging the importance of various columns, some editors consider the appearance of the newspaper on the news-stand; others think of it as opened in the reader's hands. Many editors solve the problem by devoting certain columns to certain news, *i.e.*, the last on right to local news, the last on the left to national news.

8. *Symmetry.*—Balanced and symmetrical arrangement of headlines and other front-page display is a prob-

lem that almost every newspaper has wrestled with. Newspapers in America have ranged themselves into several groups in seeking a solution, and their pages may be roughly classified thus: (1) The balanced, symmetrical page; (2) the dissymmetrical "focused" page; (3) the helter-skelter, "circus" make-up, seeking only novelty; (4) the page of contrast and balance. Some make an effort to attain symmetry; others frankly avoid symmetry and seek a changing front page. There are a few newspapers that maintain strict symmetry at the top of the front page, but make no effort to balance the headlines in the lower half.

While the newspapers that avoid symmetry can hardly be discussed in connection with the question of attaining a balanced front page, it is worth while to notice what they seek to do. The dissymmetrical "focused" front pages, instead of spreading out the news in an orderly way so as to give equal emphasis to several stories, attempt to drive the reader's attention to one spot and to center all interest in one story. They do this, not by disorderly, hit-or-miss arrangement of headlines, but by a carefully worked out scheme of concentrated display. The third class—the helter-skelter "circus" page—frankly has no scheme of arrangement at all. It simply seeks novelty and variety by scattering headlines in a kaleidoscopically changing mass each day. The fourth group usually seeks balance, but constantly varies the method of attaining it. Instead of using the same form of headlines each day, as does the first group, this class uses one-column headlines one day, two-column the next, boxes or pictures the next—but always on a careful plan.

Symmetrical front page make-up aims to display alternate columns and at the same time to emphasize the two outside columns. It is easy to obtain with seven columns or in any page which has an *odd* number of columns. In the seven-column front page, symmetrical arrangement of the top of the page is usually attained by placing display headlines in the first, third, fifth, and seventh columns, and by using less prominent headlines in the second, fourth and sixth. This method emphasizes four stories and gives excellent balance. In some cases, the headlines in the third and fifth columns, while standing out above the smaller heads, are less prominent than the first and seventh headlines. This gives symmetry while emphasizing two stories. The same balance is accomplished in many seven-column pages by the use of two-column spreads in the first and second, and sixth and seventh columns, with a displayed headline in the fourth column. When a cut is used in the seven-column page, it is usually one column wide and in the fourth column, or three columns wide in the center of the page. In the latter case, the two long heads can be balanced below it. The arrangement of the lower half of the page is usually determined by the fact that the stories under the prominent heads are the longest. The first and seventh stories frequently extend to the bottom of the column; the third and fifth extend almost to the bottom; the second, fourth and sixth are shorter. This brings small heads high up on the even-numbered columns and low down in the third and fifth columns.

Symmetry is more difficult to attain in eight columns or in any page of an *even* number of columns because two columns must be grouped together as displayed or undisplayed. Some newspapers solve it by breaking up the space with a cartoon or illustration, and almost invariably they place the cut at one side because the best front-page cut, the three-column cut, cannot be centered in eight columns. It matters not whether the cut is placed to the right or the left of the center, but different effects are attained through the choice of columns. If the cut occupies, for example, the fifth, sixth, and seventh columns, the most prominent headlines occupy the first, third, and eighth columns.

Styles of front page make-up are invented by the metropolitan press and copied by smaller newspapers, often without regard to their suitability to the paper's field. It would seem plain that the "circus" and the "focused" page, with the daily banner head, have little place in a conservative small city daily or country weekly. It is to be hoped that the community press may evolve a make-up of its own, disregarding the methods of sensation, of street sale competition, and other factors of large city journalism.

Make-up Problems of the Paper as a Whole

Many of the questions discussed above apply equally well to the entire newspaper; uniformity requires that the front page set the precedent for all succeeding pages in the matters of type, display, and general form. There are other problems, however, that are of equal importance in the physical appearance of the newspaper.

1. *Number of Columns per Page.*—Until recently most newspapers have been printed in seven thirteen-em columns per page. Within the past few years, however, it has been found that a great saving of paper can be effected by the adoption of eight columns per page, with-

out materially enlarging the sheet. The increased cost of white paper has been largely the reason. The addition of an eighth column on each page of an eight-page newspaper gives an additional 160 inches of advertising space or over 10,000 words of reading matter without increasing the paper cost. The space for the extra column is ordinarily gained by reducing the width of the margins and by narrowing the columns from 13 to 12½ ems—that is, from 2 1/6 to 2 1/12 inches. The narrowing of the columns is not noticeable to the reader and ordinarily no corresponding reduction in advertising rates is made. The extra 20 inches of space per page is therefore clear gain, so far as paper cost is concerned. Some newspapers, however, have been slow in making the change because it necessitates a rebuilding of their presses.

2. *Number of Pages and Sections.*—On small newspapers which employ flat bed presses, the number of pages is definitely set by the capacity of the press; all additional pages over the standard edition must be handled as insets or extra sections. This problem is therefore determined for them mechanically. To the newspaper which has a rotary press, the number of pages is usually determined on the basis of the amount of advertising carried. Before the war, the common proportion was from forty to forty-five per cent advertising, with fifty-five or sixty per cent reading matter. Increased printing costs have reversed the proportion; the average newspaper now devotes from fifty-five to eighty per cent of its space to advertising. In a seven-column, eight-page paper, containing in all fifty-six columns, the amount of advertising space totals some thirty

to forty columns. If the advertising department sells more than about thirty-five columns of display for any one issue, the number of pages and amount of reading matter must be increased accordingly. Ordinarily the pages are increased in multiples of four, since two-page insets are awkward. When the number of pages is increased four or eight pages, the editor must then decide whether to print the additional pages as a second section or fold them in with the main body of the paper. In some offices this matter is settled by the capacity of the press. When the paper has more than one press of large capacity, either plan is feasible, but the use of a second section doubles the speed with which the newspaper may be printed. On the large rotary presses, the increase in the number of pages decreases the output per minute accordingly; if half the pages can be printed as another section on a second press, the entire paper may be printed as quickly as one section.

In relative rank, the pages usually are: (1) Page one; (2) page three, because the eye strikes it after turning inside; (3) page 2, because it is the "turn page"; (4) the back page. If there is a second section, its first and last pages rank high. Right-hand, or odd pages, are more important than left-hand. That is why many newspapers jump stories to left-hand pages, reserving odd pages for new stories. Different offices have various ideas on this matter, as well as on the ranking of columns on inside pages.

3. *Position of Advertising.*—This is a matter that is difficult to settle because the advertiser has his own ideas about the position of the space he buys and few newspapers can disregard his wishes. With due regard for

his influence, certain phases of the question may be noted. Since the front page has become something more valuable than a wrapper, most large papers are agreed that none of its space should be sold to the advertiser. The large papers that carry advertising on the front page are rare. But on the inside pages practices differ. Some papers crowd their advertisements together so that their reading pages are kept fairly free of advertising. Others prefer to yield to the advertiser's wish to be near reading matter. In the latter case they sell two or more columns of each inside page. In the selection of the columns to sell practices differ. Some papers confine their advertisements to the last two columns to the right, reserving the more prominent left-hand side of the page for reading matter; others sell the outside columns on either side, saving the space in the center; others crowd all advertisements into the bottom of the page; still others seem to leave the matter to the printer who makes up the advertisements. The most popular arrangement is the "pyramid page" which is made up with the widest advertisement at the bottom and successively narrower ads above it, each resting against the right-hand margin. The result is an upright pyramid of ads on the bottom and right of the page and an inverted pyramid of reading matter at the top and left. Whatever the policy, however, the laying out of the advertisements should be supervised by the editorial department so that an otherwise attractive make-up may not be marred by a careless and heterogeneous placing of ads.

4. *Advertising Display.*—There has been some tendency toward limiting the amount of display in advertisements. The movement was started by James Gordon

Bennett, Sr., when he refused to allow cuts or display type in the advertisements of the New York *Herald*. Some newspapers tell their advertisers in advance what type and cuts may or may not be used, or fix a cash penalty for undue display. They realize that all attempts to increase the attractiveness and tone of their pages may be thwarted by one overdisplayed advertisement. Some newspapers refuse to use any black-face type larger than a certain specified size, requiring that larger type must be of the outline or shaded variety, which gives display without blackness. In the same way some refuse to use cuts of more than a certain blackness and forbid the use of broad, black rules or other borders. They thus require that their advertisements conform to the same scheme of tone and contrast that they have selected for their news columns. The matter of daily or frequent change of advertising copy is a problem rather beyond our discussion, but many editors are thinking about it in their attempt to make their advertisements as much a part of the reading matter of their pages as their news stories.

5. *Departmentizing.*—The basis of departments has changed in our newspapers: (1) It was formerly a matter of grouping *news* of various kinds; (2) it is now a matter of classifying *readers* and developing special departments for various groups—*e.g.*, sports, society, books. The newspaper of former days was almost completely divided into departments and special columns. Every item was classified and placed in the proper section. The news department scheme is still followed to a large extent in the more conservative of American newspapers. The objection to it, however, is that strict classification of the

newspaper's news thwarts the proper displaying of the important stories. Hence we find that the average newspaper is growing away from the news department idea and the more radical editor is abandoning it altogether. When we find that the news department scheme is maintained, we find it modified by the practice of taking out of the department the important items and leaving under the department head only the routine news. That is, the big sporting story, the society item of general interest, the unusual market story, the very important obituary, is found on the front page rather than in its proper classification. Certain departments still maintained in most newspapers are sports, society items, personals (in small papers), markets, obituaries, reviews and criticisms, editorials, etc. But the attempt to classify general news as local, state, national, foreign, shipping, railroad, police, courts, real estate, etc., has been largely abandoned, except in the case of the smallest items. The reasons for and against the news department idea depend, as do many other things in a newspaper, upon the clientele to which the editor caters. Undoubtedly the thoughtful, systematic reader, who either reads the entire paper or at least makes a point to read all news of certain kinds, likes to find items arranged in classified sections so that he can discover them all with little difficulty. The haphazard, chance reader, who scans at random seeking only the strikingly interesting or important news—the average American reader—is not willing to spend the time to read through the various departments in search of news. He likes to have the day's "specials" displayed at the top of the menu, for he wishes a few titbits rather than a complete, well-rounded meal. The editor decides the department problem on the basis of his circulation and is most likely to be thinking of *kinds of readers,* rather than of *kinds of news,* when he plans a department.

6. *The Editorials.*—The old-time American newspaper featured its editorials and gave them at least a page. Now, however, editorials have generally lost much of their prestige and in many newspapers are being maintained largely as an empty custom. Hence as the editorial section has shrunk gradually into a column or two, the page has become a problem of make-up. Since it is customary to place the publisher's announcement at the head of the editorial page, that fact, more than the importance of the editorials themselves, determines its place. The average newspaper uses a left-hand page near the center of the issue for its editorials, but since the page seldom contains more than two or three columns of editorials, the editor wonders what to do with the rest. Even if the editorials are set in larger type and wider columns, there is still half a page to fill. It is obviously no place for news, and we find a variety of practices exemplified. Some newspapers fill the remaining columns with editorials reprinted from other papers; some fill them with book and theatrical reviews; some develop a humor column and other features; some fill a large part of the space with a striking cartoon. The conservative newspaper finds these related subjects of value, but the more "popular" editor doubts their importance. Often the page deteriorates into a dead-wood section which is devoted to space fillers. The development of features that make it as interesting as the rest of the paper is an indication of enterprise. Certain newspapers, however, have demonstrated that careful make-up and some con-

sideration of content will make their editorial pages very valuable features.

The status and position of the editorial page suffered a marked change when the sensational newspapers hit upon the idea of using the editorials as circulation-builders, moving the editorials to the back page. Their idea has been taken up by many less sensational newspapers, and now one of the most conservative journals in the country uses the back page regularly as an editorial section. The change in position has also brought a change in make-up. The back-page editorial is usually set in larger type and double-measure and the entire page is put together with great care. Symmetry is obtained by using the four outside columns for double-measure editorials and filling the central portion with cartoons, anecdotes or other features. This use of the back page is valuable to the newspaper which desires to make a feature of its opinions and comments.

7. *Other Special Sections.*—Some of the modern departments that involve questions of make-up are the sporting page, the society section, markets, woman's section, obituaries.

The sporting department is maintained as a separate page or section in almost all American newspapers. It is in charge of a special editor and is given a fixed position. Some newspapers feature it by giving it the first page of the second section or by devoting to it a special four-page section on pink or green paper. The principal questions involved in its make-up are: to what extent shall important sporting items be lifted out of it, and to what extent shall other news be injected into it? Some newspapers make a practice of extracting important stories from it to be played up on the front page. Again when sports are dull, they use other news to fill up the sporting page. From an ethical point of view, other considerations are: relative amounts of local and outside sports; amateur sports encouraging physical exercise versus professional touting; relative amounts of home-made and syndicate or association material; presence of material that encourages betting or gambling; excessive publicity for professionals; material for women readers; and quality of English.

The society section usually varies in importance in inverse proportion with the size of the city in which the newspaper is published. Society news is of great importance in small cities and of less importance in large cities, although with the attempt to cater to women readers, society news has achieved a greater development in certain large cities. The make-up problem raised is whether society news should be maintained as a separate section of standard size and position, or whether it should be used as a convenient filler to utilize odd space. In newspapers that feature society news, the section is usually maintained in the same position each day under a prominent department heading. Certain journals even place the name of the society editor above it. Some develop one story each day into a "leader" and announce its content in a "blanket head" across the top of the page. The independence of the section is often accentuated by a different kind of typography. When the society editor prefers to devote the section to a few longer items, a distinguishing style of subhead is often selected for each item. When shorter items are used, they are often separated by asterisks, by classifying subheads, or even by the use of hanging indention in the set-up. Undoubtedly any variety of make-up that will make the section more attractive is of value. Society illustrations have been adopted by many newspapers, and when the newspaper cannot afford daily cuts of local social celebrities, it illustrates this page with syndicate pictures of national society lights. The society editor is usually allowed to break away from the newspaper's style sheet in the use of titles and tabooed expressions. Few social sections are so independent, however, that the managing editor hesitates to remove an important wedding notice or other significant social item to the front page.

The woman's section is a newcomer in the American newspaper because it is only recently that an attempt has been made to cater to the women readers. Its contents and make-up are, therefore, not to any great degree standardized. Each newspaper has its own ideas about the appeal to be made or is casting about blindly, keeping sharp watch for any indication of a successful strike. Certain newspapers have concluded that society news is women's news and have placed the two departments near together or have combined them. Almost every woman's section contains material on dress, fashion, and cooking. "Household Hints" is a common heading. After careful study of box-office business, some editors have placed theatrical news and criticism on the woman's page. Other journals, working on the basis that many women desire more thoughtful reading, have gone in for serious articles on woman's activities. Whether to make the section light or thoughtful is still a question. It is certain in most editors' minds, however, that the page must be typographically artistic and different from the rest of the paper; the use of illustrations, especially portraits and fashion cuts, is common with most of them.

The market section is a standard feature in many newspapers. In some cases it is merely a column, containing a general story on market conditions and closing quotations. Other newspapers, considering that this is primarily the business man's page, make a feature of it and employ a special editor to take charge of it. In such a case it is ordinarily subdivided into departments, but its articles carry the newspaper's standard headlines. The sizes of type and form of tables are often specified in the style sheet.

Obituaries are mentioned here because many newspapers devote a special section to them and make a point of including biographical sketches with each day's deaths. Typography is the only make-up question involved. The attempt is usually to condense the section into the smallest possible space, and type is chosen with this idea in mind. In some newspapers, the obituaries are printed entirely in smaller type; in others the first paragraph is in ordinary type and the sketch is in finer type. In some cases, the succeeding obituaries are separated by black-face sub-heads indicating the deceased's full name; in others a rule separates the items and the obituary is distinguished by the surname in light-faced capital letters run in the first line as a side-head.

The "Radio," automobile, and other special pages that come and go involve few make-up problems not common to the rest of the newspaper.

8. *The Back Page.*—Until recently the back page was considered a wrapper and of small importance. Most newspapers sold as much as possible of it to advertisers

and filled the remainder with unimportant material. Its real importance was pointed out by the so-called sensational newspapers that turned it into an editorial page. Other editors have devised other uses for it. One of the earliest was the back-page comic section. In 1914 a Chicago newspaper turned the back page into a second front page devoted to local news. The basic idea was not entirely new, for many small city papers had printed some local news on the back page, interspersed with advertisements. But to eliminate all advertisements from its columns, to repeat the journal's name at the top, and to give it as much attention as the front page, was a new step. Later came the idea of a full page of pictures on the last page. And so on. The importance of the back page will probably lead to further experiments.

9. *Length and Number of Stories.*—As suggested in the discussion of the front page, newspapers show a great diversity of opinion in deciding whether to print a large number of short stories or a relatively small number of long articles. The reasons for and against, as discussed above, apply throughout the paper, although it may be added that the adoption of a definite policy greatly facilitates the work of the make-up man. The consideration is one of editing. Front-page stories, handled as they are with greater care, are ordinarily likely to be worth the space they occupy. Stories on the inside pages are in many cases long simply because they are loosely written and strung out beyond the length warranted by the facts. Many can be found in almost any newspaper that would be greatly improved by a thorough boiling.

10. *Fillers.*—To what extent should the make-up man be allowed to use "fillers," two- or three-line items, to

plug up the holes in his make-up? In the most carefully edited newspaper, fillers are never used, and the make-up must come out even without them. In smaller offices, the practice is sanctioned to the extent of providing the make-up man with a galley of ready-made fillers. Jokes, anecdotes, axioms, epigrams, statistics, condensed statements of fact, advertising readers, and anything that can be crowded into two or three lines is used. Some editors use personal items as fillers or even slugs reading "Subscribe for the Leader," "Watch Our Want Ads." The use of fillers is of great assistance in make-up, but much objection is offered on the score that frequent fillers give the page a patchy appearance. Certain it is that they must be chosen with care when they are used, so that the reader may not be annoyed by inadvertently plunging into a silly joke at the bottom of a serious discussion. The practice of using fillers, while not always bad, can easily be overworked.

11. *Syndicate Material.*—With the development of syndicated reading matter and illustrations in plate and matrix form, the newspaper editor has to give much thought to deciding how much of it to use. Certain it is that by patronizing syndicates he can supply more interesting material to his readers than he can have written in his own office. He can give his readers a broader outlook on the news of the world in words and pictures than his staff can provide, and in general his syndicate material is written in better style than his staff articles. On the other hand, many of his readers who take two newspapers, may find the same material in both. Every inch of syndicate material, furthermore, crowds out an inch of local material, and to all newspapers local news

brings popularity and circulation. Many an editor spends so much money and space on syndicate material that he prints little else—part of the money put into a better local staff would improve his business. Since neither a complete exclusion nor an excessive use of syndicate material is advisable, it would seem wise to establish a definite office rule specifying what proportion of the news columns shall be devoted to each kind of material.

12. *Illustrations.*—The question of illustrating the inside pages is as important as that of pictorial art on the front page. Syndicate pictures in matrix form can be purchased more cheaply than cuts can be made, but undoubtedly they do not have the news value of the local picture. An indistinct, bleary half-tone showing the "Ruins After the Broad Street Fire," snapped by the staff photographer, is certainly worth half a dozen excellent cuts of "Vesuvius in Eruption" or "The Miraflores Locks." A smudgy half-tone of "James Jones, Rock Valley Pioneer," draws many more readers than an excellent portrait of "The Duke of Fido in Hunting Attire." But not every editor has a staff photographer, a near-by engraver, and a purse to illustrate his local news. There is also the possibility of the ever-interesting diagrams, maps, and sketches, to illustrate the news, if some one can be found to draw them.

In the selection of photographs for newspaper use certain axioms may be followed:

1. Picture should tell its own story; the reason why it is printed, its news value or interest, should be clear at a glance. Thus a mechanical device should be shown in use. The caption merely enlarges on the picture's message.

NEWSPAPER MAKE-UP 223

2. Picture should be pruned down, silhouetted, or otherwise reduced to its essentials—its story. Confusing background should be cut out.
3. Picture should contain human interest—a person—to add interest and show size of other objects. The "pretty girl" appeal, however, is overused.
4. Photograph must contain contrast for the photoengraving process will "flatten out" the picture.
5. Classify pictures as "news pictures," which must be run at once, and "feature pictures" whose interest will last for a time.
6. Pictures should not be revolting or disgusting.
7. "Natural poses" are better than stiff portraits.

Some technical considerations are:

1. For half-tone cuts, best copy is unmounted glossy photograph, 4x5 or larger. Specifications needed are: I. Width of cut in inches; II. Fineness of screen (50 to 85 lines for stereotyping; 85 to 100 for unstereotyped newspapers; 120 or finer for books and magazines); III. Edge finish (square, oval, outline, vignette); IV. Hand work (retouching, routing out, tooling); V. Name and address of sender; VI. Time at which cut is desired.
2. For line engravings, best copy is black ink or charcoal on heavy white paper. Specifications: I. Width of cut; II. Area and number of Ben Day shading, if any; III. Hand work, if any; IV. Name and address; V. Delivery time.
3. Write specifications, captions, etc., on sheet of paper and paste it lightly to back of photo. Never typewrite on back of photo.

13. *Comics.*—The great rage at present is to print a large number of so-called "comics," either in regular

series of comic strips, or as illustrations to chance jokes. They may be bought from the syndicates at a price that makes their use very desirable. A few editors scorn their use. Others look upon them as a necessary evil like the Sunday comic supplement, detesting them while realizing that they sell papers. It is certain that when a paper runs a series of good comics, many readers will turn to them before reading the front page; it is also certain that the comic back pages of many city newspapers are read in advance of the news. But on the other hand, while granting this, editors dislike to base the popularity and sale of their newspaper on such trivial features.

14. *Ease of Reading.*—This has become so important that "Easy to Read" has already appeared as a newspaper motto. All but the most conservative of American journals have accepted the idea that their pages must be easy to read. In making the decision they acknowledge that they are catering to the casual reader rather than to the thoughtful reader. They are admitting that the man who will wade through an unattractive newspaper is fast becoming unknown. Some of them are forgetting this rare creature entirely and catering entirely to the casual reader; others are trying to reach both. When the latter ideal prevails, it is not a matter of news, but a matter of type and display, a matter of putting the words in the most legible, attractive form. The problem includes many of the questions discussed above. But once the matter of typography is settled, it is as much the problem of reporters and copyreaders as of make-up man. No printer's skill will make news easy to read unless it is written and edited with that idea in mind. This involves the use of short paragraphs, the frequent use of quotation marks,

graphical figures, meaty statements, sentence emphasis, and the knack of developing ideas in headlines. If a newspaper is to be easy to read, every one in the office must coöperate.

15. *What News to Emphasize.*—Many an editor leaves this important question to the hireling who makes up—except in the case of certain front-page stories. He forgets that it may be a matter of policy so important that newspapers have won or failed by it. Too few are the offices that have a definite aim, that have analyzed their circulation, as the magazine editor analyzes his, and made a conscious effort to supply and display the kind of material desired by that circulation. Too often it is a matter of what comes into the office or is easiest to obtain. One phase of the problem involves the relative value of local and telegraph news. Successful city dailies have made a definite study of this question and follow a definite scheme in the handling and placing of city, state, national and foreign news. Few smaller newspapers have. Hence we find many small city dailies, while fighting a life-and-death battle with city competition, devoting their front pages to condensed telegraph news and neglecting or burying local events. Little thought is required to show that they cannot win, for their meager outside news is overshadowed by the columns of their city rivals. But, of course, the telegraph news is cheaper to get than local news. The matter must be decided on the basis of circulation and competition. In a town near a great city, where the city dailies early in the morning supply citizens with outside news, the only field left open to the small town daily is local news. In a town far away from a city, however, the city population is not present and the

local daily has both fields to cover. But the question is not entirely confined to small towns. Many large city newspapers are more exclusively local than the smallest country weekly. Sometimes the policy is wise; sometimes it is not. At any rate it deserves study in each individual case.

Some editors make it a rule to put on the front page each day at least one piece of news for each of the various kinds of readers in their circulation. Few editors have analyzed this aspect.

Many newspapers "play up" the same kind of news each day, forgetting the wide range of interests among their readers. A wiser policy would be to study "reader interest" and to play different kinds in turn. The daily accident or daily crime may have universal appeal, but certainly many readers are displeased with it.

Although crime and violent death may occupy relatively a small amount of space, some editors, by crowding it all on the front page, make a "chamber of horrors" of their newspaper's show window.

The effort to get a "big story" every day often distorts the news sense of the staff. Not every day has a big story, especially in smaller cities, and a wiser policy would be to emphasize properly all news available.

Because of the extreme competition in some cities, there is a tendency in evaluating news to keep the editorial eye on the opposition newspaper, rather than on the reader. After all, the paper is published for the reader, and there is no reason why each newspaper cannot do its own job as it thinks best, without so much regard to "the other fellow." Readers seldom compare the rival newspapers.

Many newspaper practices are likely to be matters of

office discipline, rather than careful analysis of reader interest. The scoop, the by-line, the "backing in" on stories that were missed, the careful parceling out of first and second day stories, the dreary following out of certain routine news, and many other matters indicate a managing editor who is more interested in keeping his staff in order than in getting out a paper to interest his city.

Some standing features, such as daily records, routine court affairs, the weather, vital statistics, obituaries, are badly handled in some newspapers. There are often readers who are interested in these features.

Because of the number of syndicates, the energy of their salesmen, and the ease of using their product, many newspapers are making excessive use of this "non-news" material. Some are developing into "daily magazines," printing more entertainment than news. At the same time, they are neglecting the valuable "local feature."

The newly acquired "leased wire" leads many a community newspaper into excessive use of telegraph news, even to the extent of "playing up" non-local news above local news.

It is seldom that a newspaper staff evaluates its product with a footrule to see just what it is giving the public. The following "measure" of the contents of a small city newspaper and of a metropolitan newspaper may suggest a possible procedure. The figures are column inches:

Small City Daily.—Exclusive of advertising, the paper contains 1,217 inches of reading matter, divided thus: news, 583; non-news (mainly syndicate), 568; editorials, 76. By source, its news is divided thus: national, 275; local, 210; state, 83; foreign, 15.

By topic, its news divides thus: sports, 119; government, 63;

markets, 60; crime, 59; education, 39; county correspondence, 36; politics, 35; agriculture, 31; society, 30; social welfare, 25; music, 20; human interest, 14; obituary, 8; religion, 6; weather, 6; labor, 5; etc.

Non-news classifies thus: special features and cuts, 158; comics, 114; serial fiction, 58; movie news, 52; children's stories, 43; cartoons, 42; verse, 19; recipes, 16; fashions, 15; health, business advice, etc.

Conservative Metropolitan Newspaper.—Exclusive of advertising, it contains 1,578 inches of reading matter, divided thus: news, 1,112; non-news, 406; editorials, 60. By source, its news is: local, 586; national, 314; foreign, 174; state, 37.

By topic, its news is: business and finance, 366; government, 160; sports, 132; politics, 118; crime, 80; society, 59; arts and science, 34; shipping, 33; social welfare, 31; education, 27; human interest, 19; churches, 18; labor, 10; weather, 8; obituary, 4; fire, 4; civil courts, 3; scandal, 2.

Non-news classifies thus: special articles, 137; "colyums," 41; comics, 34; finance, 22; children, 14; household, 19; fiction, 14; etc.

Obviously neither newspaper has studied its readers as it might and is merely following a routine and a set of rule-of-thumb ideas. The small daily shows its new "leased wire" and is tending to be "a daily magazine."

It is likely that such an evaluation of newspaper make-up and content, combined with study of reader interest, will be one of the next steps in American journalism. The business office of the newspaper has been studied scientifically; but the editorial side is still somewhat cluttered with outgrown traditions, hit-or-miss guesses, prejudices, personal notions. A psychological study of it may show the reason for much present-day popular criticism of the press. But that is beyond the range of this book.

NEWSPAPER MAKE-UP

Exercises

1. If printing laboratory is available, make-up may be practiced on the stone. Linotype matter may be obtained from newspapers after it has been used in their regular editions.

2. If no printing laboratory is available, make-up may be practiced with shears and paste-pot. Newspapers may be cut up into stories, reduced to galley form, and made up anew in various ways.

3. Design and paste up front page dummies in imitation of various well-known newspapers.

4. Dummy designs may be made of various inside and department pages, such as editorial page, sport page, etc.

5. Remaking of front pages for replate editions may be practiced thus: Take today's local paper, assume big story breaks, remake front page to get it in. Vary character of "news break," and space needed for it.

6. Cut up newspaper front pages and remake in accordance with various styles of make-up, redesigning and rewriting headlines.

7. Practice making page schedules as foundation for dummies.

8. One part of class may make up advertising schedule and dummy; another group then takes it and works out editorial dummy.

9. Get all editions of one day of a metropolitan afternoon paper and study "remaking" involved.

10. Compare make-up of city and mail editions of a metropolitan morning paper.

11. Practice selecting photographs for print and writing specifications for engraver.

12. Search standard newspapers for examples of all matters discussed in above chapter.

13. Make a foot-rule analysis of a newspaper as suggested under "What News to Emphasize."

14. Draw up a set of office rules for make-up man amplifying those under "Headline Display."

15. Day after day, study news value of banner head story in various papers, watching for overplaying.

16. Analyze reader interest of a particular newspaper and draw up office rules for front page news display.

17. Analyze a newspaper page to determine how much space might be saved by certain changes in typography.

18. Analyze the make-up of Sunday supplements and special editions.

CHAPTER VI

SYNDICATE AND ASSOCIATION MATERIAL

ONLY a small proportion of the material printed in the average American newspaper today is prepared and written in the office. The present cost of production is so great that few newspapers can afford to hire a local staff large enough to write the newspaper's entire content every day. A large portion of their material is obtained from various coöperative and commercial agencies which are able to keep down the cost for any individual newspaper by supplying the same material to a large number of papers in various localities. In some small newspapers nine-tenths of the reading matter, exclusive of advertisements, is syndicated or association material. The proportion is of course smaller in large city dailies, although most of them depend upon press associations for their telegraph news. Rare is the newspaper which does not devote at least ten per cent of its space to material secured in coöperation with other publishers.

This coöperative material may be divided roughly into two classes: association and syndicate material. Association material is primarily current news supplied daily by telephone or telegraph to enable newspapers to obtain all the news of the world without maintaining an extensive system of correspondents. It includes also local news supplied in several large cities by city press associations. Syndicate material may include almost any kind of reading matter, supplied by wire, mail, or express, in typewritten form, proof form, plate form, or in stereotype mats. This material is made up of condensed telegraph news, features, fillers, editorials, illustrations, special articles, interviews, speech reports, sporting news, biographical material, ready-made advertisements, fiction stories and serials, comics, ready-made campaigns, and many other varieties. It is supplied by various methods and various companies and enables an editor to fill up at small cost all the many columns of his newspaper which are not occupied by local news, editorials, and advertisements.

The idea behind the syndicates and associations, whatever may be their form and method, is coöperation, cutting down the cost of newspaper making by dividing it among a number of newspapers. Thereby an editor is able to publish a readable newspaper at a fraction of the cost of individual, independent operation. It would be impossible to include in this brief discussion all the various ways in which newspapers coöperate; it will be sufficient to sketch the commonest means.

I. The Press Association

If every newspaper depended upon its own resources to gather all the news outside its own city, it would need a correspondent in every city, town, and hamlet throughout the entire world. In the early days of American journalism that is what every newspaper tried to do in a more or less extensive way. But no one newspaper was rich enough to cover the entire world with an adequate network of correspondents and the result was that various individual papers were constantly getting exclusive news of great import, to the dismay of their competitors, or being scooped on important news. The system was impossible; no one newspaper could gather all the news of the day through independent action. Besides this, the system led to a costly duplication of effort. If every one of the thousands of American newspapers had an adequate system of correspondents, most of the inhabitants of the globe would be newspaper correspondents. Co-operation in newsgathering to cover the news of the world has been evolved through a system of correspondents who represent entire associations of publishers rather than single newspapers. The modern newspaper depends upon such an association for the major portion of its outside news and maintains only a few special correspondents in localities in which it is especially interested.

The association system was started in America in 1848 when several New York newspapers organized coöperatively to gather the news of the city, especially shipping news. During the Civil War, their association spread over the country to other newspapers, until now about 1,250 newspapers are members of it and its news-gathering service is world wide. The organization is known as the Associated Press and is entirely coöperative. Each member assumes the obligation of supplying to the association the major portion of the news of its locality and in turn receives the news supplied by all the other members, rewritten and condensed in accord with the change in news value resulting from distance. The cost of operating the enterprise is divided proportionally among the many members. Certain newspapers, too small to be full members, receive a daily "pony" service—a condensed version of the world's news to the extent of a few hundred or few thousand words—and pay proportionately. Until recently the "A. P." was primarily a service for morning newspapers but it now has a complete afternoon service. Although it supplies to its members all the important news of the day, its principal field is news breaking between noon and midnight, too late for the evening papers. Ordinarily it has only one member in any city and does not supply its service to non-members.

Another great American news association is the United Press Associations, founded in 1907 for afternoon papers, now serving about 900. It is a private corporation which sells its service to papers at a fixed rate. Its relation to its customers is, however, similar to that of the Associated Press to its members, and in extent and operation it is much the same. Recently it has organized a morning service, known as United News. Among other smaller press associations are the International (afternoon) and Universal (morning) News Services, operated by the Hearst newspapers and selling news to others. Among the services of the past was the Laffan Service of the New York *Sun.* There is great rivalry between the various associations, and a newspaper is as proud of a scoop secured by its association as of one made possible by its local staff. These associations take care of all American news and obtain foreign news through correspondents in various parts of the world and in coöperation with the great news-gathering agencies of other countries, such as Reuter's, Havas, Fabre, Bullier, Central News, Stephani, and other agencies.

How the Association Works

The manner in which these press associations gather and distribute news may be illustrated by the organization of the Associated Press. The entire country is divided into several main divisions with headquarters in New York, Chicago, Washington, Atlanta, Kansas City, San Francisco, and other large news centers. The division headquarters are connected by main trunk lines of leased telegraph wires, some using double or triple wire service. The heart of the entire system is New York City, and from there main trunks run to the West via Chicago, the South via Washington and Atlanta, and to various large cities of New England and New York State. The southern division has its headquarters in Atlanta, Georgia, but much of its news is filed at its two ends, Washington and Kansas City, and meets at Memphis. Washington constitutes a separate center in itself. Chicago is the headquarters of the central division and has trunk lines to the Northwest via Milwaukee and St. Paul, to the Southwest via Kansas City, to the Coast via Omaha, Denver, Salt Lake City, and to St. Louis. Located at various points on these main trunk lines and subordinate to the division headquarters are many district, or bureau, offices, which have charge of the newsgathering and distributing in their immediate vicinities. Some bureaus constitute relay points in which main trunk news is repeated, and from some bureaus go out state circuits, such as the New York state wire, the Kansas state wire, and the Michigan state wire. This press association operates 82,000 miles of leased wire in 100 main circuits and 47 state or special circuits, employs 1,000 telegraph operators, has 55 bureaus in America and 27 abroad, and serves 1,250 newspapers. Smaller newspapers receive about 15,000 words a day, while larger papers get perhaps 45,000.

In organization the division office resembles a newspaper editorial office. Into it run telegraph wires from the other division headquarters, from the district offices of its division, and from various points in its local district. The work of the office consists in receiving news from these various sources, editing it to meet the needs of more or less distant newspapers, and sending it out again to other divisions, to its district offices, and to the various papers in its district. For example, suppose that an important story is sent in to the Chicago division office from its correspondent at Springfield, Illinois. If it is of sufficient interest, it is sent in full to the eastern and southern division headquarters and to its various district offices, in slightly condensed form to far western offices, and in greatly condensed form to the newspapers of its district that receive only "pony" service. If of less importance, it is condensed for transmission to all points, except within the division. If of local interest only it is sent out only to papers within its own district. At the same time stories are coming in from other divisions that require similar treatment for further distribution. Still other stories, while being condensed for local distribution, are "relayed" through the office from east to west or west to east. All that is needed for the work of the office is a number of telegraph operators and a few editors, known as *filing editors,* who have a highly developed sense of news values. The work of district offices is similar although on a smaller basis. Part of their work is to send directly to the newspapers within the district which receive full "leased wire" or "pony" services.

SYNDICATE MATERIAL

Most of this material is handled by telegraph. Some correspondence and distribution within a small district is done by mail. Long stories, such as complete speeches, which may be obtained in advance, are often sent out to the newspapers by mail, in typewritten or proof form, subject to "release" at a certain hour on a certain date or on the receipt of a release notice by wire. In some districts, pony services are distributed by long distance telephone, by a man in the district office reading into an instrument connected with a number of newspaper offices. In each office simultaneously a stenographer, with receivers clamped to his ears, takes down the news on a typewriter. When the service is received by telegraph, each newspaper must have a telegraph operator or receive the dispatches from the telegraph company's local agent. Most of the work is done by means of wires leased from the telegraph companies, and the newspaper that has its own operator is reached directly by a "loop" from the local telegraph office. A recent development in news transmission is the Morkrum Telegraph Printer, which is operated by a typewriter keyboard at the sending end and delivers typewritten copy at the receiving end.

How the Service Comes to the Newspaper

A newspaper that gets the complete service supplied to its district receives a more or less steady stream of matter from early in the day until after midnight, and its operator takes down the matter in continuous typewritten form on numbered sheets of copy paper. Each story is headed by a separate dateline to indicate its source and its end is indicated by the mark "30" used by the operators. The telegraph editor receives it sheet by sheet, edits it to suit the style and policy of his newspaper, cuts it up into stories, and turns it over to the composing room. After it reaches his hands it is handled as if it were local copy written by the reporters, although there is so much more than he needs that much of it must be thrown away.

Although the service comes in a continuous stream, rarely is a complete story sent at one time. For the benefit of newspapers that have several editions and wish to get an edition on the press soon after the service begins, much of the important news is crowded toward the beginning. Hence early in the day, the paper receives a series of leads of important stories, each marked "More" at the end. Thus the essentials of the day's news are received first. Later in the day the remaining parts of these stories come in, labeled "Add Cincinnati Fire," "Add Springfield, Mass., Murder," "Follow Jackson Speech." Perhaps if there is much news, each story is broken into three or four "takes" arriving at various times. Later come "New Lead Cincinnati Fire," "Revised Lead Smith Trial," "Corrections for Chicago Wreck." If the news is being supplied as fast as the correspondent gathers it, the same story may have a number of revised leads as the day progresses. Expecting this, the telegraph editor holds each story as long as possible, if later developments are likely, or uses the new lead for a later edition. Frequent break-ins are made for corrections of facts and names in previous stories. More important than these are the "Bulletins" and "Flashes," cut in to hasten the service. For example, if the service is bringing an account of a football game, sent play by play from the press box at the field, the telegraph operator is likely to fall far behind in his sending, although he started sending introductory and descriptive matter long before the game started. Hence to aid the papers that are holding up extras waiting for results, the operator cuts in a "flash" at the end of each period, giving the score at that time. By the end of the game, although he is still sending accounts of plays early in the game, he stops long enough to flash the final score. The newspaper may then close its forms and save the rest for a later edition.

For example, the "flashes" of one press association reporting the nomination of a presidential candidate were (in part):

> FLASH (at 1:16 p.m. C. T.)—Madison Square Garden, N. Y.—With votes still to come on this ballot John W. Davis will have a majority. He is the first candidate to reach a majority in the convention.
> FLASH (at 1:17 p.m.)—New York decided to change its votes and give Davis 90 votes after roll completed. Illinois expected to do likewise. Both Roosevelt and Brennan asking recognition.
> ADD RUNNING (1:18)—Brennan of Illinois asked recognition to change the vote to Illinois but was informed by the chairman that he must wait until conclusion of the ballot.
> FLASH (1:18)—Iowa asked recognition of chair to swing entire vote to J. W. Davis.
> FLASH (1:18)—Iowa withdraws Meredith's name and casts 26 votes for J. W. Davis.
> FLASH (1:20)—California changes to Meredith one; Walsh 4; J. W. Davis 21.
> FLASH (1:21)—Illinois changes vote to 58 for J. W. Davis.
> FLASH (1:22)—New York changes as follows: Walsh 28; Davis 60.
> FLASH (1:22)—Davis nominated.

Cable Messages

To save cost in cabling news, messages are usually skeletonized, or "skinned," before sending, and are translated, or "unskinned," by the newspaper or press association receiving them. Methods of "skinning" change, but the following newspaper cable (in part) will illustrate:

SKELETONIZED CABLE MESSAGE

7:48 p.m. Dec. 12 BERLIN Thompsons Vienna via Budapest Quote communications strike necessary consequence long reconstruction program and Austrian governments policy said foreign minister Grunberger interview chancellor Seipel intends keep his word to unadd item budget . . . (part omitted) . . . Seipel also protecting middle classes who been among worst sufferers Austria and recognized need of educated man for something moren food unquote asked whether any prospect socialists entering government ending continual fight wherefrom whole population suffers Grumberger said saw unway admitting socialists without fundamental changes policy whereto Austria pledged by league protocols unquote Seipel referred whole problem to parliament where socialists control twofifths votes compromise yet unfound estimated sixmillion letters await delivery industrial life practically standstill—Conger.

"UNSKINNED" MESSAGE AS PUBLISHED

VIENNA, December 12.—"The communications strike is a necessary consequence of the long reconstruction program and the Austrian Government's policy," said Foreign Minister Grunberger in an interview today.

"Chancellor Seipel intends to keep his word not to add an item to the budget . . . (part omitted) . . .

"Chancellor Seipel is also protecting the middle classes, who have been among the worst sufferers in Austria, and has recognized the need of the educated man for something more than food."

Asked whether there was any prospect of the Socialists entering the Government and ending the continual fight from which the whole population suffers, Herr Grunberger said he saw no way of admitting the Socialists without fundamental changes in the policy to which Austria had been pledged by the League protocols.

SYNDICATE MATERIAL

> Seipel has referred the whole problem to Parliament, where the Socialists control two-fifths of the votes.
>
> A strike compromise has not yet been found. It is estimated that 6,000,000 letters await delivery. Industrial life is virtually at a standstill.

II. CITY PRESS ASSOCIATION

In several large cities, notably New York, Chicago, and Pittsburgh, city press associations are maintained, co-operatively or otherwise, to gather local news. For each newspaper to send men to all the police courts, fire stations, hospitals, and other routine sources would mean much duplication, but through the city association, which maintains a staff of sixty or eighty reporters, they are able to cover the city at small cost. The city press service receives its news mainly by telephone from its reporters, has it written by a few office men, reproduced in many copies on a mimeograph machine (the desk man writes his story directly on the stencil) and sends it out through pneumatic tubes or private wires to various city newspaper offices. The newspaper editor depends largely on the city press for all routine news, usually rewriting the stories, and uses his own small staff to gather other news in which he is especially interested. From the point of view of the reporter, the city press affords excellent experience in newsgathering, but little opportunity to show writing ability. It is, however, a good place for the inexperienced beginner to go to when he seeks a position in the city, for if he does well there he is sure of consideration from the local city editors.

III. SYNDICATE SERVICES

Syndicate material is supplied to newspapers mainly by commercial firms which sell their service regularly or on occasion, charging on the basis of column, page, or week. The kinds of material supplied include almost every kind of reading matter that the newspaper editor needs. Syndicate services in general may be divided into four different classes; ready-prints, plate or matrix services, copy or proof services, and picture services. Several different kinds of service may be furnished by the same company and may be combined in a weekly service of various kinds.

Ready-Prints

This name is applied to a kind of service whereby the inside pages of a newspaper are printed in the syndicate's own plant. It is intended especially for small weekly and semi-weekly newspapers and is dubbed "patent insides." In such a service, the syndicate prints the two or four inside pages of the newspaper, one side of the sheet, and the country editor prints the outside. The syndicate's pages are filled with general feature and informational material, set up in accordance with the newspaper's general size and appearance, and the content is changed for each edition. Such ready-prints cost the newspaper little, if any, more than white paper, and the editor is saved one run on the press and half the composition of his newspaper. The syndicate makes its profit from the advertising carried in the ready-printed pages.

Plate Service.

The largest syndicate service received by small newspapers is a stereotype plate service sold by the column or the page. The content of the reading matter thus distributed is written and set in type in the syndicate office; it is then reproduced in the form of thin stereotype plates which are sent out to a large number of newspapers. The plates are one column wide, about two feet long and one-fourth inch thick, with grooved bottoms so that they may be fitted upon standard bases, kept by the newspaper, and thus be made type-high. The editor saws up the plates to fit the make-up of his newspaper and after he has used them returns them to the syndicate so that they can be melted up for future use. An editor who uses much of this matter is said to "edit his paper with a saw."

Almost any kind of reading matter can be purchased in plate form. The editor may buy several columns of condensed telegraph news, shipped to him each day early enough for his edition. His telegraph equipment then consists of a hack saw and a boy to meet the afternoon passenger train and receive the daily package of plates. He may buy all kinds of feature material, long or short, miscellaneous or classified. It may be a page of farm notes or a page on health. He may buy ready-made editorials and pert paragraphs, fillers and other short items, fashion notes, architectural ideas, political résumés, any kind of reading matter he desires. The syndicate will also supply him with plate illustrations of various kinds—cartoons, photographs of prominent persons and places, sketches, maps, humorous drawings, comic strips. One of the latest developments is a page of ready-made advertisements, written and set up in better form than the editor can accomplish, and arranged for him to mortise the name of the local advertiser at the bottom. These advertisements may be classified and accompanied by suitable reading matter to attract the advertiser. All of this material is supplied in the form of plates as wide as the standard column, or several columns, if it is illustrative material. In handling it, the editor saws off as large a piece as he wants to use, slips it upon a base of the proper length, and locks it into the page form. Only a person experienced in such matters can distinguish it from material set in his own office.

Matrix Service

A modification of the plate service is the distribution of reading matter in the form of papier-mâché stereotype mats. The editor receives the mat instead of the plate cast from it. A saving in shipping cost is thus accomplished, for the mats are very light, but the editor must have facilities for casting plates from the mats.

Biographical Syndicates

There are regular services which supply biographical sketches and photographs of persons in the public eye. The sketch is printed in compact form and the picture is supplied in the form of a cut, a matrix, or a print that may be reproduced. The editor who buys such a service files the material in his "morgue" ready for instant use as soon as an obituary or biographical sketch in the daily paper is needed.

Photo Syndicates

Illustrative material for the newspaper may be purchased at small cost from photo syndicates which make a business of taking news photographs in all parts of the world and supplying photographic prints to subscribers. The editor does not ordinarily buy a regular service, but receives batches of pictures at regular intervals, from which he may select those which he wishes to use. He pays for as many as he keeps and sends the rest back. Most of the news-feature pictures that appear in newspapers are obtained in this way, as shown by credit lines. In smaller newspapers, however, they were purchased in plate form from companies which bought them from photo syndicates.

Story Syndicates

A large amount of the fiction and serial stories carried by newspapers and small magazines is purchased from syndicates which make a specialty of this material. It is sold in typewritten or proof form, and the purpose of the syndicate is to divide up the author's price among a number of publishers. The plan was started a few years ago by a New York magazine which made a business of syndicating to Sunday newspapers the excess of good material that came to it from its contributors. A large part of the content of the Sunday supplement is obtained in this way. Many authors now sell syndicate rights on their works, as well as the right of publication in one magazine.

Syndicated Sunday Supplements

With the growth of the special illustrated Sunday supplement, many schemes have been invented to supply newspapers with the large amount of material needed. One of them is the syndicated Sunday magazines which the newspaper uses as a special supplement of its Sunday paper. Some newspapers print these Sunday magazines in their own plants, or buy the exclusive use of them, but the majority of the newspapers buy their Sunday magazines from a syndicate which supplies them ready printed. There are of course several Sunday magazines and only one newspaper in any city buys the same magazine.

Weekly Syndicate Services

A combination of the other kinds of feature service is the daily service designed especially for city newspapers of fair size. It consists of a daily bundle of printed pages containing enough reading matter to fill several newspapers and the stereotype matrices of a large number of pictures to illustrate it. The service contains news articles, special features, newsy interviews, editorials, jokes, sporting news, special department material, fillers, comics, cartoons, news photographs, national society news, fashion notes, health notes, material for special campaigns, and many other kinds of reading matter. The service is supplied to only one newspaper in any one city and, were it not for the necessity of publishing some local news, the editor could make his entire newspaper out of the syndicate material. Some of it, in fact, is as newsy and interesting as his telegraph news and can hardly be distinguished from the matter which he receives by wire. The entire service, supplied six days a week, costs him about as much as one good reporter. He clips out what he wishes to use and sends it directly to the composing room.

Exercises

1. Obtain from local press association representative carbon copy of one or more days' complete report. Make thorough study of it and of the selection made by the local newspaper.

SYNDICATE MATERIAL

2. Obtain from various syndicates, complete sets of services, study them, and note newspaper use of them.

3. Practice handling the stories brought in "takes" and "flashes" by the press associations—using carbon copy of daily report.

4. From the press association obtain an "unskinned" cable story, mimeograph it, then "skin" it and edit it for use.

5. Compare in two newspapers of same day, using same press association, the use made of various articles in the report.

6. Study all the syndicate matter in a newspaper, noting credit lines, etc.

7. Measure a newspaper with a foot-rule and find out how much, in column inches, is obtained from: (1) local staff work; (2) special correspondents; (3) press association; (4) syndicates; (5) other sources. Reduce figures to percentages.

8. Compile a morgue from syndicate material, especially pictures.

9. Make a study of the ready prints, or "patent insides," of a country weekly newspaper.

10. Study the stereotype plate matter ("boiler plate") in small newspapers.

11. Read some exchanges (papers from near-by cities) seeking: (1) local ends for the home paper; (2) ideas for make-up of departments and for display; (3) hints or tips for local features; (4) editorial comment for reprint; (5) tips for the managing editor; (6) miscellany for reprint. Edit copy for use.

12. Practice in receiving "pony" telephone service may be obtained by installing an extension on an office telephone, in another office. Toe-button to cut out transmitter, as well as head phones, may be obtained from telephone company. One student may dictate to another, reading daily newspaper.

CHAPTER VII

REWRITE AND FOLLOW STORIES

AMONG the various duties assigned to the desk man in the average newspaper office, there is more or less original writing of various kinds. A fair portion of the newspaper's content requires no newsgathering and hence may be written by a copyreader or some other office man. Some large offices hire special "rewrite" men to do this office writing, but few staffs have such a minute division of duty. The average copyreader must be as ready to dash off a story from facts telephoned in by a reporter as to edit copy, as skilled at writing an obituary from facts dug out of the morgue as at writing headlines.

One special form of writing, which often falls to the hands of the desk man, consists of preparing the various kinds of rewrite and follow stories that constitute the foundation of each day's issue. This "rewriting" results from the fact that any newspaper regards as its news field only one half the time that elapses between issues. The field of the morning newspaper is from about four o'clock the previous evening to four o'clock in the morning. The rest of the twenty-four hours, from four A. M. to four P. M., is the field of the evening paper. Whatever happens in the newspaper's own field of action is considered material for original newsgathering. Whatever happened in the preceding twelve hours was supposedly

REWRITE AND FOLLOW STORIES

covered by its predecessor. Yet, since many newspaper readers buy only one paper a day, the morning paper cannot utterly disregard the events recounted in the previous afternoon paper, and the evening paper must present a summary of the news printed in the morning paper which appeared since its own last edition. This "rehashing" of slightly old news results in the special kinds of news story known as the rewrite, the "boiled" story, and the follow-up, or follow, story.

The first step in the preparation of each day's issue is this rewriting. In some offices it is called "laying the foundation," and it is almost always done by some desk man or subordinate editor. In some small offices the city editor does it. The man who lays the foundation arrives long before the rest of the staff and devotes himself to reading the newspapers that have appeared since the last edition of his own paper. He scans them carefully and clips out all items that deserve mention in his own paper. Some items he sets aside to be rewritten; other items he saves for the city editor to follow up; still others he designates for boiling. Sometimes he does the rewriting himself; in other cases he gives the task to another office man. In such case, he indicates by an underscored word or two the new element to be emphasized. The follow items he lists in the city editor's assignment sheet.

The idea behind the writing of all of these various kinds of "rehash" stories—rewrite or follow—is to give the account a new slant or a new feature. The writer has in mind, not only the reader to whom the item is news, but also the reader who has seen the previous account. The difference between the two kinds of "rehash" story is that the rewrite contains nothing more than was in the original story, while the follow story presents later developments and additional facts. The rewrite is based entirely on the first story; whereas the follow requires additional newsgathering.

I. The Rewrite Story

The rewrite story, as suggested above, is nothing more or less than an old story retold from a new point of view, rejuvenated by a different treatment that makes it appear new. The rewrite man gives it this new twist by looking through it for a new feature, a new beginning. He writes a new lead on the old facts, playing up the new feature that he has decided to emphasize, and rewrites the entire story in accordance with the new point of view. The result contains no new facts but appears new. It is usually shorter, also, since the rehash is not worth as much space as fresh news.

In seeking this new feature, the rewrite man looks through the old story for some fact or element that the original writer failed to elaborate or emphasize. If the original story played up the cause of the fire, he emphasizes the property loss or some other striking element. Perhaps he finds only a possibility of showing the relation between the story and some other event—it may be the third murder in two days. Perhaps the story gives him an opportunity to begin his rewrite with the next probable development. He shows the firemen searching the ruins, the police scouring for the robber, or the arrested culprit in the magistrate's court. These expedients failing, he may begin his story with some subordinate item expressed in more striking terms. The following are examples of rewrite leads:

REWRITE AND FOLLOW STORIES

Reckless driving was the charge made against Samuel Johnson, carpenter, 367 N. Mills street, who was arraigned in municipal court this morning. He was severely censured by Judge Malcolm Smith for failing to slow up while passing the Lincoln school and running down a 4-year-old boy.

This is the third time Johnson has appeared before Judge Smith for reckless speeding and the judge said (and so on for several paragraphs including the judge's remarks).

REWRITE

"I advise you to quit driving an auto."

This advice was given to Samuel Johnson, carpenter, 367 N. Mills street, who was arraigned in municipal court this morning on the charge of reckless driving.

FIRST STORY

Collision between a jitney bus driven by John Hanson and a private automobile at Mayner avenue and Newhall street at noon yesterday caused severe injuries to one youth and six other high school boys. They were hurled many feet through the air.

REWRITE

George Bandell, age 15, son of the president of the first national bank, was thrown from his seat in a jitney bus yesterday and severely injured. The bus collided with a private automobile at the corner of Mayner avenue and Newhall street and seven high school boys, including Bandell, were hurled through the air.

The newsiest beginning of a rewrite story is usually: (1) a feature that was overlooked in the original; (2) a feature that was buried; (3) a forecast of the next development; (4) the relation to other events; (5) the local end; (6) the cause or motive. The rest of the rewrite story is a retelling of the original story in condensed form. The writer takes care, however, to use new expressions, to reverse the order, and to emphasize other angles.

Four "Musts" for a rewrite story are:

1. Must be shorter than first story, from one-third to one-half of original length.
2. Must base its interest on new feature or angle.
3. Must be written in better style, because it has less news value.
4. Original story must be entirely rewritten—every paragraph, every sentence. Some careless workers simply write a new lead and paste to it some paragraphs of the former story; the best offices do not consider this adequate rewriting.

II. Boiled News Items

The writing of what may conveniently be called the "boiled story" takes care of much of the rewrite material in many large offices. To handle all the material of a previous edition in rewrite stories would take up so much valuable space that much fresh news would need to be omitted or condensed. To save space the rewrite man must either throw away many important items or condense a large number of them to the briefest possible terms. The latter practice has long been common in many offices, and its result is a column or two daily of rehashed material in the form of short items. Ordinarily these items are grouped together under a general heading, such as, "City News in Brief," "Do You Know That—," "The City News Ticker," "Tabloids," "Grist from the Day's Grind," etc. The articles may be classified as telegraph or local, state or national. Sometimes a small headline precedes each item; sometimes the items are separated by short rules and distinguished by a few words in capital letters in the first line.

The writing of such items is an art that requires long practice and a highly cultivated sense of news values. To condense a long story to one or two sentences means that only the most significant facts may be included and that every word must count. Decided emphasis must be placed on the feature, and usually the feature played up is not the one emphasized in the first story. Although the items are short and to the point, they always give an identification of the person concerned, address, time and place. The following will illustrate.

> Falling over a fence around a newly laid cement sidewalk, Roger Ostermoor, aged 47, 841 Seventh street, broke his arm and two ribs last night.

> Fire damaged the two-story frame carpenter shop of Carl Goodsole, 165 W. Fifth street, yesterday morning. Damage is $4,500.

> The Madison police are searching for Mrs. Emma Hasward, who escaped from the Whitehall insane asylum Wednesday night.

Traffic policemen will wear white caps after June 1, according to Redford Bladen, chief of police.

Two persons were slightly injured when an automobile belonging to Small Smith 736 West avenue, ran into a telephone pole last night.

The man who committed suicide by throwing himself in front of a Central passenger train Monday night has been identified as William Sand, 293 Maquard street.

Dancing in public parks will be the subject of discussion at the regular meeting of the Citizens' club tomorrow.

Sixteen military organizations in the city have petitioned the major to use his influence to keep picnic parties out of Armory grove this summer.

James Lungwith and Fred Naazur were fined $25 in court yesterday for carrying revolvers. They declared that they had $43 and needed protection.

Because he allowed his 13-year-old daughter to sell postcards and gum on the streets, Henry Grover, a peddler, was arrested yesterday on the charge of violating the child labor law.

III. The Follow Story

The follow-up, or follow, story is not always written by the desk man. When additional newsgathering is required the story is turned over to the city editor and is handled by a reporter as an assignment. But since the additional material may frequently be obtained by one or two telephone calls to the news sources indicated in the story, the rewrite man often handles the follow.

The first step in the writing of a follow story is to look over the clipping upon which it is to be based, to discover what phases of the story may be followed up, what subsequent developments may be expected. If it is an accident story, the rewrite man may look for more complete data in regard to the fatalities or injuries, the present condition of the victims, the fixing of the blame. If it is a robbery story, he looks into the resulting pursuit, capture, or trial, or, in the case of a public institution, its present financial condition. A murder story affords follow possibilities in the pursuit, capture, or trial hearing of the criminal, the present conditions of the victim of attempted murder, the unraveling of the various phases of the mystery surrounding the crime. Suicide offers inquiry into the disposition of the body, the present condition of the victim if the attempt was unsuccessful, the disposition of the victim's estate or the action of relatives. Storms, floods, and other disasters offer follow possibilities for special reportorial assignments. Often the best follow-up is an interview with some of the persons concerned or with some of the authorities who have the case in hand. Once the rewrite man has decided what elements in the story offer follow-up possibilities, he must decide whether to turn the matter over to the city editor or try himself to get the necessary information for the follow over the telephone.

The writing of the follow story involves characteristic problems. It cannot be treated in exactly the same way as a news story because it does not contain strictly fresh news and is written for two different kinds of readers—the man who read the previous story and the man who did not. Hence it involves the presentation of the subsequent developments, plus a synopsis of the original account. The most interesting part is its method of recalling the original incident so as to enlighten the new reader without offending the old with reiterations.

The lead of the follow-up story usually begins with the subsequent developments, stated in newsy form. After this it runs into a résumé of the gist of the previous story with an elaboration of the facts in the case. It is to be noted that this involves the use of the definite article and a reference to the matter which suggests that the writer is merely recalling the previous event. Thus, although the first story referred to the accident as "a fire which destroyed," the follow recalls it as "the fire which destroyed." But in spite of this suggestion of recalling the incident, the rewrite man takes care to elaborate the previous facts and identify the case so fully that the new reader does not feel that he has missed anything. For example:

FIRST STORY

Propped against a telephone pole, the body of 6-year-old Arthur Wendzog, 268 Water street, was found apparently strangled to death at 5 A. M. this morning.

FOLLOW STORY

Two stained rags are the only basis on which the police now hold out hope of obtaining a clue to the murder of 6-year-old Arthur Wendzog, 268 Water street, who was found strangled to death in an alley near his home yesterday morning.

After the lead, the first two or three paragraphs are devoted to the elaboration of the new developments, for they are of greatest interest to all readers. The rest of the story is then a synopsis or summary of the material in the clipping on which the follow is based. The summary involves a general reversal of all the material in the first story and usually some condensing.

Exercises

1. Study rewrites and follows in successive editions of newspapers in the same field. Trace each story separately.

2. Read a local morning paper "to lay the foundation" for the afternoon paper—or vice versa. Clip and separate all local copy into these groups: (1) to be rewritten; (2) to be boiled down to "Locals"; (3) to go to city editor for follow up; (4) to go into datebook; (5) to be killed. Write all the stories of first two groups.

3. Practice making rewrites based on stories in local papers.

4. Practice boiling stories to a paragraph; make a column of such items from local paper.

5. Practice writing follows by assuming new developments in local stories.

6. From a pile of city newspapers, prepare a column of "Humor and Pathos in the News," by rewriting human interest stories into "Tabloids" of less than thirty-five words each.

7. From a pile of exchanges, write half a column of two-line, three-line, and four-line "time" fillers for make-up.

8. Clip miscellany from exchanges and prepare for reprint, with headlines and credits.

PART II
THE MECHANICS OF PRINTING

CHAPTER VIII

TYPE

A KNOWLEDGE of type—its nature, measurement, possibilities, and limitations—is absolutely necessary for success as a newspaper desk man or editor. The close relation between the mechanical department and editorial staff makes this so. Half the work of publishing a newspaper is nothing more or less than a printing job, and the desk man, acting as he does as director of the printers who are doing the work, should be able to talk their language and to understand their work. It is not necessary to be able to "stick" type or to operate a linotype machine, but it is necessary to know the problems that the typesetter and linotype operator face. Unless the desk man understands type, he cannot successfully edit copy, write headlines, direct make-up, or intelligently suggest changes in design.

To understand the printer's work, the desk man must know (1) the various ways of measuring type matter and their interrelation, (2) the names of the various sizes, (3) the uses of the various sizes, (4) the various styles of type and their uses, (5) the various families of type, (6) the way in which printers set type by hand, (7) the operation of the various composing machines, (8) the additional furniture and equipment used in putting together pages, and (9) the language of the printing office, so that he can specify type and indicate his wishes with a fair degree of certainty that the printer will understand his specifications. This would appear very complicated, but a study of the principles of the printer's work and a few visits to the composing room will lay a good foundation for the development of a thorough knowledge. No one, however, should hope to learn all there is to know about type; it is one of the largest subjects in the world.

Inelasticity of Type

The first and hardest thing to learn about type is its absolute inelasticity. "Type is not made of rubber," as the printers remark. The statement sounds reasonable, but the man who is used to working with longhand or typewritten manuscript sometimes fails to grasp it. He has an unconscious feeling that another word can be crowded into this line or another may be extracted from that without making any material difference. He doesn't realize that every individual letter and space is a separate piece of metal of definite size and that they must fit together with microscopic exactness. A page form is made up of thousands of these tiny pieces of metal fitted together so perfectly that, after pressure has been applied to the four edges of the form, the entire page of type may be handled as one piece without a single piece of metal falling out. It is like a complicated puzzle and every part of it must fit within a hair's breadth; one piece too large or too small will break the even pressure and allow part or all of the form to collapse.

The student must grasp this idea at the outset before going further with the study of type. If necessary he must go to the composing room and try to fit together a few lines of type to see the application of the principle.

After that he will never again call for a few letters of pica type in a brevier line or try to crowd an extra letter into a "fat" headline.

The Single Piece of Type

Every piece of type is a piece of metal with three dimensions. It is a rectangular stick with a flat base, four flat sides, and a flat top on which a letter or character is raised in high relief. The names of the various parts of the type are: the raised character is the *face;* the flat top on which the face stands is the *shoulder;* the body of the piece of type of which the shoulder is the top is called the *shank.* On the bottom of the type is a *heel nick* which gives the type two feet to stand on; in the front side of the shank is another nick which tells the printer, by feeling, which is the bottom of the letter; extra nicks are sometimes cut in the front to distinguish certain small capital letters that may easily be confused with small letters. In the form, the type stands firmly on its flat base, held in an upright position by other pieces of type pressed against its four sides. A number of such pieces of type set together in this way form with their tops a flat surface containing raised characters which press ink into the paper when the form is placed on the press. The fact that in each type the shoulder is slightly larger than the face affords white space about the printed letters. If one type projects above the others it cuts through the paper or raises it away from the other types; if too short it does not touch the paper; if one piece of type is too small in its other dimensions, it falls out of the form; if too large it bulges the line and other types fall out.

How Type Is Measured

Of the three dimensions possessed by every piece of type, only two are considered in type measurement. The third dimension—the height of the shank from base to top—is the same in all type—0.918 inch. That is, it is the same in all American and English type, although it varies in other countries. The two measurements that must be considered are its width and height as one looks at its end—in other words, the height and width of the letter as it appears on the printed page. This is the only height that is considered in subsequent discussion. Furthermore, the width and height that concern the printer are not those of the raised letter, but those of the shoulder itself—the square end of the type which supports the raised letter. This square shoulder is slightly larger than the letter itself, so as to afford white space between letters and lines and to allow for the varying size and shape of different letters. In other words, since some letters are larger than others in the same font and some extend above or below the general line, the printer must consider the dimensions of the shoulder on which the letter rests. Thus, although *h* is taller than *o* and *p* extends below the line, the shoulders of the types which print *h, o,* and *p,* in the same font, are of the same height, and the printer's measurements deal with the size of the shoulder.

Of the two dimensions of the shoulder, furthermore, the height is the more important. If a line of type is to be straight, all the type in it must have the same height, but there need not be any such regularity in width, so long as the lines come out even at the end. Therefore, although in any given font all the type is of the same height, there is great variation in width. In other words, *m* and *i* are

TYPE

the same height, but not the same width. The *m* type is as wide as three *i* types placed side by side but it fits in the same line because its height is the same.

It is therefore evident that type measurement in general is just a measurement of the height of the type as it appears on the printed page. In the modern point system, to be discussed later, the height of the letter is taken to be the distance from the line formed by the bases of all the letters to the top of the shoulder. The difference between two sizes or two fonts is simply a difference in this dimension.

Old Methods of Measuring Type

Until very recently there was no definite, universal system of type measurement. Various sizes were designated in general by a series of names—type approximating one-sixth of an inch in height was called *pica;* type of about half that size was call *nonpareil*, etc. But the various sizes varied in different type foundaries and there was no uniformity of size. Pica type made by one foundry might be noticeably larger than pica from another; brevier from one foundry could not be used in the same line with brevier from another. Hence there was endless confusion in the printing offices. If an office had two fonts of minion and the "printer's devil" mixed them up, both fonts were useless until sorted again. Printers were continually forced to "bodge" with cards to make types justify and line.

Not until 1886 was this confusion ended by the establishment of a uniform system of type measurement in all American foundries—a system which all printers now know as the point system. French type founders began work on a uniform system as early as 1737 and had worked out a plan generally adopted throughout Europe before 1800. In America no attempt to correlate the type of various foundries was made until 1822, and the first definite step was taken by a Chicago firm of type founders which lost its plant in the great fire of 1871. Their system, with some modifications, was adopted by the American Type Founders' Association in 1886. It is now universal in America, but it does not correspond with the European point system. The system is somewhat complicated, also, because it is not metric or decimal, but is simply a correlation and adjustment of former sizes to a systematic plan of measurement. The old pica type of one foundry which happened to be about 1/6 inch tall was taken as the basis and called 12-*point* and other sizes were correlated with it. The standard pica of the point system is, to be exact, 0.16604 inch.

The Point System

The unit of measurement in the point system is the *point*, or 1/72 inch. All sizes of type are designated in multiples of this point. Eight-point type is thus 8/72 inch high; 10-point type is 10/72 inch high; 72-point type is 72/72, or 1 inch high. As the point system is the measurement of the shoulder of the type, it allows for space normally shown between lines set *solid*, without *lead* between the lines. Thus nine lines of 8-point type approximately fill 1 inch; twelve lines of 6-point occupy the same space; an inch will accommodate 10.2 lines of 7-point type. On this basis, the number of lines of any size of type a given space will accommodate can be determined.

TYPE

Names of the Various Sizes

As the adoption of the point system was only a readjustment of old sizes to numerical measurement, many of the old names are still used in connection with the new system. The new 12-point is the same size as the old pica and therefore is now known as 12-point or pica; similarly the old name brevier is applied to the 8-point. The following is a list of old names now in use and their point sizes; each is set in the size designated:

POINT SIZE	NAME	POINT SIZE	NAME
4	Brilliant	10	Long Primer
4½	Diamond	11	Small Pica
5	Pearl	12	Pica
5½	Agate	14	English
6	Nonpareil		
7	Minion	16	Columbian
8	Brevier		
9	Bourgeois	18	Great Primer

Body type is usually made in 5-, 5½-, 6-, 7-, 8-, 9-, 10-, 11-, 12-, 14-, and 18-point. The usual display sizes above 14-point are 18-, 24-, 30-, 36-, 42-, 48-, 54-, 60-, and 72-point—in general, they run in 6-point jumps up to 60; in 12-point jumps above 60. Some series have also 20, 56, 96, and 120. The smallest sizes are *excelsior* (3-point), sometimes used in fractions, and *microscopique* (2½-point). There are many other names such as *Paragon* (20), *double-pica* (24), *Canon* (48), but they are rapidly giving way to the newer point designations.

Standard Line

Although the original point system, applied only to the height of the letter, certain type founders are now using it in connection with the width of the letter. That is, instead of allowing the *set-width* of the letter to be whatever the face happens to make it, they change the set-width enough to give it a point measurement. The advantage of the system is that with all letters cut in widths which are exact multiples of the standard unit, the point, it is easier to justify the lines—to fill them exactly. The position of the face on the shoulder, also, was until recently variable in different fonts and sizes, and types of different fonts, although of the same point height, would not *line* together, that is, some letters were nearer the top of the shoulder. This difficulty has been overcome by the adoption of the *standard line* in most American and some English foundries. In all type cut on the standard line the distance from the bottom of the shoulder to the base of the letter is the same and type from various fonts will line together. It is to be noticed, however, that there are two standard lines, one for body type and another for display type. Type cut on the display line is designated as the *lining series* and cannot be used in the same line with standard line body type.

Uses of Various Sizes

The sizes commonly used in newspaper work are nonpareil, minion, and brevier. Agate is taken as the standard of measurement in advertisements, but it is seldom actually used; advertising space is sold by the *agate line* and fourteen agate lines equal an inch of advertising space. Bourgeois, long primer, and small pica are the types most commonly used in book work. Larger sizes are most frequently used in display only.

The special uses of the various sizes are as follows:

Diamond is the smallest type regularly made and is used only in small Bibles and prayer-books. Pearl is sometimes used for the same purpose and finds some utility in notes and references in small dictionaries. Agate is sometimes used in market reports in newspapers and for similar purposes. Nonpareil is the smallest type that can possibly be used in book work and even then it is used only for footnotes, indices, etc.; some newspapers use it for very unimportant stories. Minion is commonly used as body type in large newspapers and occasionally as a subordinate type in book work. Brevier is the body type most often seen in small newspapers as well as in cheap book editions; it is commonly used in all printing work when a small type is desired. Bourgeois (pronounced bur-jois) is the type commonly used in magazine printing and in double-column books; it is a readable type but is too small for long lines in book work. Long primer is most frequently used in book work; newspapers also use it for important articles and editorials, especially in bold face. Small pica is the type of rich editions in which space is not important. Pica is the standard unit of measurement for column widths and printing furniture, but it is seldom used except as display or in very rich book work. English is now a display type only although it finds some use in Bibles and other church books for pulpit reading. Great primer, except as a display type, is used only in children's books and large quarto volumes.

Column Widths

In our study of type measurement, we found that the width of individual letters need be taken into consideration only in connection with the length of lines. As the letters vary greatly in width, printers have found it convenient to adopt one letter, the *m*, as the unit of line measurement. The *m* is used in preference to any other letter because in any font the shoulder of the *m* type is exactly square. For example, in 8-point type, which is 8/72 inch high, the *m* is 8/72 inch wide. Column widths and line-lengths are therefore designated in "ems." Ten ems of 8-point type is 80/72, or 1-1/9 inches, long. Typesetters are usually paid space rates and their work is estimated on the basis of one thousand ems of the type they set, regardless of the space it fills. Although one thousand ems of nonpareil fill only about half as much space as one thousand ems of pica, the printer is paid the same for each.

In measuring column widths and printing space in general, however, the pica or 12-point em is used as the standard unit. The pica em is a convenient unit because it is 12/72 or 1/6 inch wide. The 2-1/6-inch column commonly used in newspapers is designated as 13 ems wide, whether it is set in 6-point or 8-point. Other spaces are designated accordingly as 18 ems, 21 ems, 25 ems, or whatever the case may be, and the length of the line can be figured out on the basis of 6 ems to the inch. To avoid confusion, it is customary to specify in "ems pica"; thus, 8-point Roman, 15 ems pica. An easy way to become familiar with the system is to do a few problems in figuring space on the basis of printing measurements; for instance, how many lines can be used and what line-length should be specified to fill a space 4 inches wide and 7 inches high with 9-point type?

Variation in Width of Type Face

It has probably been noted that there is much variation in the width of the same letters in different styles of type, although the height of the letters is the same. The 30-point letter *O* used in the usual newspaper headline is decidedly narrower than some other 30-point *O* used in an advertisement. This is because the proportion between the width and height of letters is not the same in all type. Every different font and family has its own proportion, and the proportion may vary within the same font. The reason is that every style of type is made in three or four different widths to suit special purposes. There is no definite system of measuring the various proportions, but special names are applied to various widths. The type in its common form is designated as *standard width*, narrower type of the same size is called *condensed*, wider type is called *extended*, and the narrowest is known as *extra-condensed*.

EXTRA-CONDENSED 10-POINT TYPE
CONDENSED 10-POINT TYPE
STANDARD 10-POINT TYPE
EXTENDED 10-POINT TYPE

Variation in Body Size

Although the size of type is measured by the size of the body rather than the size of the letter, there is some variation in the relation between the two. The variation results from the fact that it is often desirable to increase the space between lines, and the type founders make up small type on larger bodies to save the printer the trouble of placing strips of metal, or "lead," between the lines of type. In specifying such type, the printer must give two sizes—the size of the type face and the size of the body. When he calls for 8-point type on 9-point body, he is given a type of the usual 8-point face on a body large enough to give an extra 1/72 inch between each pair of lines. Many fonts are regularly made in this way because their design calls for wide spacing between lines. The 8-point on 9-point body size is common in small newspapers, and 10-point on 12-point body is frequently used in magazine work.

Styles of Type

Certain general kinds and styles of type are so commonly used that they deserve mention here. The kind of type ordinarily used in reading matter is called *body type*, as distinguished from *display type* used in headings and prominent lines. The common body type in use in American newspapers and magazines is designated as *Roman*. In its commonest form it is called *thin-faced* Roman; when it is heavier and blacker it is known as **bold** or **black-face** Roman. Any kind of type, in the same way, is called **bold** when it is heavy and black, and most styles are made both in thin-face and bold. Type that slants toward the right is known as *italic;* it may be thin-faced or bold italic and is usually found in every font. Besides the regular capital and small letters, most fonts also contain another style called *small capitals*—they are capitals of the same height as the small letters of the same size.

This line is set in thin-faced Roman
This line is set in black-faced Roman
This line is set in Italic
THIS LINE IS SET IN CAPITALS AND SMALL CAPITALS

Type Families

One step beyond the standard styles, which are a regular part of every font of type, is the classification of type into great families designed at various times by different type founders. Certain of the designs go back so far into typographical history that they may be classified in general as *old style, antique, modern,* and *fancy* faces. Old style is characterized by short *serif* (cross-marks at the ends of strokes), long connecting fillets between the serifs and main strokes, and small figures. The lines of old style are frequently wavy and broken in imitation of the imperfect work of early type makers. Antique type has bolder serifs and a uniform line with little shading. Modern type has longer serifs, shorter fillets, greater shading, and large figures.

A proper classification of type divides it first into *groups* (such as Gothic, Roman, script, black letter, etc.); within the groups are *families* (such as Caslon, Cheltenham, Bodoni); families are divided into *series* (such as Caslon Bold Condensed); series are divided into *sizes* (such as brevier, or 8-point). One of the great groups is the *Gothic* which is characterized by extreme plainness and lack of ornamentation; it is the "block letter" of sign painters. It appears in many styles and has been much used in headlines. The various kinds of *script* type make another group which imitates handwriting. In American offices, the type of some foreign countries and of older times is called *black letter;* it imitates medieval copyists and includes *Old English, German, Tudor, Missal,* etc. To learn the vast range of type faces and styles, as well as their classification and names, it is best to study the catalogues of the type founders. It is well to be able to identify the commonest of them.

Printer's Furniture

Pieces of wood or metal used to fill space are called *furniture*. Printer's equipment also includes many other pieces used to print lines or other kinds of impressions. Most of it is now made in accordance with the point system and is measured in points or ems pica. Thin strips of metal used to increase the space between lines of type are known as *leads* and are 2 points or 2/72 inch thick. When a single lead is placed between each pair of lines, it is said to be *leaded*. If two 2-point strips are used, it is *double-leaded;* wider leads are called *slugs*. Without leads, it is said to be set *solid*. A *reglet* is a wood strip (6- or 12-point) used in spacing. The blank pieces of type used between words are *spaces* A wider space, used for indention, is a *quad;* it may be 1-em (*mutton* quad), 1-en (nut quad), 2-em, 2-en, etc. (One *em* is twice one *en* in width.) Spaces vary in width and it is through this variation that the printer takes up space to make lines the same length—they are the only elastic elements in typography. After the printer has set up about as many words as a line will hold, with average spaces between them, he adjusts the length of the line by substituting thinner or fatter spaces in each position; this operation is called *justifying*. Printers sometimes justify by *letter-spacing* between letters.

Any strip of metal that prints a line is called a *rule;* it is made of brass and its thickness is measured in points. The long rules between newspaper columns are called *column rules* and rules below incomplete or squared-up articles are *cut-off rules*. Sometimes cut-offs print wavy lines. The common rules used in newspapers are *hairline, 2-point,* and *6-point.* If a newspaper is printed with the rules upside down so that the flat bases strike the paper, the effect is called *turned rules.* Some rules, called *double rules,* print fine parallel lines; others, called *perforating* rules, cut a row of small holes through the paper; others print a line of *leaders. Borders* are decorative rules or series of metal pieces, like type, that may be used as a frame about type matter. When a frame made up of simple straight rules is used in the newspaper it is called a *box.* A border made of asterisks is a *star-box.* Pieces of cut-off rule below banner heads are *dingbats.* Short lines between articles and headline decks are *dashes*—they are usually 3-em, 5-em, 7-em, etc. All of these are made of brass, type metal, or wood. Wood is used largely in filling up large blank spaces, for every fraction of space must be made snug and tight. Some large letters and cuts are also made of hard wood to save weight, since a square foot of type matter weighs about thirty-seven pounds.

Other Typographical Terms

Many of the terms which the typesetter uses are derived from the names of his implements. For instance, he measures his work by the *stickful*—the amount of type which may be placed in the *composing stick* which he uses. The stick is a three-sided metal tray, about as large as the palm of the hand, with one side adjustable to match varying line-length. When full, it holds about two inches of type matter—reckoned as one hundred and fifty words of newspaper type. Each stickful is in turn transferred to a long metal tray called a *galley*. As the first *proof*, or impression, is taken of the type while it stands in the galley, this proof is called *galley proof*. The operation of taking proof is called *pulling proof*. Corrections are made by *revising* the type matter as it stands in the galley. The type with which the hand compositor works is distributed by characters in the various compartments of a *case*, or flat tray. The sections, or *boxes*, vary in size according to the relative number of types stored in them and they are unlabeled for they are arranged in the same way in all cases and the printer learns their position just as a typist learns his keyboard. It is not necessary for the printer to look at the type, for the position of its box tells him what letter it is and the nick in its shank indicates the bottom of the letter. Capitals are laid out in one case and small letters in another; since the first is ordinarily placed above the latter, it is called the *upper case*—hence capitals and small letters are called *upper case* and *lower case* letters respectively. Each case contains a *font* of type, that is, a complete assortment of a certain size and style of type, including some 275 different characters and a definite number of each character. A complete font includes Roman small letters, small capitals, capitals, figures, punctuation points, and accented letters, italic small letters, capitals, figures, points, and accents, fractions, commercial signs, and "peculiars" which include marks of reference, braces, dashes, leaders, spaces, and quads. A *ligature* is a combination of letters on one shank, such as ff, fi, fl, ffi, ffl, ﬆ, æ, œ. *Logotypes* are entire words cast on one shank—not extensively used at present. The number of types of each character in a font is determined on the basis of a definite *scheme*, corresponding to the

TYPE

relative frequency of various letters in ordinary reading matter. A size of the font may thus be designated by the number of letters *A* in it. When a foundry catalogue lists a certain type as "19A $1.20, 36a $1.30, $2.50," the printer knows that the font will contain nineteen *A* types, thirty-six *a* types, and other characters in proportion.

The manuscript which the printer follows in setting type is called *copy*, and each piece of copy as he receives it is a *take*. The copy indicates not only the content but the style and face of type to be used and other specifications. After the pressmen or stereotypers have used the type, the printer must *distribute* it among the proper boxes of the proper cases. Type purchased, cast, or arranged in letter groups ready for the cases is called *sorts*. If at any time in the process of composing or making up the type becomes mixed, the result is *pi*. Discarded and broken type is thrown into the *hell-box* to be melted up. Offices which have type-casting machines throw all type of 12-point or less into the hell-box to save distributing it. If in distributing the printer mixes the type of various cases so that many *wrong-face* letters appear in proof, the result is called *dirty case*.

I. How to Specify Type

All copy intended for a printer must contain certain marks to indicate the type to be used and the manner in which it is to be set. These marks are usually written on the upper left-hand corner of the first page and inclosed in a circle to indicate that they are not to be set up. As the marks usually refer only to the body of the copy, separate marks must indicate the style of the headings.

When all the headings are alike, one mark opposite the first or at the top of the page suffices, but any variation in heading type must be indicated by other marks, in circles, in the margin of the copy beside the heading concerned.

Complete type specifications on any manuscript include name, style, and size of type to be used; length of lines; and general arrangement of paragraphs and lines. Thus a piece of copy might be marked: "8-point Bodoni Script, 15 ems, solid, indent paragraphs 2 ems." If the printer has only one style of body type, as is frequently the case, "7-point Roman, 13 ems, leaded, indent paragraph 1 em." If a special 10-point on 12-point body is desired—"10/12 Roman, 21 ems, solid, hanging indention 1 em."

In a newspaper office it is not usually necessary to mark all copy. The standard column width, usually 13 ems, will be used unless otherwise specified. If the newspaper's ordinary body type is 8-point Roman, the compositor will use that unless directed to use something else. Special display is all that the newspaper desk man marks specially but he must mark it in the language of the printer. Thus space between the lines is specified by marking "lead" or "double-lead"; heavier type is marked "bold face," or "Bl. face," or "all caps," or "Sm. caps"; two-column lines are secured by marking "double-measure, 12-pt. bold caps"; other display may be called for by "hanging indention, 1 em," or "center 11 ems"; a frame around the type body is specified as a "Box."

More careful specification is required in the marking of heading type. A type might be marked "12-pt. Caslon Bold Condensed, centered," or "14-pt. Light De Vinne Extended, all caps, flush at left." In the newspaper office, the necessity of specifying for headings is saved by the use of numbers for standard headlines. The composing room and editorial office both have a schedule containing models of the newspaper's common headlines, their numbers, and the type and arrangement. When the desk man marks a headline "No. 8," the printer, by referring to his schedule, knows at once the kind and size of type to be used.

The best way to learn type and its specification is to obtain the catalogue of a large type foundry and study the faces and names. Printers know their type by the names given by the founders, and each type case is indexed with the name of the type within it. But, since no office has in stock all the types listed in the catalogue, it is useless to specify a special face without first investigating the styles in the printer's cases.

II. Some Handy Tables

Display available in linotype matter is: Box (made of rules); star-box; white margin (formed by indenting each line 1 em on each side); leaded or double-leaded; double-measure (two-column lines); half-measure; hanging indention (all lines except first indented); bold face or italic (depending on machine); all caps; caps and small caps; larger body type.

Suitable column widths for various sizes of type are the following:

```
5-point type  .....................10 to 14 ems pica wide
5½-point type .....................10 to 16 ems pica wide
6-point type  .....................12 to 18 ems pica wide
8-point type  .....................12 to 26 ems pica wide
10-point type .....................18 to 36 ems pica wide
```

Number of lines of type per inch in various common sizes, solid or leaded, are:

Type Size	Set Solid	2-Point Leaded
5-point	14 lines plus	10 lines
6-point	12 lines	9 lines
7-point	10 lines plus	8 lines
8-point	9 lines	7 lines plus
9-point	8 lines	6 lines plus
10-point	7 lines plus	6 lines
12-point	6 lines	5 lines plus

Approximate number of words per square inch in various sizes, solid or leaded, is:

Type Size	Set Solid	2-Point Leaded
5-point	69	59
6-point	47	34
8-point	32	23
10-point	21	16

Approximate number of words per newspaper line (12½ ems pica) in various type:

- 5½-point type ....9½ words
- 6-point type ....8 words
- 8-point type ....7 words
- 10-point type ....6 words
- 12-point type ....4½ words

Exercises

1. Make a thorough study of type—its groups, families, series, and sizes, in a type catalogue—both founder's and composing machine type.

2. Practice identifying type faces and sizes in newspapers and magazines. Learn the names of typographical symbols found.

3. Memorize and practice using old names of type sizes.

4. Analyze the typography of a particular newspaper.

5. Visit printing offices and study machines and materials.

6. Work problems in estimating type matter for various spaces, including column widths, number of lines per page, etc. Master the point system and its use—and the use of ems pica.

7. Practice writing type specifications for various kinds of matter found in newspapers and magazines.

8. Plan type pages and layouts, drawing up diagrams, with complete specifications.

9. If printing equipment is available, students should set up the matter they have designed.

10. This chapter may well be taken up in connection with proofreading.

CHAPTER IX

PRINTING PROCESSES

BECAUSE newspaper development has been largely made possible by the invention of labor- and time-saving devices for the printer and because no desk man can intelligently direct a printer unless he understands the processes by which written copy is quickly reproduced in thousands of printed papers by the mechanical staff, this chapter is devoted to explaining the machines and processes that are in common use in modern newspaper plants. No attempt will be made to explain the mere mechanical aspects of the machines; that is the concern of the inventor and the repair man. It is the principle behind the various mechanical processes that the desk man needs to know, as well as the possibilities in speed and output. To understand these principles it is more important to know the historical development of any machine, the various steps which led to its invention and the problems involved, than to be able to identify each lever and gear in the latest model. It is one thing to stand bewildered beside a machine and hear the operator explaining that the matrices are no good and the what-you-call-it lever is worn; it is a more valuable thing to know what the machine does and in general how it operates.

Five Branches of Invention

There are five branches of mechanical invention that make the modern newspaper possible. (1) One is mechanical type composition. Until inventors worked out machines that would do the work of the hand typesetter, all newspapers were greatly limited in size and speed of production. Until a machine was produced that could compose thirty to forty words a minute, every office was kept down to the comparatively slow pace of the hand compositor. (2) Another great branch has been the development of the rotary printing press with its increased speed and size of output. (3) Between these two processes is the invention of stereotyping which made the rotary press possible, and (4) electrotyping, a finer modification of it. (5) An important subsidiary process is that of photographic engraving, a process which has brought illustrations within the reach of every newspaper. Without these five processes, the modern newspaper with its many interesting illustrated pages, its vast circulation, and its multiple editions would be impossible.

I. Mechanical Type Composition

To understand the mechanical substitute for the hand compositor, it is necessary to understand the basic principles of type making, for the machine that does the "typesticker's" work is a type maker, rather than a typesetter. No composing machine in common use at the present time handles or sets ready-made type; every one makes new type for every word it composes. To understand its principle, therefore, it is necessary to know the steps which led to the development of the type-making machine.

There is nothing new in this modern custom of making type in the printing office. All printers made their own type until about the middle of the sixteenth century—but they made it by hand. Not until about 1550 did type founding become a separate trade. One of the first type founders in England was Joseph Moxon, who established a foundry in 1659. Another was William Caslon of the next century. Binney and Ronaldson were among the first type makers in America, for the trade was not introduced on this continent until late in the eighteenth century. All of these type makers, who established the faces and fonts that we know today, made type by hand for it was not until the middle of the past century that machinery was invented to aid their work. The first successful type-making machine and the progenitor of the machines now in use was invented by an American, David Bruce, in 1838.

The Making of Type

Since the beginning of type making in 1450, the process has been one of casting, of forcing molten metal into a mold. For every individual letter and character the type founder must have a separate mold, and each piece of type must be cast separately. The mold must be small and deep, with the letter cut in bas-relief in one end. That is the basic principle of all type founding, whether by machine or hand, and of the mechanical composing machines.

Since the shanks of various letters are alike in general shape and size, the part of the mold that must be changed for different letters is the bas-relief of the character—the *matrix*, as it is called. Until very recently, the making of this matrix was done by hand. The first operation was to cut a *counter-punch*—a piece of steel with the letter carved in relief on one end. This was done by marking the outlines of the letter on the steel and cutting away the metal around the letter; the counter-punch is an exact steel duplicate of the finished type. The next step was to drive this counter-punch into a piece of soft steel to make a bas-relief of the letter—a *punch,* as the type founders call it. When this bas-relief has been smoothed and finished, it is the matrix of the type mold. Every step in this process must be repeated for each of the 275 letters and characters in the font to provide a matrix for each letter. The first punch-cutting machine was invented about 1885. Much of the matrix making is now done with this machine or by electrolysis, by plating the counter-punch with copper, peeling off the copper film and backing it up with soft metal to form a matrix.

The mold of which the matrix forms one end consists of two blocks of steel with a square groove in the side of each so that the two when put together form a rectangular casting box. As some letters are wider than others, the mold must vary in the direction of the set-width. In the old process of casting type by hand, the workman fitted a matrix in one end of a type mold of proper size and then with a spoon poured it full of molten metal. To drive the metal firmly into the matrix he gave the mold a vigorous upward shake as he poured the metal. Each type required a repetition of this process. The type was then dressed down for the removal of superfluous metal, especially the jet at the open end of the mold, a groove was cut in the base so that it would stand firmly on its feet, and a nick was cut in one side to guide the printer in setting it.

Type-Casting Machines

The type-making machines of today do only the casting part of the process. Their molds and matrices are previously made by a punch-cutting process as described above. By the use of a plunger in a pot of molten metal, they automatically do the work of the spoon and the shake employed by the hand type caster. Most of them also trim and finish the type. Their advantage is speed; they cast type fifteen or twenty times as fast as a hand-workman—from 3,000 to 10,000 types an hour—and turn out a better product. But these machines, while they are the fathers of the composing machine and are used in some newspaper offices to cast "sorts" for the type cases, can do no more than continue casting the same letter over again until the matrix is changed. To convert them into composing machines, we need to equip them with some means for changing matrices automatically so that they will cast any letter as it is needed, and set it in its proper place in a galley. Then we shall have a typecasting and composing machine that will do the work of the hand compositor.

Type-Setting Machines

Long before any attempt was made to remodel the type caster for use as a composing machine, inventors tried to solve the problem of mechanical composition by designing a machine to set ready-made type by machinery. At first sight, it would not seem difficult to work out a machine with a series of grooves or boxes to hold the various letters and a keyboard with wires or levers arranged to release the proper types and allow them to slide down into a galley in proper sequence. But there were two obstacles to be overcome. One was the justification of the line—the filling in of space between words to make all the lines the same length. The other was the redistribution of type. The typesetting machine was of little value unless it did away with the slow process of distributing type. On these obstacles the idea of mechanical typesetting broke. As early as 1822 typesetting machines were patented; the first practical one was brought out in 1853 but it required hand justification; another in 1870 solved the distribution problem but did not justify. Although practically abandoned today, these mechanical typesetters did good service in newspaper work during the middle of the past century Their inability to distribute type printers made up for by melting up the type as fast as it was used and casting new ready-sorted type on a rotary type-casting machine. The highest development of the mechanical typesetter is the unitype which is used to some extent today; it distributes type automatically but requires hand justifying. About 1890 a machine was invented which set, justified, and redistributed type but it was too costly for practical use. It is probably fortunate, however, that these machines failed, for their failure brought the development of the type-casting and composing machine with its perpetually new type and other advantages.

Type-Casting and Composing Machines. The problem involved in remodeling the type-casting machine into a mechanical compositor, as indicated above, consisted in devising some way to fit a different matrix into the casting box as each letter is needed and to set the type in the galley. The problem has been solved in a number of different ways in various machines but only two are used to any great extent in the newspaper office—the linotype and the monotype. An explanation of the principles incorporated in these machines will illustrate the workings of the others. These two machines must not, however, be confused with the type-casting machines which many newspapers have installed to cast "sorts" for the cases. The type casters, which are really the machines of the type foundry, do not change matrices in response to the operation of keys and do not set the type that they cast.

The Linotype Machine

The linotype machine derives its name from the fact that its inventor solved the problem of casting, setting, and justifying type by casting an entire line of type in a single piece. The output of the machine is not a series of separate pieces of type, but a slug which has on its edge the faces of the various letters that make up a single line of type. It is as if the printer had set up the various pieces of type in a line and fused them into a single piece of metal. It operates by means of a line of previously assembled and justified matrices.

Its inventor, Ottmar Mergenthaler, began work on the machine about 1876 and put it into commercial use in 1886. Now it is used by thousands of newspapers, many book publishers, and other printing firms. The original machine has been developed and improved by many successive patents, but its basic principle has remained unchanged. The machine is operated by a keyboard, very similar to the keyboard of a typewriter, electric or other power is required to operate it, and a gas flame keeps its pot of type metal in molten condition.

The basic idea of the Mergenthaler machine is to bring a series of type matrices, corresponding to the various letters required by the printer, into line to form a composite matrix for a mold that casts a bar of metal just the size of a line of type. Its operation involves

(1) the assembling of the matrices, (2) the pouring of the molten metal, and (3) the redistribution of the matrices for later use. All of this, including the justifying of the line, is done automatically, as the operator presses the keys, and the finished line-slugs are deposited in a tray in proper order.

The type matrix of the linotype is a flat piece of brass about 1½ inches long and ¾ inch wide. One end is cut away in a triangular notch with grooves and nicks to guide the distributor. The letter mold, or matrix proper, is on one edge of the matrix. The matrices, of which there are a number for each character on the keyboard, are stored in a magazine at the top of the machine. Separate channels are provided for the matrices of the various letters with gates operated by the keyboard, so that when the operator presses a key the corresponding matrix slides out of the magazine, down a channel in front of the machine, and takes its place in a line beside the keyboard. As successive matrices reach the line, they hang side by side with their type molds in a horizontal line on one side. At the end of each line, the operator moves a lever and the machine does the rest; meanwhile the operator is composing the next line.

After the operator throws the lever, the line of matrices which constitute one line are automatically moved away to the left to take their place in front of a horizontal casting box located in a large wheel. The casting box is just the size of a line-slug and open at front and back; it is really just a horizontal slit in the solid wheel. When they reach the casting box, the line of matrices with their separate type molds form its front surface. From a pot behind the wheel, molten metal is forced into the casting box by a plunger, in sufficient quantity to fill the mold. The metal cools and hardens as the wheel containing the casting box slowly revolves over a knife to trim the bottom of the slug, and the finished line-slug is pushed out into a galley at the end of a quarter revolution. Meanwhile a long arm reaching over from the back of the machine has carried the line of matrices to the top of the magazine and deposited them in an automatic distributor. They hang on the distributor rod by the fourteen nicks in the V-shaped notch at the end of each matrix and are moved along the rod above the magazine by a slowly revolving screw. Each matrix has a separate combination of nicks fitting in certain grooves in the distributor rod, and when it reaches its place a break in certain grooves allows it to drop from the distributor and slide into the proper compartment in the magazine, ready to be used again in a later line.

Line justification is accomplished by wedges between the matrices. Whenever the operator strikes the space bar in the keyboard, a long, thin wedge moves into the line and hangs loosely between the matrices that compose the words on each side. As the operator throws the lever at the end of the line, the wedges are automatically driven down so as to take up extra space and crowd the matrices closely together. The line is thus filled out with equal spaces between the words before the slug is cast. The justifying wedges are not returned to the magazine but hang in line beside it ready to drop into place.

All operations of the machine are automatic. The operator simply keeps the motor running and the metal hot, presses the proper keys, and throws the lever at the end of each line. A power-driven belt is also used to bring the matrices down from the magazine so that only a slight touch on the key is required. While the operator is setting one line, another is in the casting box and the matrices of another are being distributed in the magazine. If he presses the wrong key or makes any other mistake, he can rectify it by picking out the matrix or rearranging all the matrices of the line as they hang beside the keyboard. Once the line is cast, however, he must reset the line and make a new slug to rectify an error; the old slug he puts back into the melting pot. In the same way, all proof corrections, however slight, must be made by setting new lines to take the place of faulty lines.

Since all the matrices in the machine's magazine are for the same size and face of type, it is quite evident that the machine in its simplest form is limited to one font. Bold-face type of the same font is provided for by the use of matrices with two molds and a device to bring the proper mold into use. But the two faces of the same font are as great a variety as can be set with one magazine. This inconvenience has been overcome by the development of machines with interchangeable or multiple magazines. Linotypes are now built with two, three, or four magazines and corresponding range of variety; in others the magazines are interchangeable so that the operator can change from 7-point to 8-point by removing one magazine and slipping another into its place. In this way the machine has been developed until it is now able to set almost any face or size of type in common use; recently machines have been brought out which set type large enough for newspaper headlines or irregular slugs for use in display advertising.

Besides its speed—about 8,000 ems per hour or 35 words per minute—and the fact that only one operator is required to run it, the linotype has certain other advantages and disadvantages. The line-of-type idea is a decided advantage in newspaper work because line-slugs are easier to handle than individual pieces of type and facilitate rapid make-up. On the other hand, the fact that new lines must be cast to rectify errors makes proof revision of linotype work rather difficult and costly. This is offset, however, by the fact that every line is made of absolutely new type and the type is cast only as needed. A few bars of type metal piled in a corner take the place of the extensive type cases of former days. After the slugs have been used for printing, they are thrown back into the melting pot and transformed into new lines. Age and wear in the machine result in bad alignment and hair-lines between letters because the brass matrices, becoming slightly worn, do not fit sufficiently close together to keep molten metal from being forced between them to form ridges that show up as minute lines in print. The linotype machine costs about $3,500, and a new set of matrices costs about $75. The linotype equipment of a large newspaper, including from ten to fifty machines, involves a considerable investment.

The Monotype Machine

The Lanston monotype is selected for study in this connection because it represents an entirely different principle of mechanical composition and is coming into extensive use in American printing offices. For reasons to be pointed out later, it finds little use in newspaper offices but is used by many magazine and book publishers. It is an American machine and was put into commercial use about 1899.

The characteristic feature of the monotype is that it casts a separate piece of type for each letter and sets up the type in a galley, justified ready for use. It is the ultimate development of the basic idea of the casting machine as pointed out above, since it accomplishes the necessary change of matrix in the type mold automatically. Another characteristic feature of the monotype is that it consists of two separate machines—a keyboard and a type caster—which may be operated at different times and in different places. The output of the keyboard is a perforated paper roll, like a player-piano roll, which is later used to guide the operation of the type caster in making and setting type to correspond with the copy.

To set up copy on the monotype, the operator manipulates the keys of a large keyboard, much like the keyboard of a typewriter, but, instead of printing the words on a sheet of paper, the keyboard simply punches holes in a roll of paper about five inches wide. Compressed air supplies the power to revolve the roll and transmit the pressure of the keys. Each letter, as its key is pressed, is represented by two small holes in the paper roll; as will be seen later, the two holes supply motion in two directions to the matrix-grid of the type caster. Each succeeding pair of holes is below the preceding pair on the roll. The keys on the right-hand bottom rows punch only one hole each, but all the others punch two; 225 variations are possible.

Justification is accomplished by another perforation at the end of the line to regulate the size of spaces between words. When the operator nears the end of a line, the fact is indicated by a bell and a cylindrical scale above the keyboard which revolves as the composition progresses. When he has set enough words to fill the line, the scale tells him what justifying keys to strike—it has kept account of the number of spaces between words and the total amount of space left to be divided. The scale is in the form of two numbers and justification requires the pressure of two keys in the two rows of red keys across the top of the keyboard—one key in each row to correspond with the two numbers indicated on the scale. The resulting perforation sets a uniform width for all the spaces cast in that line. The justification holes come after the letter holes of the line, on the roll, but they precede the line in the type caster for the roll runs backward in the second machine.

The monotype keyboard may be placed in a quiet office far from the composing room and operated by a stenographer. Its paper rolls may be stored away for any length of time, may be used as many times as desired, or may be kept by the author as a duplicate of his work to save composition in later editions. One keyboard may supply rolls for several type casters or, as is more often the case, several keyboards may be used to keep one type caster busy.

The type caster is like the type-making machines used by the type founders, except that instead of one letter-matrix, it has many, arranged to be brought into position in the type mold automatically as they are needed. In the type caster there is a separate matrix for each letter and character in the font, all of uniform size and fitted together in one flat matrix-grid. This is a block of metal about four inches square and one inch thick, ruled in 225 small squares like a miniature checkerboard with a letter mold in each square. When the machine is in operation, this matrix-grid shuttles about above a stationary casting box so that now one letter, now another, forms the end of the type mold. As the grid moves about, the mold automatically changes size to provide for the varying set-width of the shanks of different letters. Behind the mold is a pot of molten metal with a plunger that forces a jet of metal into the casting box and fills the mold for each successive letter. Water circulating through holes in the casting box hardens the metal instantly, and the type is pushed out of the mold and into line in a galley. As each line is filled it is pushed down in the galley to make room for the next.

The shuttling of the matrix-grid is guided by the perforated roll made by the keyboard. The grid has motion in two directions—forward and backward, to right and left. One of the pair of holes in the roll regulates the first motion, the other controls the second. The movement in one direction, by the movement of a metal wedge in the side of the casting box changes the size of the mold to suit the letter. The machine is operated by compressed air and guided by air escaping from small tubes through the holes of the paper roll—just as the player piano is guided by air escaping through holes in the music roll. As each pair of holes comes over the mouths of the tubes, springs give the grid a combined motion in two directions and it is stopped by two vertical plungers, actuated by the escaping air, at the proper place to bring the desired letter-matrix under the mold, the size of the mold is changed, molten metal is forced into the mold, and the finished type is pushed into the galley. The entire operation is done so quickly that the machine casts and sets type at the rate of 150 to 180 a minute. At the same time, the justification holes in the roll adjust the set-width of the spaces for each line, so that spaces of the right width are cast and set between the words and each line comes out exactly even. When not in use in setting composition, the type caster may be used to cast "sorts" for the printer's case.

As the matter composed by the monotype consists of galleys of individual types, rather than line-slugs, errors are corrected and proof is revised just as if the matter had been set by hand. Once cast and set, the type can be removed or changed to any extent desired without recasting, a case of the same type supplying the needed letters. This, added to the fact that each type is new and fresh, is a great advantage in some kinds of printing work. It is not so convenient for newspaper work, on the other hand, as the line-slugs of the linotype, because individual pieces of type must be handled with greater care and are harder to make up in page form. The fact that monotype composition requires two operations and the ribbon runs backward in the second makes it difficult to divide copy into short takes for rapid handling and lessens the usefulness of the machine in the newspaper office.

Greater variety of face and size is possible on the monotype than on the most improved linotype. All that need be changed to alter face or size is the small matrix-grid bearing the type molds. The printer may have in stock as many grids as he desires and the change from one to another requires but a moment. The matrices, also, do not wear and result in disalignment or hair-lines as in the linotype. The ribbons are interchangeable and can be used to set any face desired; this is accomplished by a standardization of set-widths of letters, a change especially evident in Old Style faces. The same ribbon may be used in setting any desired size of type if the line length is changed proportionately. Some of the large machines are arranged to perforate two ribbons at once, one for small type and narrow measure, the other for larger type and long lines. The operator may thus compose type for a de luxe and a popular edition at the same time. The most important mechanical fault that appears in monotype work is honeycombed type which results from overheating the type metal and consequent bubble-holes which may cause the type to break down in the press.

Other Composing Machines

In addition to the linotype and monotype, there are several other automatic type-casting machines that are used to some extent in the United States. Among them is the junior linotype, a machine which casts lines of type like the linotype by means of long matrices suspended on endless wires encircling the machine. Since the original Mergenthaler patents have expired, other machines, including the intertype, the linograph, etc., have been brought out on lines similar to the linotype.

Whatever the machine, its possibilities do not go beyond the work of the hand typesetter; its output is type or slugs set up in long galleys, and subsequent hand make-up into page form is necessary just as if the type had been set by hand. If the machine casts and sets individual types, they must be handled with as great care as hand-set matter; if it casts line-slugs they must be arranged and locked up in the form. No machine has been devised to take the place of hand work in make-up, and every office, no matter how many typesetting machines it has, must also have some practical printers to do this work. Since the most versatile machine, also, is limited in variety of size and face of type, much display in any publication must be set by hand in the old-fashioned way.

II. Stereotyping

The process of stereotyping is the making of metal plates to reproduce the pages of a publication after the type has been set, arranged, and locked up in page form. For the rotary press, these reproductions must be in the form of semicylindrical plates that will fit the rollers of the press. That is, the flat-page form with its myriad type faces protruding from the top surface must be reproduced in a curved plate with the same type faces on the outside surface, as if the flat-page form were bent backward over a barrel. As high-speed web presses are used by all large newspapers, stereotyping is a necessary part of the newspaper's mechanical work.

The problem of stereotyping is to make an impression of the page form in some plastic material that can later be hardened and used as a mold. Various methods of stereotyping differ largely in the kind of material used as a mold. The first method, which was invented about 1802, employed plaster-of-paris. This or clay was used in all stereotyping for many years, but it was not entirely satisfactory because it could not reproduce engravings and was too slow for newspaper work.

The Papier-mâché Matrix

The papier-mâché process, which is the common process of today, was invented in France in 1829. It receives its name from the fact that the plastic mold used is a sheet of papier-mâché made in alternate layers of thick, unsized paper and tissue paper, pasted together. The mold is called a matrix, or *mat* (in England, a *flong*), and looks like a sheet of heavy cardboard with a smooth surface. When it is moistened it becomes soft enough to take a perfect impression of all the individual pieces of type as it is pressed into the surface of the page form. After it has been baked, it may be used as a mold for molten metal. In practical use, the taking of the impression and the baking of the mat are done in one operation. With the wet mat laid on its surface, the page form is run under a heavy roller, then placed in a press and subjected to heat and pressure at the same time. In about four minutes the form is taken from the press and the mat is removed, ready baked for use. Every large newspaper office has several stereotyping presses, heated by steam or electricity, and regulated so that the mat may be baked as quickly as possible without melting or crushing the type of the form. The mat will not only reproduce type and line engravings, but coarse half-tones as well. After the baking, any large blank spaces in the mat are backed up with small pieces of cardboard to keep them from yielding under the weight of the molten metal and allowing the spaces to fill so that they "print up" in the press. In most offices the raw stereotype mats are made by hand, built up of heavy paper and tissue paper rolled and pasted together, but recently a rotary flong machine has been perfected that makes as many mats in an hour as half a dozen men can make in a day.

Casting the Plates

The work of taking the type impression and baking the mat is only half the process of stereotyping. To make a plate from the mat, the stereotyper must place the mat in a mold and cast molten metal into it. For the curved plates used on web presses, the mat is bent forward and placed in a semicylindrical casting box. The mat forms the outside surface of the plate mold and the casting box supplies the other surfaces. When the molten metal has cooled, the result is a semicylindrical plate with the type faces on the outside surface. This plate must then have its edges trimmed and its inside surface milled or shaved to remove superfluous metal and make it fit the press roll. In small offices this process of casting and trimming plates is done by hand. Larger offices have machines which cast, trim, and cool the plates at the rate of three or four a minute. These machines, of which the autoplate is the best known, have a melting pot as large as a bathtub, two, four, or even more plate molds, and automatic shavers and trimmers to cut the plate into finished shape. The autoplate combines the four operations required in hand casting—a slow task because the plate must cool before it can be handled—and accomplishes the same work in three-fourths of a minute. Other machines are the autoplate junior and the multiplate. Ordinarily several plates are made from each mat, for if the newspaper has several multiple presses, it makes perhaps as many as twenty stereotype plates for each page, clamps them all on the rolls, and runs all its presses at full capacity on the one edition. In that way it prints its entire edition of many thousand copies in a very short time. Without the process of stereotyping to reproduce pages it would need to set up type and make up each page many times to secure enough duplicates. For the small rolls of duplex presses, page plates are made in the form of complete cylinders, instead of the usual half-cylinders.

Other Uses for Stereotyping

The production of page plates for rotary presses is not the only use made of stereotyping in modern newspaper work. Since the process provides a cheap way to produce duplicates of type and cuts, it more than anything else has made possible the extensive syndicates that supply a large part of a newspaper's make-up at less cost than that of setting up the material in the office. As a large number of plates may be made from one mat, the process provides a cheap and convenient way of storing and shipping type impression. Through the process, the syndicate becomes really a coöperative enterprise to divide up the cost of setting type and making engravings—the heaviest item in printing. Once the type is set and the mat made in the syndicate office, many stereotype duplicates can be supplied to newspapers at a fraction of the original composition cost, and many newspapers, especially small ones, buy much of their reading matter and many illustrations in this form. There are a number of syndicates that supply not only feature material but news as well so that a small newspaper within a few hours' express distance from a large city may buy its daily telegraph news in this form, thus saving the cost of telegraph tolls, writing and editing, as well as type composition. The editor who prepares his newspaper in this way is said to "edit with a saw," because he receives the plates in long galley strips, known as "boiler plate," and saws them up to fit his make-up. To save shipping expense the plates are cast about one-fourth of an inch thick with grooves in the bottom so that they may be locked upon a standard base and made "type high." The newspaper keeps the thick, heavy metal bases in its own office and receives by express only the thin top plates.

Many newspapers cut shipping expense still further by owning a small mold for casting stereotype plates and purchasing only the papier-mâché mats from the syndicate. The mat is so light that it may be forwarded by mail and when it arrives in the newspaper office only a few minutes are required to slip it into the mold and cast a plate from it. This is the method ordinarily employed by syndicates that supply feature material with illustrations. If the material is such that the newspaper may wish to use it again at some later time, the mat is filed away in the office. This is especially true of portraits of prominent persons and pictures of places and things that repeatedly come into the public eye. The newspaper files the portrait mats in its "morgue" of biographical material and thus has a portrait ready for instant use. Since certain syndicates now make a specialty of portraits in mat form, many newspapers keep their morgues up to date by purchasing a regular portrait-mat service.

Stereotyping has its faults as well as its advantages. Because of the possibility of imperfect work in the making of the mat or the plate, stereotyped material does not give the clear-cut printing impression of type. It is seldom therefore used in high-grade printing, such as book or magazine work. In the reproduction of half-tone engravings, the papier-mâché mat is too coarse to reproduce the minute dots of fine-line cuts and therefore requires the use of very coarse half-tones. But withal, stereotyping is a necessary link in the chain of inventions that have made possible the modern newspaper.

III. Electrotyping

Electrotyping is a more costly but finer substitute for stereotyping. It is a method of reproducing type and illustrations by electrolysis. It came into use about 1850 and is now extensively used in fine printing. The fundamental idea of the process is the same as that of stereotyping—to take an impression of type matter and use it as a mold for casting plates. But the mold in this case is of copper and is made by electrolysis, much like the process of silver-plating.

The type form or cut to be electrotyped is first reproduced in wax by the simple operation of placing the form under a sheet of wax and subjecting it to pressure in a steam press. The resulting wax mold with the impression of the form on its surface is then given a coat of graphite, iron filings, and a weak solution of copper sulphate, to make it an electrical conductor. A piece of copper imbedded in its corner makes the electrical connection. The mold is then suspended in a solution of copper sulphate under the action of electric current for an hour or two. By electrolysis a thin film of pure copper is deposited uniformly over its surface. When the copper film is about 0.005 inch thick, the mold is removed from the solution and the copper film is peeled from its surface. Zinc chloride solution is then brushed over the back of the film and sheets of tin foil are laid over it and melted down into the film. The copper sheet is then backed up with molten lead. The finished plate is slightly over one-eighth inch thick and must be mounted on a base to be type-high. It is no more nor less than a copper-plated stereotype of the original form. The process produces only one electroplate, but the plate is thinner and lighter than the type form and has a copper printing surface.

Electrotyping is commonly used in book publishing and to some extent in magazine publishing since it results in a very fine printing impression. In book work it is especially valuable because the thin electrotype plates may be stored away between editions more compactly than type forms and save keeping costly type tied up in idleness. These advantages offset the high cost. Electrotyping is used to a large extent in advertising. To insure good make-up in their advertisements, many concerns prefer to supply ready-made electrotype plates, commonly known as "electros," to newspapers and magazines than to trust to the type supply and skill of unknown printers.

IV. Printing Presses

All of the mechanical typesetting and stereotyping machines would be of little use to the modern newspaper if the high-speed perfecting press had not been invented. It alone makes possible the tremendous circulation of city newspapers; without it daily circulation would be measured in thousands rather than tens and hundreds of thousands for, whatever the circulation, it must be printed in an hour or two. The huge mass of machinery called a rotary web perfecting press, capable of printing and folding 100,000 or more eight-page newspapers an hour, seems beyond the understanding of any brain except that of a skilled machinist, but its basic principles are easy to grasp if one remembers that it is the climax of a mechanical development toward a single goal, simple enough in itself. The idea of the designer of a multiple rotary press is identical with that of the maker of the first wooden hand press; both were seeking to build a machine to do the same thing at the greatest possible speed. The fundamental idea of presswork is (1) to spread ink on a type form, (2) to lay a sheet of paper over the form, (3) to press the paper firmly upon the type so that it will receive an inked imprint, and (4) to remove the printed sheet. This is the simple operation that a printing press must perform, and every step in its development has been toward designing a machine that would perform this operation better and at higher speed.

The Hand Press

The first printing press, such as that used by Gutenberg when he began to print from movable types about 1450, was the simplest possible solution of the problem and continued to be used, with slight modification, for three hundred and fifty years, until after 1800. This first kind of press was built of wood and consisted of a flat bed, on which the type form was placed, and a platen above with wooden screw and wheel to press the paper into the type. The pressman inked the type with leather pelt-balls and laid each sheet of paper on the form by hand, but the press was an improvement over the former practice of taking an impression with a mallet and a block of wood. This first press had little advantage in the way of speed over hand imprint, but it furnished a more even impression with less care on the part of the pressman. The first improvement, which came about 1550, was a metal screw and a movable bed, or *rounce,* arranged to slide on a greased track so that the form could be brought out from under the platen for inking. About this time some one added to the movable bed a hinged *tympan* with a *frisket* hinged to it—a cloth-covered wooden framework which served as a holder to keep the paper from flying off the form as the bed was pushed into position under the platen. The next step was to add a series of levers to the screw to give greater pressure. This improvement came in the Blaew press, invented in 1620—a wooden press capable of turning out 200 to 350 "pulls" per hour, or about 100 to 150 copies of a four-page paper. This was the kind of press used by Benjamin Franklin, and its use required nine separate hand operations for each impression. The first iron hand press was the Stanhope press which was built in England in 1798 and had a more complicated system of levers to turn the screw. With twelve hand presses of this type, operated by twenty-four men, the London *Times* in 1814 got out its edition of 10,000 copies in about six hours. In 1816 an American brought out the Clymer Columbian press which had no screw, but secured pressure through a series of levers. This was supplanted in 1822 by the Smith press which used a simple toggle-joint in place of the complicated levers. The final development of the hand press came in the Washington hand press, which had a simplified toggle-joint and a bolted frame to secure greater strength. It has a windlass to move the bed, an improved tympan and frisket, and automatic ink rolls, but it is little faster than the first wooden press of 1450. Many a famous American newspaper began publication on a Washington hand press, and many offices, especially engraving plants, now use it as a proof press.

The First Power Presses

When steam power came into use, press designers went to work on power presses, but their first efforts met with the obstacles of securing the continuous motion that power requires. It was necessary to give the press moving parts. Power could be used to draw the bed back and forth, but to adapt it to applying pressure on the platen at the right time and to handle paper was more difficult. The first power press, which was brought out in 1810, was merely a modified hand press with a toggle-joint operated by a cam to drive the platen down upon the paper. In 1814, Koenig's steam press carried the modification further and printed 1,000 impressions per hour. The idea was further developed in the Treadwell and Adams press of the '20's by making possible feeding at both ends. These presses were built mainly of wood with a power-operated platen in the center and two beds that shuttled in from the two ends. With four men to lay on sheets and four more to remove printed sheets, such a press printed 4,000 to 5,000 impressions an hour.

The Cylinder Press

But in these presses too much time was wasted in the raising and lowering of the platen. The next idea developed was the use of a cylindrical platen which rolled over the type form. The idea was worked out in various ways with a stationary bed or a stationary platen. The first press of this kind was the Koenig press of 1813 which had one large cylinder that made three impressions for each revolution, stopping after each impression for the bed to return. It is to be noted, however, that the bed of this press was moved by a rack-and-pinion system so satisfactory that it continued in use until very recently. In 1814, Koenig built a press with a small continuously moving cylinder; by placing two cylinders side by side and transferring the paper from one side to the other by means of tapes he made it a *perfecting* press— that is, it printed both sides of the paper. Napier's press of 1830 brought in smaller cylinders and grippers to assist in feeding paper sheets. Before the middle of the century, Hoe and Co. had developed various types of cylinder presses that are still in use. This is the type of press known in American printing offices today as the *flat bed* press. The *stop cylinder* idea came back in 1852 in lithographic presses.

But even this type of press was too slow. Each sheet of paper must be fed in by hand, limiting the speed to about 2,000 impressions per hour, and the reciprocating motion of the bed made useless any attempt to increase the speed by the development of automatic feeders. Improvements have brought the cylinder press up to the highest speed that can be attained in printing directly from type in a flat-page form, but the flat-bed press must be fed by a skilled pressman and is too slow for newspaper work.

PRINTING PROCESSES

Type Revolving Machines

To attain greater speed it is obviously necessary to eliminate the reciprocal motion of the bed, to substitute for the flat bed a cylinder revolving in one direction. This requires that the type be placed on the circumference of the cylinder—a difficult problem—but the next step in press design was the application of this idea. In 1848, the London *Times* installed a press, called the Applegate Machine, which was arranged so that the type form could be placed on the curved surface of a cylinder. The printing cylinder was 5½ feet in diameter and stood with a vertical axis; its surface was not an exact curve, but was made up of a number of flat surfaces each as wide as a column. The type was secured in these flat surfaces by V-shaped column rules. Each column therefore presented a flat surface and "overlays" on the impression cylinder were necessary for perfect imprint. The press had eight impression cylinders, grouped about the central printing cylinder, and with eight men feeding in sheets of paper, it printed 10,000 copies an hour. Only one of these presses was contructed because in the meantime there had been built in America, in 1846, the Hoe Type revolving machine, which carried out the idea with greater perfection. Its type was held on the surface of the cylinder by V-shaped rules, but the arrangement was such that the flat surfaces were eliminated and the type surface was a perfect curve. The first of these Hoe type-revolving presses was built for the Philadelphia *Public Ledger*, and had four impression cylinders, giving an output of 8,000 sheets an hour printed on one side. Later type-revolving presses with as many as ten impression cylinders were built, increasing the capacity to 20,000 an hour. Several New York dailies used them. But these presses were far from the ultimate goal sought, since they required one man for each impression cylinder to feed in sheets of paper and the highest speed that a feeder can attain is about 2,000 sheets an hour. They also printed only one side of the sheet at a time. The fact that the type was held by columns partly accounts for the headline styles of the day—vertical display in many one-column crosslines, rather than the modern horizontal display in banners and spreads.

Web Paper and Stereotyping

The problem to be solved then was one of feeding the press and its solution was difficult as long as individual sheets of paper had to be used. In 1861, however, improved machines in the paper mills made possible the making of paper in continuous rolls and the development of stereotyping offered a substitute for the type-revolving idea. Papier-mâché stereotyping had been used in book work since 1829, but it was not until 1861 that it was developed sufficiently to reproduce pages of newspaper size. With the curved stereotype plate it was possible to substitute small cylinders for the huge type-revolving cylinders and to increase the output of the press by adding more printing cylinders. As all the motion was continuous, it was also possible to print from a roll of paper, rather than on separate sheets. With the development of impression cylinders that lessened the "offset" on the back of the paper, it was easy to run the sheet continuously from one printing roll to another so as to print it on both sides. Thus the rotary web perfecting press was evolved. *Web* is the name applied to the roll of paper, and *perfecting* means "printing on both sides." The only problems that remained were those of cutting and folding the sheets.

The Rotary Press

The first web perfecting press in England was the Walter Machine built for the London *Times* in 1862. It had a single long roll to which the paper was returned for impression on the reverse side and used cutting cylinders to separate the sheets. The newspapers were delivered flat and no folding machine was attached to it until about 1870. In America, the Bullock web press was built in 1865 and had an automatic folder; it received its paper from a roll, but cut it into sheets before the paper reached the printing cylinders. Hoe and Company improved the cutting and delivery process in 1871 and developed the speed of this single roll rotary to 18,000 copies per hour. In 1875, the same company devised a rotating folder of greater speed which prepared the way for future developments; all later rotaries printed the paper before cutting it. The printing press had now reached the stage of operating at high speed with no hand work and its future development was simply one of refining and adding to its mechanism.

The huge web perfecting press of today, reduced to simplest form, consists of a roller with two, four, or eight stereotyped page plates on its circumference, a platen roller to press the paper against the printing plates, an ink roller revolving against the plates, and a continuous sheet of paper running between. Such a set of rollers prints, of course, only one side of the paper, but the paper may run on through a similar set a few feet away at the same speed for reverse impression. If each roller carries four page plates, four pages are printed on each side of the paper as it passes through the two sets of rollers, and the result is an eight-page newspaper. If each roller carries eight plates, the two sets print sixteen pages. Just beyond the printing cylinders is a folding machine that automatically cuts and folds the paper into separate newspapers as fast as it comes out. Suppose, however, that the press is built with two pairs of printing rollers receiving paper from two webs and feeding the two streams of paper into the same folder. The result is a multiple press that will print papers of twice as many pages or will print twice as many papers of the same size. Thus the capacity of the press can be increased *ad infinitum* by the addition of more sets of printing rolls. For color supplement work, the paper may be run through several sets of printing rolls, each printing a different color on the same page.

Multiple Rotaries

The first step in the development of the multiple rotary was the Hoe Double Supplement press built in the early '80's. It had one eight-page and one four-page printing roll and folded and pasted the various sheets together. In 1887, the first quadruple press, a combination of two simple rotaries, appeared; it printed 48,000 eight-page papers per hour. The sextuple was evolved in 1889 by the combination of two double supplement presses in one. It prints 90,000 four-page papers, or 72,000 eight-page papers, or 48,000 twelve-page, or 36,000 sixteen-page, or 24,000 twenty-four-page papers an hour. It has three double rolls, two folders, and uses about twenty-six miles

PRINTING PROCESSES

of paper an hour. The next step was the octuple, with four eight-page rolls—just twice the quadruple—and a capacity of 96,000 eight-page, or 60,000 twelve-page papers an hour. Two of these were then built together in the double octuple for color supplement work, with a capacity of 96,000 four-page papers in several colors an hour. The later double sextuple press has twelve eight-plate cylinders and prints 96,000 twelve-page papers in black, or 48,000 sixteen-page papers in color each hour.

These various combinations are built in special forms to suit the individual purchaser. There is no standard design, but there are three general arrangements of rolls. (1) The two parts of the quadruple or sextuple may be built at right angles to each other with the folder between; (2) the various sets of rollers may be placed in two or three decks, one above the other; (3) or they may be placed in tandem, one behind the other. One form is called the *straightline* because of the direct course of the paper through the press. A more recent form is the *duplex* which uses smaller rollers and cylindrical page plates. Because of the large size of the newspaper page, the multiple presses are very large affairs, costing many thousands of dollars, but they alone make possible the tremendous circulations of today. A battery of several multiple presses, all printing from duplicate stereotype plates, will print the largest newspaper's entire edition in a very short time.

Other Kinds of Presses

Modified rotary presses are now used to a large extent for printing magazines and books. The only difference is that each revolution of the printing rollers prints thirty-two or sixty-four magazine pages instead of eight newspaper pages. There are, of course, many variations in the construction of rotary presses and many different models; it is possible here to give only the basic principle. Many steps also have been omitted in the description of the development of the high-speed press. There are many other kinds of presses working on slightly different principles that have not been mentioned although they are in common use. One of them is the well-known job press which is an ingenious machine using a flat form and flat platen.

Offset Printing

Offset printing is a kind of press work whereby the impression on the paper is made, not directly from the surface of the type or printing plate, but by means of a transfer of ink from the printing surface to a rubber surface and then to the paper. It was invented about 1884 and further developed by the construction of the rotary offset press in 1906. The process is based on an accident that occurs every day in the printing office— when a printer feeding a high-speed job press misses a sheet and carelessly allows the press to print on its platen. If he does not at once put on a clean platen, the next sheet inserted receives an impression on both sides, one from the inked type and the other an *offset* from the ink deposited on the platen. An English publisher casually noticing that the offset impression was more attractive than the direct impression, received the idea which has since developed into offset printing. The process is a mechanical duplicate of this printing office accident with the direct impression omitted and a rubber platen inserted

PRINTING PROCESSES

in place of the paper or composition platen used in direct printing.

In the rotary offset press, the roller which carries the printing surface prints directly on a roller with a smooth rubber surface. The inky image thus deposited on the rubber roller then becomes the printing surface for a sheet of paper pressed against its surface by a second platen. This results in a richer and smoother print than is ordinarily obtained by direct impression. Further, it furnishes a means of printing from various kinds of printing surfaces at the same time. Formerly relief, intaglio, and lithographic printing required separate presses and different kinds of presswork. But it matters not what kind of plate is used in the offset press, the rubber roller takes ink from one as well as another.

"Make-ready"

As many newspapers are still printed on flat bed presses, many newspaper men confront the old problem of "making ready" which has delayed many an edition. As even the most perfect type does not give an absolutely level surface, it must be brought to a perfect plane after it has been placed on the bed of the press. This involves pasting pieces of paper, or *underlays,* under low areas of type, or *overlays* upon the part of the platen that bears on the low areas. Especially in the making ready of pages containing cuts is the work arduous. Make-ready requires more time than stereotyping, and careless make-ready always results in uneven impression. Some make-ready is required on a rotary press, although most of the unevenness of the type surface is eliminated when the pliable mat is placed in the mold.

"Fudge"

Fudge printing is an interesting phase of web press work used by newspapers that make an effort to print extras containing up-to-the-minute news. As it takes about seven minutes to make a stereotype plate, even after a page form has been remade to include later news, and several more minutes to place the new plate on the press, the newspaper is driven to various mechanical expedients to have a sporting extra with a full account of the game ready for spectators as they leave the field or a market extra containing closing quotations in the street as soon as the stock exchange closes. Fudge is one of these expedients. A fudge plate is a front-page stereotype plate with a blank space of varying size in the upper right corner—perhaps there is also a blank space where the banner headline should be. As the paper passes over the fudge plate this space on the front page receives no impression. But further on in its course the paper passes over a small roller, called the fudge roll, which contains just enough type to fill the blank space. The fudge roll has no stereotype plate, but has ingenious clamps to hold linotype slugs on its surface. Only a moment is required to stop the press and change these slugs, and the news can thus be brought up to the minute without delay. To facilitate the use of fudge in extras, some newspapers have a linotype machine and a telephone or telegraph operator in the pressroom. Changes in the banner head to accord with the changing news are accomplished in the same way. Because the fudge is on a separate roller, also, it can be printed in red or green ink to emphasize its content. Another expedient is a type-high blank space in the plate in which the final score can be stamped with a steel punch.

Ready-Prints

In connection with presswork, the ready-prints used by many country newspapers may be mentioned. To save composition and presswork, many country editors purchase their paper from syndicates with one side of each sheet already filled with feature articles and other general material. The editor prints his local news, advertisements, and editorials on the other side of the paper, and folds it so that the ready-printed material is inside. He is saved not only all the composition of the inside pages, but one run on the press as well, and the ready-print costs him little, if any, more than white paper. Because the ready printed pages are always folded inside, they are often dubbed "patent insides."

V. Engraving

Until about 1880 the only illustrations available for newspaper use were wood-cuts—pictures laboriously carved by hand in hardwood blocks, chalk plates, and similar makeshifts. Wood-cuts were costly because they required skilled workmanship, it took much time to make one, and the resulting print was not highly artistic. Hence few newspapers printed pictures except small stock cuts used mainly in advertising. The situation was entirely changed in the eighties when the photo-engraving process came into commercial use. Cheap, attractive illustrations are now within the reach of any newspaper.

Line Engravings

The simplest photo-engraving is the line engraving which reproduces an illustration consisting of a white background and black lines with shadings of fine black lines and no tones or smooth masses of shading—a pen and ink drawing is a good example. Such a picture has only two tones, black and white. The making of such a cut is accomplished by a process almost as simple as the making of a photograph. The picture that is to be reproduced is placed in a strong light and photographed on a sensitized glass plate in a large camera. When this plate has been developed it is used as a negative to "print" the picture on a sheet of zinc or copper whose surface has been covered with a sensitized coating, just as a photographic print is made on sensitized paper. Treatment with ink after a water bath develops the plate, removes affected parts of the sensitized coating, and leaves on the metal plate lines and areas of coating corresponding to the black lines and areas in the original drawing. After the remaining coating has been built up with a coating of dragon's blood, a red substance that clings to the sticky lines, and hardened, the metal plate is immersed in a nitric acid bath which etches, or eats away, the unprotected areas and leaves the coated lines untouched. The plate, after proper cleaning, thus bears on its surface the original drawing in relief as clean-cut as if engraved by hand. This plate is then a line engraving that may be used to print the picture on paper. But it prints only black lines without tones. Because it is usually made of zinc, it is commonly called a *zinc etching*.

Half-Tone Engravings

The half-tone engraving is a modification of the line engraving whereby the blackness of the impression is broken up into contrasting tones. It is obvious that when only black ink is used in printing, an unbroken area will print nothing but solid black. To produce a gray or a lighter tone with black ink, the printing area must be broken up into small spots of varying size to shade into the white surface of the paper. This is what the half-tone process does—it breaks up black areas into fine points.

In principle the half-tone process is based on photographic methods similar to those of the line engraving; the chief difference lies in the use of a screen to break up the solid black areas. When the negative is exposed in the camera, a screen is placed in front of the negative to break up the light. The screen consists of two clear glass plates with fine parallel lines ruled on their surface with a diamond or acid; one plate is ruled horizontally and the other vertically so that together they make a grating of fine cross-lines. The result of the exposure is a negative in which the unaffected coating consists of a series of small dots. When this negative is used to "print" on a sensitized metal plate, the same effect is produced. Etching of this plate produces an engraving whose surface is made up of hundreds of small points varying in size according to the tones of the original picture. There are of course many variations in the practical application of this process, but this is its principle in simplest form. For ordinary work the half-tone plate is made by stripping the film from the negative and laying it on the metal plate instead of "printing" its form on a sensitized coating.

Using the Cuts

The line engraving is ordinarily made on a zinc plate and the largest areas between the lines are *routed out* with a cutting tool to prevent "printing up" in white areas. It is used for printing cartoons, line drawings, and all illustrations that consist of black lines. The plate is about one-fourth inch thick and is tacked upon a wooden block to make it type-high. Its size is governed by the distance from the camera's lens in the production of the negative.

The fineness of the half-tone is regulated by the fineness of the screen. For newspaper work when stereotyping is necessary, a coarse screen is used, a screen with from 60 to 100 lines per inch. This produces an engraving with relatively large points on its surface, and the black dots that compose its tones are plainly visible on the printed page. Such plates are usually made of zinc. For finer work, a screen with from 100 to 160 lines per inch is used and the points and dots become so small that they can hardly be seen. For such engravings zinc is too coarse-grained and copper plates must be used. Coarse zinc half-tones are used most in newspaper work because they are cheaper and the stereotype mat will not take an accurate impression if the lines are closer together than 60 or 80 lines per inch. The finer copper half-tones are used for printing that is not stereotyped. In some cases a fine half-tone is used in stereotyped work by leaving a hole, or mortise, in the stereotype plate and setting the original engraving into it.

Make-ready

When the original type and cuts are used in the press, making ready involves evening up the cuts with overlays or underlays to "bring out" the tones. In very fine work the pressman may spend several days making ready. In

PRINTING PROCESSES

stereotyping, an overlay of stiff paper is usually placed on the mat over a cut to press the mat firmly into it. A fine cut when properly made ready will reproduce with black ink the delicate shades of the original photograph.

Both zinc and copper cuts are mounted and handled in the same way. Their cost is based on a price per square inch. In newspaper work their size is specified in column width for the size of the drawing then determines the vertical dimension; in all work in fact only one dimension need be given and a cut of almost any size may be made from one drawing by relative enlargement or reduction. For the best half-tones, clear-cut glossy photographs are required; for the line engraving a drawing with much contrast is necessary.

Color Engravings

Colored pictures are printed by means of a development of the photo engraving process requiring a separate line engraving or half-tone for each color. Since all colors are but combinations of the three primary colors, red, yellow, and blue, three plates properly shaded and overlapping in mixed areas, will reproduce all the known colors and combinations of colors. There must be a plate that contains all the blue areas, a plate containing the red areas, and another the yellow. To reproduce the picture with these three plates, each must be printed with colored ink successively on the same sheet of paper. Often a fourth, or black, plate is added to bring out the shading and tone.

The production of the three plates requires three successive repetitions of the photographic process through different colored glass filters. The colored picture is first photographed through a filter which excludes all but red rays and the red components of mixed rays and produces a negative of the red areas. This process is carried through to completion and a corresponding "red" plate is made. Then the process is repeated for the "blue" plate, then for the "yellow" plate, and finally without a filter for the "black" plate. The four cuts must then be mounted on separate bases and carefully trimmed so that their separate impressions coincide, or register, in printing. The printer then places his yellow plate in the press and prints with yellow ink; then he substitutes the red plate and runs the same pages through the press again printing with red ink—and so on. The result of the four impressions is a colored reproduction of the original colored picture. It is to be noted, however, that the filter used is not of the same color as the ink to be used but a combination of its *complementary* colors; the filter used in making the "blue" plate is therefore orange. In making colored half-tones, also, the print is not made by stripping the film from the negative but by direct photographic printing to insure perfect register of the minute dots which constitute the half-tone surface.

The engravings may be either line engravings or half-tones, although the latter are usually used. Newspaper color work, the Sunday supplement, is frequently done with etchings printed on a rotary press; the various color plates are mounted on different cylinders and the web runs through them in succession. For finer work, however, half-tones are used. The finest work requires four color plates, as explained above, but much color printing is done with three, or even two, plates. The absence of one of the primary colors is compensated by the use of simpler color mixtures that approximate the tones of the original picture. Color plates are very costly because of the great skill and care required in the making; the four plates for a picture of magazine page size may cost as much as one hundred and fifty dollars.

The Ben Day Process

The Ben Day process is a method of imitating half-tone work in the background of line etchings. By means of a special film through which ink is rubbed on the drawings or on the metal plate, before it is etched, a stippled effect of uniform black dots or fine rulings is produced in the shaded areas without the use of a screen in the camera. It finds its commonest use in the making of sketches and detailed drawings for newspaper and other publications and is valuable because it saves the draughtsman the work of shading dark portions of his drawing with a pen. The artist merely draws the outlines of his sketch and specifies Ben Day shading in certain areas. There are many varieties of Ben Day stipple work and the draughtsman orders them by number from the engraver's chart.

Rotogravures

With the invention of the rotary photogravure press in 1906, intaglio printing of illustrated supplements has come into common use and many American newspapers now have such presses. The photogravure is merely the reverse of a line engraving, made by a similar photographic process with grooves and hollows in place of raised lines. Its presswork requires the wiping of the plate after it has been filled with ink. When printed on a rotary press it is called a rotogravure. In such a case the film stripped from the negative is not placed on a flat copper plate, but on the surface of a large copper roller which constitutes the printing surface after it has been etched with acid. One side of the roller passes through an ink bath which fills the impressions in the intaglio engraving, the surplus ink is cleaned away with a knife, and the ink is lifted out by the paper which passes over it. After the picture has been printed, the copper roller is turned down in a lathe to remove the engraving. Although merely a reversed line engraving, the rotogravure is given the tones of a photograph by the varying depth of the engraving and the use of transparent ink. It has been used with greatest success with brown ink which gives varying sepia tones. A recent combination of rotogravure and color printing is known as the "coloroto."

Other Kinds of Engravings

The subject of illustrative printing is a large one, constantly changing and developing. The practical processes of today may be divided into four general groups on the basis of the kind of plate used: relievo, intaglio, lithographic, and collotype.

Relievo, or relief, printing is the name applied to all processes which employ plates whose printing lines and areas are raised so as to receive the ink and press it into the paper. The group includes all printing from type, electrotype plates, stereotype plates, wood engravings, half-tone engravings, and line engravings. In each of these the printing, or inked, surface is in relief. It is the kind of printing in common use in all newspaper, publication, and job work.

PRINTING PROCESSES

Intaglio printing is a designation applied to all processes which employ plates whose printing surfaces are in bas-relief—the lines and surfaces which represent the picture are grooves or hollows cut into the plate. In the process of printing with intaglio plates, the grooves and hollows are filled with ink, the surface of the plate is wiped clean, and when the plate is pressed upon the paper the ink is transferred to the paper by absorption and remains in the form of ridges or raised surfaces. An illustration is the engraved visiting card whose ink may be felt with the finger. This class of printing includes copper and steel-plate engravings, stone engravings, acid etchings, aquatint etchings, mezzotint engravings, music engraving, photogravures, Rembrandt photogravures, Renaissance photogravures, and others. The various names designate the material used in the plate and the process by which it is engraved.

Lithographic printing includes all processes which employ flat surfaces to which ink is applied directly in the form of the design desired and absorbed by the paper when the impression is taken. That is, the picture is drawn in absorbent ink directly on the surface of a flat plate and transferred to paper pressed upon it. The work may be done in black or in colors. The commonest illustration is the colored lithograph for advertising purposes. Stone plates were originally used in the process but now, for finer work, aluminum, zinc, and other kinds of plates are used, and various processes have been developed as substitutes for the hand work necessary in the old-fashioned stone lithograph.

Collotype printing is a development of lithographic printing in that it employs an unetched surface, but its surface is a film of sensitized gelatine which receives ink and transfers it to paper. This is the least common of all methods of reproducing pictures and is used only for very fine work.

The Newspaper Art Department

The art department is a common part of most large newspaper plants of today. Sometimes it consists of a staff photographer with a dark room in the office; sometimes it includes a number of artists and draughtsmen; some newspapers also have facilities for making their own engravings. The work of the art department consists in making and retouching photographs, drawing decorative borders around photographs, making sketches, diagrams, maps, and other illustrative or decorative material. One kind of work consists in making layouts of pictures—groups of photographs interwoven with decorative borders and sketches. As the photographs must be reproduced in half-tones and etchings must be made of the pen work, a layout usually consists of several cuts. To make such a composite picture, the artist does the pen work, borders and sketches, on a large sheet of paper leaving blank spaces here and there for the photographs. He then numbers the photographs to correspond with the spaces and indicates the size to which the photographs are to be reduced. The engraver then makes the separate cuts and puts the layout together. Color work is done in water color or even oil. Attached to the same department are cartoonists and comic artists who provide the newspaper's pictorial humor.

Exercises

1. Trace out in a daily newspaper and in various magazines the work done by various machines and processes discussed above.
2. Inspect machines in printing and engraving plants.
3. Illustrative material may be obtained from companies that manufacture these machines.
4. Engravers will supply illustrations of various kinds of cuts, screens, color proofs, etc.
5. This chapter may well be taken up in connection with make-up.

CHAPTER X

SMALL PUBLICATION WORK

THE handling of small publications—student newspapers and magazines, local "boosting" monthlies, association quarterlies, house organs, propagandist pamphlets, and other small periodicals—can hardly be considered a regular part of the newspaper desk man's work. But since a newspaper is always associated with a printing office, sometimes a job office, a newspaper man is expected by the general public to know all about printing and publishing work and to be well fitted to take charge of publications. Whenever any body of people determines to issue a publication, it instinctively turns to a so-called "journalist" for advice or assistance. If there is a school of journalism nearby, the first impulse is to ask advice of the instructor or one of his students. In college circles, most student publications are handled by students of journalism who are studying to be newspaper men. Since there seems to be this close relation in the public mind between newspaper work and the ability to edit any small publication, it is well for the newspaper man or journalism student to know something about it.

This discussion will be by no means a conclusive treatment of publishing work or a handbook for the prospective publisher. It is merely a group of convenient methods and systems, classified for reference, and the readiest answers to some of the problems in small publication work. Some of the methods are new; others are as old as printing. They were gleaned from work in large magazine offices and from bitter experience with small publications. Added to the material in preceding chapters, they may suggest a starting point for the inexperienced "editor and business manager." Much of the discussion is intended especially for the editor or teacher-adviser of student publications in college or high school, whether they are working with the newspaper or magazine form.

I. Planning the Publication

The first step in launching a publication is to design its physical make-up. Before the editor approaches a printer for terms or issues a call for "copy," he must have a definite idea of the size, make-up, general appearance, and reading-matter capacity of his publication. Too many young editors leave the consideration of these matters until they have gone to the printer for terms, and the result is that the printer, in order to get down to brass tacks, designs the publication for them. It is then the printer's publication. If the editor will plan it and visualize it in advance, he can make it his own publication, and incidentally he will receive better terms and treatment from the printer because of the knowledge of the job he evidences.

Cost Considerations

The style and appearance of the publication must in general suit its purpose. It may be modest or bizarre, cheap or rich, small or large. These conditions are to some extent determined by the money at the editor's disposal, but in most cases a handsome publication costs no more than an ugly one if the editor knows how to make the most of his money. Pleasing appearance depends upon paper, type, size, and make-up. Of these, paper affects the cost most, because paper is usually the largest item. But with proper knowledge, the editor may choose a paper of moderate cost and make it appear rich by his selection of size and typographical make-up. To do this, however, he must know paper sizes and the basis on which paper is judged. Pleasing typography costs no more, in general, than ugly typography if the editor knows how to select type and can adjust his selection to the printer's stock, knowing whether to call for machine or hand composition. Size has little to do with the cost if the editor knows how to utilize paper of standard size with the least waste and how to economize on press work, the second largest item in cost. With a clear understanding of the purpose of his publication, the editor may obtain a pleasing make-up without materially increasing expense.

The Capacity Problem

The planning of the publication involves also an estimate of the amount of reading matter it is to carry. The editor should have a fairly clear idea of the number of articles and their length before he attempts to design make-up. He must know approximately the space that must be devoted to advertising and the position of the space. That is, he must suit his design to the capacity required. Some of the problems he must face are as indicated in the following discussions:

1. Size of Pages

The Usual Sizes.—The general page size is determined mainly by the purpose of the publication and the manner of its distribution. For some purposes the smaller sizes— 5 x 7½ or 6 x 9 inches—may be chosen. These sizes are easy to read, easy to mail, and are the largest sizes in which the type-matter may be set in single columns. Larger sizes —8 x 11, 9 x 12½, etc.—require double columns. The largest practical size, 11 x 14, requires three columns. Magazines are at present tending toward larger pages, about 8½ x 12, to accommodate more decorative page make-up and to enable them to sell advertising space next to reading matter. In choosing the page size, the editor must consider the weight of his paper, for a larger page requires heavier paper.

Standard Paper Sizes.—Exact page size cannot be selected until the paper has been chosen, since a variation of half an inch may involve a serious waste of paper. Book paper is made in standard sizes but it is not always possible to get all sizes in the paper chosen. The standard sizes are as follows:

22 x 28 inches	28 x 42 inches
24 x 38 "	32 x 44 "
25 x 38 "	36 x 48 "
26 x 40 "	

After the general page size and kind of paper have been selected, the exact page size may be figured from the paper size best suited to give the required number of pages with the least press work. The exact page size is determined by dividing the two dimensions of the white sheet by the number of folds, as will be shown later. In figuring these dimensions, the editor should allow for a trim about one-fourth inch at the top, bottom, and one side of each page after the paper has been folded. A good appearance will usually be assured if a standard proportion of about 5 to 7½ is followed. Another rule is to make the diagonal of the page twice its width. These details the editor can work out with the printer when he chooses the paper, if he has a general page size in mind, but he should not attempt to decide the size of the type body of the page before he knows exactly how large his pages are to be.

2. Number of Pages

How Press Work Affects Size.—The chief consideration in deciding the number of pages is the number of "runs" on the press. Given the page size and the approximate number of pages desired, it is necessary to figure the exact number of pages on the basis of the size of the printer's press. To explain, a small booklet is not printed page by page on small sheets of paper, but a number of pages are made up into one form and printed all at once on a large sheet of paper. The paper is then folded and trimmed into finished form. For example, a sixteen-page publication would be divided into two eight-page forms. Eight pages would be printed on one side of the sheet and the other eight on the reverse. The operation of printing each form is called a "run on the press." And it is the number of runs on the press that has much to do with the cost of the publication, not because of the time required for actual printing, so much as the time consumed in making up the forms and making ready on the press.

Methods of Folding.—To understand how press runs are reckoned, it is necessary to understand the methods of folding that printers employ. Obviously a single leaf of paper printed on both sides is the simplest form of press work; it carries two pages but cannot be bound into

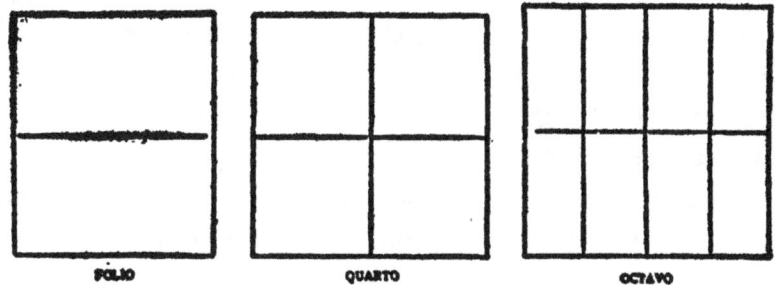

EXAMPLES OF FOLDING

a book. The next step is to print two pages on each side and fold the sheet once; the result is called a *folio*—it has two leaves or four pages. If the sheet is folded twice it is called a *quarto;* four pages are printed on each side and the quarto contains four leaves or eight pages. Three foldings gives the *octavo*, with eight pages on each side; it has eight leaves or sixteen pages. The next step is twelve pages on a side, or *duodecimo*, containing 24 pages; this is rarely used in modern printing. Above duodecimo, the number of pages is indicated thus: 16mo, 32mo, 64mo. Mo or ° means in each case the number of *pages* on one side of the sheet or the number of *leaves* in the finished book. A complete table would be as follows:

```
Unfolded .......... single sheet .....  1 leaf,     2 pages
folio   ..............  1 fold .........  2 leaves,  4 pages
quarto  ............  2 folds.........  4 leaves,  8 pages
octavo  ............  3 folds.........  8 leaves, 16 pages
16mo    ..............  4 folds.........  16 leaves, 32 pages
32mo    ..............  5 folds.........  32 leaves,    pages
64mo                    folds..........  64 leaves, 128 pages
```

Reckoning Number of Pages.—It will be seen then that the number of pages in the booklet must be a multiple of *four*. An odd number of pages is impossible, and a number not divisible by four means a pasted inset of one sheet. Beyond this, the question is determined by the size of the printer's press. If our pages are so large that the press cannot print more than eight at one time, our publication must be made in octavo form. That means that two runs, the smallest possible number, will give sixteen pages. We would hardly select twelve pages, for that would require four runs—a folio and a quarto, each requiring two runs—and the extra press work would cost more than the composition of the four pages saved. If sixteen are not enough, it is best to enlarge to two octavos, or thirty-two pages, for any enlargement requires two extra runs and we may as well get as many pages as possible out of the press work. Our octavo publication will then economize press work if its total number of pages is some multiple of sixteen—16, 32, 48, 64, etc.

Ordinarily, however, if the pages are of fairly small size the printer's press will accommodate a 16-page form and the 16mo is the cheapest size to select. As 16mo carries 32 pages, the publication's number of pages should be some multiple of 32 for greatest economy. When we go beyond octavo, however, the number of pages increases so fast that composition cost goes ahead of press cost and it is economical to increase the number of runs instead of the number of pages. For instance, 48 pages— one 16mo and one octavo—would be cheaper than 64, although four runs are necessary in each case. However 44 pages would not be cheaper because it would require one 16mo, one quarto, and one folio—six runs on the press. Forty pages would require one 16mo and one quarto, but the quarto run would be a costly waste of press work.

It will be seen therefore that some knowledge on the editor's part will go far to save needless press work. In brief, it is usually wise to plan the publication in octavos—multiples of 16 pages—or in 16mo, multiples of 32. Any growth in the publication's size should be in octavo at least, for quartos are wasteful. This figuring is upset sometimes in a printing office that uses duodecimo forms, which lead to the use of multiples of 12 pages. The duodecimo, combined with octavo or 16mo, gives greater elasticity. Printers sometimes handle quartos and octavos by printing the entire eight or sixteen pages on both sides of a large sheet and cutting the sheet in two.

The mechanical working out of this press work can be learned only in the printing office. The arrangement of a 32-page form so that the pages will be in their proper places looks to the editor like a complicated task, but the practical printer works it out from a chart that is a part of his stock in trade. The folding is done by hand or by a folding machine. After folding the booklet is stitched on a wire stapling machine and the pages are cut by trimming off three edges. When the run is more than 16mo, it is customary to cut the sheet in two before folding so that the paper will not bunch along the folded edges. The editor's only part in the proceeding is to insist that the printer make up the form with care so that the margins of the finished pages will be of equal width.

3. Paper

How Paper Is Selected.—Paper must be chosen with reference to these points: weight, strength and body, surface, durability, color, and cost. The weight is usually determined on the basis of the size; the larger the page, the heavier the paper must be. Heavy paper gives the publication a richer appearance but it also increases the mailing cost—sometimes a serious item. In choosing weight, the editor must take care to avoid paper so light and transparent that black type shows through it. Strength and body are almost synonymous with general quality; the stronger and more brittle a paper is, the better its quality—and the greater its cost. Weight has little to do with quality for a heavy paper may be too soft and flimsy to stand press work and folding. It is well to test quality by tearing a corner of the paper or by "rattling" it to see how brittle it is. Surface must be chosen with reference to typography and illustrations. Soft paper prints deeply and hard paper receives only a surface impression. The relation of surface to typography will be discussed under Type, but here the kind of illustrations must be considered. Zinc engravings print well on almost any paper, but half-tones, especially fine copper cuts, require a smooth, hard surface. Durability is of little importance to the small publisher unless he is concerned with a publication that will have future value. Color is more important than is generally supposed because absolutely white paper is rare. Almost all paper is slightly tinted to conceal imperfections. Some papers have a slightly bluish tint; others more of a cream color. The choice between them depends upon the kind of cover chosen and the effect desired. By specifying ink slightly

SMALL PUBLICATION WORK

off the black and delicately tinted paper, the editor may obtain a pleasing color scheme without additional cost. The cost is determined by the other considerations, and, if the editor has a clear idea of his publication, he can usually find what he wishes in moderately priced papers. The editor should ask to see the sample booklets sent out by the paper manufacturers and, when unable to choose between two kinds, should ask the printer to fold a sample sheet of each into the form of the finished publication. Paper is retailed by the pound, and the weight given in the sample book is the weight of a ream (500 sheets) of that size. If a sample is marked "25 x 38, 60 pound," the meaning is that 500 sheets of that size weigh 60 pounds. If the same paper is sold in large sheets, however, its weight is listed higher; thus, 25 x 38, 60 pounds, may be the same paper as 28 x 42, 70 pounds.

Really to know how to judge paper, however, it is necessary to know something of the manufacture of paper, what it is made of, how it is made, and the various kinds on the market.

Paper Materials.—Paper is made of wood-pulp, wood-fiber, rags, or esparto grass. Rag paper is rarely used for anything except writing paper, and grass paper is mainly used for wrapping and other rough uses. The common printing papers are the wood-pulp and wood-fiber, sometimes called mechanical and chemical pulp. Of these the latter is the better because the wood in it is in long shreds that knit together and give greater strength—it is also more costly because the fibers are separated in the pulp by chemical, rather than mechanical means.

How Paper Is Made.—The general steps in paper making and their effects on the finished product may be described briefly. The ingredients in the paper, rags or wood, are first chopped into small bits, mixed with water or chemicals, beaten, cooked, and reduced to a pulpy semi-fluid mass. In hand-made paper, this pulp is spread out in sheets on wire screens, but hand-made does not concern the small editor. The paper that he will buy is made by machinery. The semi-fluid pulp is poured upon a slowly moving belt of wire cloth that vibrates meanwhile to spread the pulp into an even layer over its surface. If the belt vibrates only in one direction, the paper is not so good because its fibers all lie in one direction. This quality may be discovered by an attempt to tear the paper first one way and then the other. If the top wires in this belt all run one way, with some perhaps higher than others, the paper receives a series of parallel impressions and is called *laid* paper. A belt woven in the form of a grating, on the other hand, produces the mesh appearance seen in *wove* paper.

As the wet pulp passes along on the wire belt, it goes under a roller, called the *dandy roll*, which squeezes the water out of the pulp. The dandy roll has a wire cloth surface and the nature of its weave produces the laid or wove effect on the upper side of the paper. It is the dandy roll, also, that puts in the *watermark* by means of raised letters or figures on its surface.

Judging Paper Surface.—Surfacing is accomplished by means of huge steel rollers, called *calenders,* through which the paper is run. Once through the rollers produces *machine-finished* paper. More rolling produces surfaces ranging through *calendered* to *supercalendered.* Each rolling makes the paper harder and smoother. Some paper is covered with *sizing* to fill the pores and keep ink

SMALL PUBLICATION WORK

from spreading. Other paper is filled, or *loaded*, with clay or some similar substance, to give it smoother surface. Other paper is *supercoated*, and still other paper is *enameled* on one or both sides. *Plate* paper is that which has been subjected to great pressure to produce a smooth surface on both sides without filling. Among the unsized papers are *copperplate* and various craft papers. *Antique* paper is a thick, porous paper that has received only light calendering, or none at all. The list of surfaces as they range from rough to smooth is: antique, egg shell, news print, machine-finished, English finish, calendered, sized, supercalendered, coated, enameled, plate, etc. *Deckle-edged* is a name applied to paper that has not been trimmed but bears the natural rough edge produced by the rubber deckles that keep the paper from falling off the wire cloth belt. As half-tone engravings require smooth paper, it is better to choose for them something at least as smooth as calendered paper, on the basis that the finer cuts require smoother paper.

4. Type

Size of Type Page.—The first consideration in the matter of typography is the size of the type page with reference to the size of the paper page, and it is impossible to determine the size of the type page until after the paper has been chosen. Then the type page must be designed with regard to uniform margins on all sides. It is well to allow generous margins, even if this involves sacrifice elsewhere, for they give richer appearance. The smallest margin that can be used with success is ¾ or ⅞ inch; from that the margin may go up to 1¼ inches with good effect. Certain unusual effects are produced by unequal margins—wider at the bottom and outside than at other edges—but this treatment requires corresponding richness in typography and paper.

Column Widths.—Shall the publication be set in one, two, or three columns? This is almost automatically decided by the size of body type selected. The extreme column width employed in modern printing is about 40 ems pica, or 6½ inches—and this only with large type—for longer lines are difficult to read. Therefore if the type page is wider than 6 inches it must be divided for any type With average body type the maximum line length is much shorter. In the case of 7- or 8-point type, the best column widths are from 13 to 18 ems pica, 2-1/6 to 3 inches. With 9-point type, the column may safely be 21 ems pica, or 3½ inches, wide. With 10- or 11-point, especially when it is leaded, the width may run to 27 ems, or 4½ inches. On the other hand, the narrowest practicable column for any type is 12 ems, or 2 inches; the narrowest for 9-point is about 18 ems; the narrowest for 10-point is about 21. Columns narrower than these require much running over of words from line to line. (See tables in Chap. VIII.)

Page Diagram.—The easiest way to figure column widths, etc., is to lay out the page in diagram form. First cut a sheet of paper to the exact size of the finished page. Then with ruler and pencil draw the outlines of the type page, allowing proper margins. Lower the top line enough to allow for the folio head. The result is an exact diagram of the type page and its dimensions can be measured off with a ruler. Its width or line length should be translated into ems pica for the printer—six ems equal one inch. Its height may be translated into number of lines of type by dividing the height by the number of lines per inch of the type selected. For example, if the diagram shows the type body to be 4 inches wide by 6 inches high, the length of lines will be 4 (inches) x 6 (ems per inch) or 24 ems pica. If 12-point type is used, the number of lines will be 6 (inches) x 6 (lines of 12-point per inch) or 36 lines. If more than one column is used, one em should be allowed for column rule between. When small type on larger body is used, the number of lines must be figured on the body size—thus there are only six lines of 10/12 type in an inch although the type face is only 10/72 inch high.

Selection of Body Type.—Body type must be chosen with regard to size, blackness, and style of face. The above discussion will indicate the size of type best suited to given column widths. In general, however, the best sizes for small publication work are 9-, 10-, and rarely 12-point. For fine work, it is better to adopt a small face on a large body, as 9/10 or 10/12, than to use a large face. The same effect may be produced by leading small type. Blackness of type should be chosen with reference to paper selected. Since soft, rough paper receives a deeper impression than hard, smooth paper, it is best to use fine-cut type on hard paper and blacker type on soft paper. Sharp type also goes best with half-tone cuts. As regards face, standard Roman type is best suited to most publications and easiest to obtain. Pretty effects may be obtained by the use of antique, old style, or some decorative face, but when an ornamental type is chosen, the design of the entire publication must correspond with it. It is often possible to obtain some modern decorative face, such as Bodoni, for example, in all sizes from body to display, and the use of the same family throughout gives a neat appearance. The final decision will however probably be based on the printer's stock and machines.

Selection of Other Type.—Display type must be chosen with regard to body type, just as in newspaper make-up; headings and titles should match reading type. The use of very black titles with light-face body type, or the opposite, ordinarily shows bad taste. The tendency of the present day seems to be toward smaller, lighter display type, since white space gives as great display as much ink. The sizes of type ordinarily selected for titles are 12- to 36-point. Whether in capitals and small letters, or all capitals, depends on the length of the title, but it is well to select two or three standard headings to be used for various purposes throughout the publication. Unless the editor has a natural feeling for typographical display, he is wise to select his titles from the same family as his body type or from some family of similar cut and decoration.

With the question of display type goes that of folio heads and other details. Folio heads are page headings, including page numbers, that are repeated at the top of each page. They may be of ordinary type or, better, of some lighter face. The capital or small capital of the body type makes a good folio head. The editor must also decide the kind of rules to be used under and over the folio head—or the omission of rules. If authors' names are to be set at the head of the articles, it is well to set them in black-face capitals and small letters of the body type. If they are placed at the end of the article, small capitals of the same type are good. All of these details are mentioned because it is well for the editor to decide them in advance.

SMALL PUBLICATION WORK

Kind of Composition.—Whether the publication is to be machine- or hand-set depends largely on the printer's facilities. More faces are available in hand-set work, but delay may accompany this advantage. Ordinarily hand-set work makes proof correction easier than linotype work, for the resetting of line slugs to make revisions requires successive proofs until all errors have been eliminated. Monotype work does away with these difficulties, but few job printers have these machines. Before the final decision on the matter is made, it is well to see a sample of the printer's machine work to judge the age and condition of the machine.

Type Specifications.—When all matters of typography have been settled, it is well to make up a schedule of the various kinds of type and to repeat type specifications in every succeeding piece of copy. Specify in each case, not only the size and face of type, but the column width; in the margin opposite each title, repeat the size and face to be used. Many annoying misunderstandings will be avoided if this course is followed.

5. Illustrations

The average small publication is limited, in the matter of illustrations, to zinc etchings for line drawings and sketches, and half-tones for reproductions of photographs or wash drawings. It is well to use copper half-tones and specify a screen of about 150 lines per inch. In specifying sizes it is necessary to give only one dimension, for the other is determined by the size of the picture and the usual specification is width since the cuts must accord with column widths employed. It is well also to work out a page design before ordering cuts.

Engravers charge by the square inch for these cuts on a definite schedule that may be obtained from the nearest house. To insure the best cuts, drawings should be in black ink on white paper and photographs should be clear-cut, glossy prints. Obviously the size of the drawing or photograph has little to do with the size of the cut since it may be reduced or enlarged at will. When the cuts come from the engraver it is well to examine the engraver's proofs carefully and to insist that the printer use great care in making ready on the press (see Chap. V).

6. The Cover

A cover for the publication more than pays for itself in the improvement of appearance that it gives. When the outside page is printed on the same sheet and folded with the rest of the pages, manifold troubles arise. Unless the folding is absolutely accurate the printed matter is seldom centered perfectly on the page, and unless inking is perfect there is a constant variation in impression. If the cover must be dispensed with, some of these difficulties may be avoided by the use of very little printed matter on it and the elimination of any semblance of a border that may accentuate bad folding. The chief reason for a cover is to supply heavier outside pages to give form to the booklet. To accentuate this, a paper of different color and texture may be chosen. Ordinarily cover paper is inexpensive, but the cover adds extra cost for it requires separate press work. Hence it is well to limit the printing upon it to the two outside pages so that the extra press work may be reduced to one run. The pretty effects produced with a cover that laps over the inside pages is offset by the cost of extra trimming and binding—for with such a cover the two parts of the publication must be trimmed separately before binding. As for the printed matter on the cover, it is best to use as little as possible and to set it in relatively small type. If the publication must carry a list of officers, the names of the editors, or the table of contents, it is wise to place them on an inside page. All that is usually needed on the cover is the name of the publication, the date, the volume and series number, and perhaps some special announcement of its contents—perhaps the names of leading articles in a small box. If a very decorative cover is selected, it is well to have an electrotype or cut of it made to avoid any possible typographical errors in succeeding issues; a mortise may be cut in the electro for contents and date or they may be placed at its top or bottom. The question of advertisements on the cover will be discussed later.

7. The Title Page

The position and content of the title page are rather well established by custom. If an entire page is devoted to this purpose, it should be the first right-hand page in the book. A great saving of space can be effected, however, by reducing this material to a title heading at the top of the first page of reading matter. When a list of editors, officers, or contents must be included, a good plan is to devote the top of the first right-hand page to title heading and the bottom to this additional material. As this matter is set in display type it is wise to select type to correspond with the title type used throughout and on the cover. Here again white space makes better display than large, black type. In content, the title heading should include the name of the publication, the name of the publishers, the publication office, the number of issues per year, the price per issue and per year, the volume and series number, and the date of the issue. The names of the editor and business manager should be included here. If the publication is mailed as second class matter, the title heading should carry a notice reading: "Entered as second class matter on—(date of entrance)—at the post office at—(city and state)—under the Act of Congress, March 3, 1879." This is also a good place for copyright notice if the publication is copyrighted. Some small editors also include a list of advertising rates and other notices, but these may usually be dispensed with. Large magazine and newspapers usually place this material on the editorial page, but the first page is a better position in a small publication since it rarely has a distinct editorial page.

This material is mentioned here because much of it is required by the postal authorities. In addition, the publication must carry at stated intervals an announcement of ownership sworn before a notary. It is well to consult the local postmaster in regard to the postal laws before venturing upon such an enterprise. Copyright is secured by sending two copies of the publication and a small fee to the Copyright Bureau, Washington, together with proper blanks obtained from that office.

8. Advertisements

Where to Place Them.—The position and make-up of advertisements must be determined at the outset. The small editor will find himself almost forced to yield to the advertiser's desire to be near reading matter and should plan make-up accordingly. A good method is to devote left-hand pages to advertising, beginning at the back and working forward through the booklet as far as necessary. If all advertisements are kept on left-hand pages back of the book's center, a maximum of 25 per cent of the space will be devoted to advertising—a good ratio—and all advertising space will face reading matter. The question of selling the back page and the two inside pages of the cover to advertisers is a serious one. It is usually possible to charge a higher rate for these positions but little is gained for the extra press work will destroy the profit. The advertisement on the back page also injures the appearance of the small publication far more than the price can offset—clean covers give distinction.

Uniformity in Appearance.—Matters of typography and make-up should be settled before any advertisements are accepted. More and more publishers are limiting the size and blackness of type in advertising display, especially near reading matter. A good plan is to refuse to use in ads larger or blacker type than is employed in the largest title. The printer should also be urged to confine himself to one style of type throughout, preferably the style used in reading pages, and to obtain all display through small type offset with white space. Illustrations allowed in advertisements should strictly accord with the rest of the make-up—no black cuts should be permitted. Many advertisers will call for fancy borders about their ads, but the appearance of the publication will be greatly improved by the use of the same kind of border for every ad—perhaps a single heavy rule. This will secure uniformity and give all advertisers a fair chance in attracting notice. It would not be wise to announce such a policy in advance, for the average advertiser does not give the matter a thought, and the balky advertiser can usually be convinced by a proof of a well-set ad conforming to the editor's policy. The typographical rule is needed mainly to govern the careless printer who has a weakness for large type and for the nearest case.

9. Dummy Model

After the editor has decided on the make-up, it is well to make a *dummy model* to guide the printer and settle misunderstandings. To make such a dummy, the editor should obtain from the printer a sheet of the paper chosen, folded, trimmed, and stitched in final form with cover attached. On each page he should draw the outline of the type matter to show its size and position, the line length and number of lines. At the top of each page he should indicate the content of the folio head, on special pages he should mark the extreme limits of space to be occupied in display, and on various pages the amount of space to be left for headings. A line about the advertising pages will show the standard border size. Throughout he may indicate the kind and sizes of type to be used in various places. When finished, the dummy will be a complete working model of each issue. One copy may be given to the printer and another may be retained by the editor as it will prove of great value in estimating space and paging proof. It will form a part of the printer's contract like the drawings which an architect attaches to his building specifications.

Sample of Publication Design.—As an example of design and its problems, the following will illustrate the working out of a small publication for a special purpose. It was a small monthly designed to combine greatest artistic effect with low printing cost. A large page, about 9 x 12, was chosen for its possibilities in illustration and artistic page make-up. Thirty-two pages were selected because the printer's press could handle that size in two octavos. For economy a cover was dispensed with and a heavy paper was chosen to make up for its absence. The paper used was a calendered book paper, slightly cream in color, 36 x 48 inches in size, running 110 pounds to the ream. After folding and trimming, the pages were 8¾ by 11½ inches and had uniform margins of ⅞ inch on all sides. Hand-set body type was chosen because the printer had only a worn-out Junior Linotype and in his cases was a large stock of the Bodoni family. The 10/12-point Bodoni Book was selected as body type with 12, 18-, 24-, and 36-Bodoni Bold for headings. There were also a few fonts of script and italic of the same family so that the one style of type could be used throughout. Headings were to be set in 24-point capitals and small letters and in 18-point capitals, with an occasional 36-point heading on an important article. Light-face 12-point capitals were to be used in folio headings. No type larger than 24-point was to be used in advertisements and each was to have single-rule border.

The front page outside carried the name in a box, 3 x 6¾ inches, near the top; this was drawn up and reproduced in a zinc etching. The volume and serial numbers and the date were in small type below it. The rest of the page was blank save the title of the leading article in 36-point capitals and small letters in the center below the cut. Page 2 carried an advertisement. Page 3 had the board of editors and publisher's announcement in a box at the top and an announcement of the succeeding issue below. Page 4 carried a layout of photographs or a cartoon. Reading matter began on page 5 below a title heading. From this point through page 15, each page was in two 27-em columns, set in 10/12 Bodoni Book with no column rule; each column had 56 lines and each page carried about 1,100 words. Each article heading stretched across the entire page and consisted of a title in 24-point bold capitals and small letters centered, the author's name in 10-point capitals and small letters, and a three-line summary in 10-point italics, indented 4 ems on each side. The first word of each article was a 24-point initial. All articles began at the top of right-hand pages, extended through either two or four pages, and if necessary were broken over to the back. Thus the best article lengths were approximately 2,000 and 4,000 words. Illustrations were ordered in single and double column widths and each page was treated as a separate problem of make-up. Pages 16 and 17 were devoted to editorials, set in 10/12 Bodoni Book, in two 25-em columns, and each page was surrounded by a single-rule border. The editorials were short and separated by three asterisks; each began with a 24-point letter. These pages were the exact center of the book.

Back of page 17, all reading matter was set in three 18-em columns. The headings were of the same design but in smaller type. All advertisements of full-, half-, or quarter-page size were placed on left-hand pages; their make-up was begun at the back and was never to go further forward than page 20. Advertisements sold by the column inch were placed in the last column to the right of the reading pages, as near the back as possible. The pages back of page 16 were used for articles breaking over from the front, for unimportant material, for departments, and miscellaneous reading matter. The design afforded a magazine of great capacity at small cost, and a great flexibility of make-up. The uniformity of typography gave it great richness.

Specifications of a Quarterly.—Ideas for a smaller publication may be suggested by this description of a periodical designed for best appearance at least cost. A small page, 6 x 9, was selected so that it could be mailed in envelopes. The paper inside was a cheap antique since no illustrations were used; it was also cream-colored and as light as could be handled on the press, because the publication was not entered as second class matter and it was desired to keep the mailing cost down to 1 cent per copy—meaning that the copy, cover, and envelope must not weigh more than 2 ounces. The lightness of the paper required a cover—cheap stock of a light-brown color. The size chosen was thirty-two pages because the printer's press handled a 35 x 48 sheet and could print the entire booklet in two 16-page runs. A uniform modern face of type was selected for all reading matter and display as the printer had a fairly complete stock of one family. All reading matter was set in 10/12-point type, 27-em columns and 42 lines per page with side margins slightly less than ¾ inch and broader margins at top and bottom. Less type on the page would have improved the appearance but sacrificed capacity. All headings were set in 12-point black-face capitals and the author's name was in 8-point capitals and small letters. Some unimportant material was set in 8-point type. Folio heads were 10-point light capitals, with single rule above and double rule below.

The outside cover carried simply the name, date, volume and serial number, and a box at the bottom containing a brief list of contents. All other cover pages were blank. The first page inside had the title heading at the top and a box containing officers' names at the bottom. The three inches of space between was devoted to the beginning of the leading editorial. From that point on articles succeeded each other continuously, beginning where they would, although an attempt was made to place headings near the tops of pages. No articles were allowed to end at the bottom of right-hand pages, but a few lines were always carried over to lead the reader to the next title. Beginning with page 18, all left-hand pages were devoted to ads, sold in full, half, and quarter pages, set in uniform type not to exceed 24-point, and boxed in a single-rule border. In the special number each year that carried the convention program, the program was carefully divided into sessions and placed on the right-hand pages in the back—a page to a session. This pleased advertisers and enabled the editor to charge higher rates in this issue.

II. Handling the Copy

Exact Length Important

As soon as the publication has been designed and the contract let to the printer, the editor is ready to begin turning in copy. The work of designing should have indicated the most suitable article lengths, and the editor should establish certain lengths for certain purposes. Whoever his contributors may be, he will find his work simplified if he asks for a definite number of words when he calls for copy. Instead of asking for "a short article," he should ask for "a 2,000-word article" or "3,000 words on the subject." The length should be determined on the basis of the number of words carried on each page.

Form of Copy

All copy should be typewritten before it is given to the printer. If the author does not type it, the editor will find that the cost of typewriting will be saved in mistakes avoided. It is much easier also to estimate space that typewritten copy will fill. The copy should be double- or triple-spaced on one side of the paper and should have liberal margins for corrections. Before giving it to the printer, the editor should edit it as carefully as the newspaper desk man edits reporter's copy to avoid changes in proof. For the sake of uniformity, he should establish definite rules of typographical style, punctuation, spelling, and grammar. These matters may be treated in accordance with suggestions in Chapter II, athough the small editor must exercise greater care in altering the content of articles. Every piece of copy should bear type directions at the head of the first page. These should be indicated in printing office terms, inclosed in a circle, and should include the size and style of body type, the column width, and the size and style of various display lines, also whether underscored material should be set in bold or italic type. In tabulated material, a diagram or model should indicate the form.

Proof Corrections

When the material is in type, the printer will supply galley proof, which should be corrected carefully in accordance with the suggestions in the chapter on "Proofreading." It is well to have some one follow copy so that changes in content may be noted. When a change of content due to the printer's error is noted it should be marked "See Copy" to avoid charge for correction; other extensive changes not in accord with the copy should be recorded so that the correction bill may be checked. After the galley proof has been returned, it is well to read a revise to see if corrections have been made. In linotype material it is necessary to see successive revises until all mistakes have been eliminated, for the new line-slug may have another error. After all errors have disappeared, two proofs should be supplied for use in making a page dummy, which will be described later.

Copy Record

As all the copy for an issue is rarely turned over to the printer at the same time or handled together, the task of keeping track of it is a complicated one. To simplify this, the editor will find a "copy record," in some such form as that below, of great assistance. A separate record should be kept for each issue and the several columns indicate the progress from copy to finished form, with the dates entered to serve as a check on a dilatory printer.

Name of Article	Estimated Length in Number of Words	Copy Rec'd	Copy Sent to Printer	First Proof Rec'd	Rev. Proof Read	Length in Type Lines
Smith's paper..	3,000	3/14	3/15	3/18	3/20	300
Book reviews..	1,000	3/15	3/15	3/20	3/22	100
Programs	1 page	3/12	3/12	3/18	3/20	42

Diagram of Make-up

As the galley proofs pile up on the editor's desk, it is a bewildering task to take account of the space they will

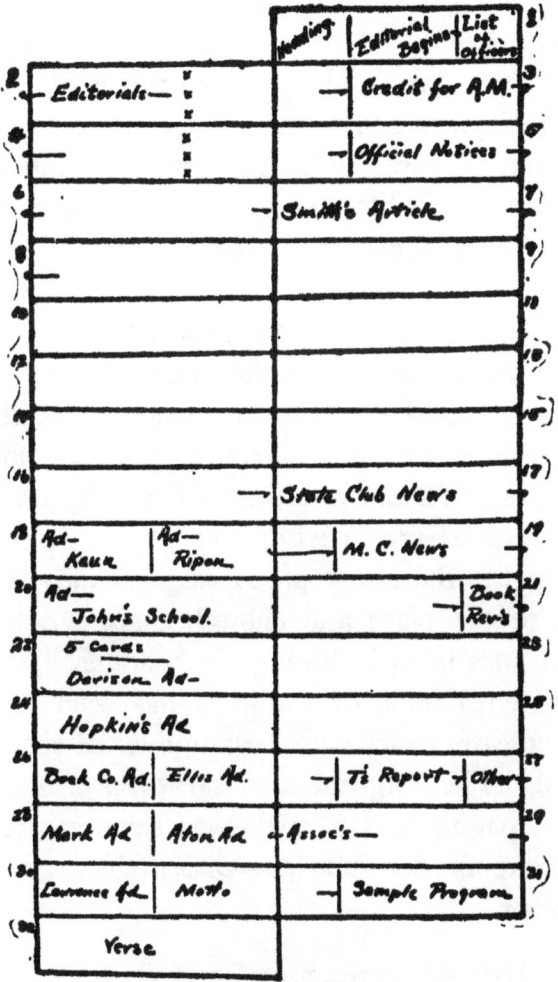

MAKE-UP DIAGRAM

fill, and some system must be devised or the editor will find himself on press day with several pages too few or too many. A diagram that expresses the editor's ideas of the finished make-up in graphic form will simplify the problem and make easier the puzzling task of paging. The preceding diagram is one that works successfully and is simple to draw and fill out. In the outline, each page is represented by an oblong space, with the page number in the corner. The pages in the left-hand column are left-hand pages and those in the other column are the pages that face them. The advantage of this system is that it enables the editor to see opposing pages in proper relation. Pages 1 and 32 stand out alone, because no pages face them.

After the diagram has been drawn, the first step is to indicate on the proper pages the material whose position in the book is fixed, *i.e.*, the title pages, advertisements, etc. Then it is possible to see graphically how much space there is to fill and to estimate it exactly on the basis of the number of lines of type per page. As each piece of copy reaches the revise proof stage, it may be entered up in the proper place and enough space is left for the number of lines in it, including the heading. Just before press day, when most of the copy has been set up, the diagram indicates exactly how many lines of space remain to be filled. The diagram then serves as a model to be followed in paging and furnishes an easy way to try out various make-up possibilities—easier than cutting and pasting proof.

III. Making the Page Dummy

Paging Proof

A page dummy is an exact working model of a finished publication to guide the printer in making up galleys of type into page forms. The printer can, of course, page the type without a dummy, if the consecutive order of articles is suggested to him, but it is well for the editor to follow the example of magazine editors and work out make-up themselves. This must be done if any attempt is to be made to obtain artistic make-up, which involves treating each page as a separate problem. The dummy is made by cutting the galley proof into page lengths and pasting it on sheets of paper that indicate the finished pages. The easiest method is to bind up enough sheets to give the required number of pages—*i.e.*, sixteen leaves give thirty-two pages—number them in order, write the proper folio head across the top, and paste on each page the proof of the type matter that is to appear on that page. The sheets should be large enough to allow for corrections and directions in the margin. If a diagram has been made up in advance, the task is a simple one; without a diagram, it is a matter of cutting, pasting, and fitting until things come even. A good plan is to paste proof on a copy of a previous issue.

Problems in Paging

Certain principles must be followed in making a page dummy. The first of these is to make each page exactly the same length; if the make-up allows forty-two lines of type, forty-one or forty-three lines on a page will cause unattractive unevenness. The printer may make up for it by leading out short pages, but that is not good practice. In counting the number of lines, the editor must make due allowance for inserts in smaller or larger type and for each heading; the proof will indicate how much. When the dummy is complete, he must insist that the printer follow it to the line, for an extra line carried over in one place will mean a line carried over on every page following. All instructions may be indicated in the margins and a chance is offered to catch errors missed in former proofs.

Position of Article Headings

The problem involved in the placing of article headings is concerned with making each page attractive and at the same time with carrying the reader through from page to page so that, when he reaches the end of one article, the heading of the next is before him. Some editors prefer to place all headings at the tops of pages and to make up for varying article lengths by leaving the bottom of the last page blank when the article does not fill it. In such practice, it is customary to begin all articles on right-hand pages to carry the reader through and to facilitate clipping. This method often involves the use of fillers or break-overs and is ordinarily too wasteful of space for the small publication. A better practice is to place the articles in consecutive order without regard for the position of the headings—at the top of the page or the middle, on the left or right. The reader is carried along by the few lines of the preceding article carried over. This system makes attractive pages and economizes every inch of space. It is harder to make up, however, for some attempt must be made to keep headings above the middle of the page and some juggling of article is involved.

Page Breaks

Another question is the typographical one of breaking from one page or column to the next. It is considered bad form to break a word from one page to the next and equally bad to leave a partial line—the first or last line of a paragraph—at the top or bottom of a page. The editor must avoid it either by juggling the articles, or, better, by asking the printer to rejustify a line or two in order to crowd back a word or make an additional line. Many paragraphs, it will be found, end in one-word lines which offer elastic points where a line of space may be saved by a small amount of rejustifying in the preceding lines.

Page and Form Proofs

After the editor has submitted his page dummy and the printer has made up the pages, it is best to ask for a page proof of the entire publication for a final checking up of folio heads, page numbers, and all the work of paging. When this has been revised, the publication is ready for the press. Even then, careful editors go to the printing office on press day to see a form proof or the first sheet off the press. Besides furnishing the last chance to catch errors, it gives an opportunity to see if all pages are right-side-up and in proper place. If the sheet is folded and trimmed it is possible to examine the uniformity of the margins.

IV. THE BUSINESS MANAGER'S WORK

There is so much variation in the financial conditions behind small publication work that it is impossible to discuss the business end of the work in great detail. There are, however, certain ideas and methods that will assist the small editor in his business problems, whatever may be his financial backing.

1. Advertising

Dealing with the Advertiser.—If the publication is to carry advertising, the matter of handling it involves similar problems in all cases. The questions regarding its position, typographical and other limitations, and make-up, have already been discussed. Its character and amount will be determined by the nature of the publication. The matter of soliciting advertising must be determined by the conditions of the work. Whether it be solicited in person or by letter, however, one or two things are always true. Whatever the character and circulation of the publication may be, the editor will find it wise to analyze the appeal of his publication, the reason why it is a good advertising medium, and formulate this appeal in concrete statements that will attract the advertiser. He then has a "talking point" like the salesman of goods. His publication is more than likely to be a class publication circulating among readers of a certain kind, and will appeal to a limited degree to all advertisers who wish to reach this class. But, more than that, there is usually some reason why this publication will supply a cheap and effective way of interesting and reaching this class. It may be the only publication in a large territory going to this class; it may be the official organ of the class; it may be published as a means by which the class of readers exchange notes. Some thought on the subject will open up larger advertising possibilities than were at first imagined. And in all cases advertising space should be thought of by the editor as a commodity of value, a kind of goods that he has for sale. In no case should advertisers be asked to buy space as a favor or a duty—they should be offered a definite amount of valuable publicity at a proportionate price. If the editor knows his field, he can often express in figures the cost of circularizing the field by letter as compared with the cost of reaching these customers through his publication. On this basis, his advertising becomes a business proposition. His soliciting letters should carry that feeling and should state the value of his space in brief, concise language. Very often when it is hard to convince an advertiser and point out the appeal, it is worth while to write an advertisement embodying the editor's ideas and even have it set in type to show its value.

Checking Advertising Returns.—After the space is sold it is wise to follow it up with an idea of discovering what returns it is bringing to the advertiser and of increasing its "pulling power." The use of a "key address" in the ad will enable the advertisers to know exactly what business is resulting from it. In most cases, also, it is wise to request a change of advertising copy with each issue as the constant change gives the advertisement the character of reading matter. Nothing is so dismal to advertiser or editor as standing cards, unchanging from issue to issue. The change does not involve extra cost since a printer charges about as much for holding the ad in type as for resetting it.

Size of Advertisements.—The division of advertising space depends upon the publication's make-up. If small pages are used, it is best to sell space by full, half, and quarter pages. With larger pages the space may be sold by the column-inch, meaning an inch high and a column wide. Newspapers sell all their space by the inch at the rate of fourteen agate (5½ point) lines to the inch, but such a practice in small publications results in difficult make-up. The prices charged are usually based on what the editor thinks he can get, or on a fair division of cost between subscriptions and advertising. The foundation is the price of the full page. The standard among national magazines of general circulation is $1 per page per thousand circulation—the page being about 7 x 10 inches and containing about 16 column inches. This means that a magazine of 120,000 circulation may charge $120 per page. With a class circulation, the small editor may charge relatively more because his circulation is intensive —every reader is a possible buyer of the class of goods advertised. He uses his page rate as the basis of his schedule but he does not ordinarily divide his rates exactly in proportion to the division of space. The small ad is not so valuable as the large ad, in that it offers less room for display and discussion, but to a certain extent it attracts almost as much notice. Hence a half-page ad is worth more than half as much as a page ad, and a quarter-page of space is worth more than half as much as a half-page.

The Rate Card.—A sliding scale of rates is therefore necessary to include all sizes that the editor wishes to sell. A certain discount should also be given for contract ads that are to run more than one time, and an extra rate should be charged for special positions, such as cover pages and the first page after reading matter. All of these should be figured out in advance and embodied in a printed rate card to be inclosed in all letters soliciting advertising. The printed card indicates to the advertiser that the editor is businesslike and is treating all advertisers alike. A suggestive sliding scale of rates for a small class publication is illustrated here:

SMALL PUBLICATION WORK

ADVERTISING RATES

Full Page	$15.00
Half Page	8.00
Quarter Page	4.50
One column	8.00
Inch (single column)	1.50

(Cover pages 20 per cent extra)

Dimensions: Size of page, 6 x 9 inches. Two columns. Column length, 7 inches; column width, 13 picas (2 1/6 inches).

Forms close 15th of month previous to publication date.

Terms: Cash with order or satisfactory references. Accounts payable quarterly. Ten per cent discount on annual contracts. All advertising next to, or facing, reading matter.

Rates Subject to Change without Notice

In the above card the scale is based on the price per page per single insertion, which results in a lower page rate on contracts. It might be figured out more completely on the rate card on the basis of a *minimum* price per page (say $20) on any contract:

	Four Insertion Order	Two Insertion Order	Single Insertion
Full Page	$80.00	$42.00	$22.00
Half Page	44.00	23.10	12.10
Quarter Page	24.00	12.60	6.60
Column Inch	8.00	4.20	2.20

This scale has a minimum rate of $20 per page on the greatest discount—for four insertion order—and gives

5 per cent. increase for two insertions and 10 per cent. increase for one insertion. It illustrates the way in which large magazines figure their advertising rates. A typographical model for the rate card may be obtained from any magazine.

Advertising Contract.—Although an advertiser's letter ordering space is almost as good as a contract, many small editors feel that it is safer to use a contract. An advantage of the system is that the contract forms a convenient record for filing in the office; if it is printed on a card of convenient size it may be filed in a card catalogue which serves as a handy record of the ads to be carried in each succeeding issue. If it carries in addition a place for recording the acceptance of proof and of payment, the card file saves much bookkeeping. The following is a suggestive model:

Publisher, Sample Magazine, ...192..
    1234 First street, City, State.
        Please insert advertisement of the undersigned, to occupy ...., commencing............
for which........agree to pay $......................

Proof Submitted   Proof O.K'd   Paid

Saving of printing is accomplished by printing the contract on the back of the rate card, since both must be inclosed in letters soliciting advertising. Duplicate contracts are of little value unless the advertiser pays in advance.

Proof to Be Submitted.—As indicated in the record spaces on the contract card, the editor submits proof of the advertisement before it is published. He sends a printer's proof to the advertiser, as soon as the ad is in type, and delays publication of the ad until it returns with O. K. or corrections. Much difficulty will be avoided at times if these accepted proofs are filed with the advertiser's correspondence.

Billing the Advertiser.—When the advertiser's bill is sent to him, it is well to send him a marked copy in the same mail so that he may be sure the ad was published. Some advertisers wish two copies for their office files. Because of the large number of bills to be sent out each month, it is wise to have a printed bill-head; it is likely to receive prompter payment. Needless to say, also, no one should try to run a publication, however small, without a printed letter-head carrying the editor's name and office of publication. In fact, the smaller the publication, the more necessary is the letter-head, not because advertisers distrust the editor's honesty, but because they wish to be sure that they are buying space in a bona fide publication.

System and Methods.—All of these suggestions will indicate that the advertising branch of small publication work must be conducted in a businesslike manner. No matter how small the publication, the editor must convince the men with whom he is dealing that he is thoroughly businesslike. Money spent on proper letter-head and other printed matter, as well as on typewritten correspondence, will be more than repaid in added prestige and business. Each magazine has a system of its own for handling these matters and advertising managers are usually glad to supply a beginner with samples of their printed matter and an explanation of their various systems. They are often especially glad because they realize that the slipshod business methods and cringing solicitations of many small, insignificant publications are doing much to retard the development of advertising business on a modern basis.

2. Circulation

Wrappers or Envelopes.—The most serious problem in connection with small publication circulation is that of wrapping and addressing. If the magazine is of small size, 6 x 9 inches, the best wrapper is a cheap manila envelope, large enough to hold the booklet without folding, and printed with the name and address of the publication in the upper left corner. If it is mailed under the second class rate, it should carry the words—"Entered as second class matter in the post office at ———." It is also wise to print under the name, "Postmaster:—If not delivered please notify publisher and postage will be sent for return." This aids in eliminating dead addresses on lists. If the publication is too large for envelope mailing, the best substitute is a flat manila wrapper rolled around the magazine and pasted. It may be large or small, printed or blank. The wrapper can be handled more quickly than envelopes, but results in a tightly rolled magazine. A bulky publication may be mailed flat in a wrapper, but there is danger that the wrapper will be torn off in the mail.

Addressing.—There are several ways of disposing of the addressing problem. If the circulation is small, less than 500, the cheapest method is to address the envelopes by hand, with pen or typewriter. A large circulation requires the use of an addressing machine. The simplest kind of mechanical addresser is some form of the "mustang mailer," a contrivance used by many newspapers. It requires a printed list of names and addresses on tough colored paper and operates by cutting and pasting one name each time it is pressed down on a wrapper. For its economical operation the circulation lists should be set up on the linotype machine and kept in type form in galleys; each month, after corrections have been made, the printer takes a proof of the galley for use in the mailer. The chief objection to this method is that the pasted slip is small and indistinct. The next best mailer is some form of the stencil mailing machine. There are other kinds of automatic addressing machines but many of them are too costly for the small publisher; he must use the facilities which the printer has or he can borrow. In cities the printers are likely to have mailing machines but in smaller towns the editor must rely on the mustang or hand addressing.

Subscription Lists.—The work of keeping track of subscriptions is greatly facilitated by the use of a date or some other sign on the address slip or stencil to indicate the date on which the subscription expires. Some system must also be adopted for classifying the names on the lists. They may be arranged alphabetically or, better, by states or cities. With such a classification and the expiration date, the editor can easily keep his lists up to date by going over the lists after each issue and throwing out dead names.

Subscription Blank.—Methods of developing circulation and following up expired subscriptions are outside this discussion, but, if a subscription blank is used, the following is a good form. It should be printed on a piece of paper that may be slipped into a letter and should carry at the head the name and address of the publication.

> Gentlemen:—I am enclosing one dollar ($1.00) for one year's subscription to the Sample Magazine, beginning..............................
> Name .... Street ....
> City .... State ....

Postal Rates.—Mailing rates depend on whether the publication may be entered as a second class periodical. If it is not admitted under this rate, it must be mailed as third class matter at the rate of "1 cent for 2 ounces or fraction thereof," and stamps must be affixed to each copy. This often makes necessary some consideration of paper weight. If the weight of each copy is slightly over two ounces, it is better to reduce its size or the weight of the paper than to pay 2 cents on each copy. The weight may be determined in advance by having the printer make up a dummy of the paper selected, of the exact size and with cover attached. If the weight is slightly over the mark, lighter paper or cover or greater trim may reduce it—sometimes an extra $\frac{1}{8}$ inch trimmed off one edge will save 1 cent per copy in mailing. The envelope must of course be considered in the experiment and, if the weight is close to the mark, it is well to have the postmaster weigh a copy and give his official sanction. When the circulation is large enough to warrant it, the postmaster may save the editor the work of affixing stamps by allowing him to print "1 cent paid" on the envelope and pay in a lump sum.

The Second-Class Rate.—Permission to mail under the second-class periodical rate is obtained by application to the postal department through the local postmaster. He will require the editor to fill out under oath an application blank containing a long list of questions concerning the nature and business of the publication. If the postmaster thinks, after reading the blank and examining the editor's books, that the postal authorities are likely to honor the application, he forwards it to Washington with two copies of a current number of the magazine. While negotiations are pending, he may if he wishes allow the editor to deposit a sum of money equivalent to the third class rate and to mail an issue or two carrying the note, "Application for entry as second-class matter at the post office at ——— pending." If the entry is allowed, the amount in excess of the second-class rate is then refunded. This rate is granted only to a publication that fulfills the following conditions: It must be issued regularly at stated intervals, as frequently as four times a year, bear a date of issue, and be numbered consecutively. It must be issued from a known office of publication. It must be formed of printed paper sheets, without board, cloth, leather, or other substantial binding, such as distinguish printed books for preservation from periodical publications. "It must be originated and published for the dissemination of information of a public character, or devoted to literature, the sciences, arts, or some special industry, and having a legitimate list of subscribers: Provided, however that nothing herein contained shall be so construed as to admit to the second-class rate regular publications designed primarily for advertising purposes, or for free circulation, or for circulation at nominal rates."

In brief, the second-class rate is intended for bona fide

periodicals and every attempt is made to close it to advertising publications. To this end, the editor is questioned concerning the amount of advertising he carries, whether his space is open to all advertisers, the relation of his paid circulation to his total circulation, and the intent of the publication. Some leniency is occasionally shown to publications with small circulations and much advertising, on the basis of their intent. All small editors make an attempt to get this rate not only because of its cheapness—1 pound for 1 cent—but because second-class matter is mailed by the pound without stamps and the extra expense involved in the "or fraction thereof" phrase in the third-class rate is eliminated. The editor simply delivers his edition, wrapped and addressed, at the post office; it is weighed in one mass, and he pays by the pound in monthly or quarterly payments. The admission to the rate gives a certain amount of prestige in the eyes of advertisers, since it indicates that it is a bona fide periodical with a paid circulation.

3. The Printer

No small publisher should attempt to do business with a printer without a written contract specifying not only the price but the character of the work. The contract should give the kind and weight of paper, the size and number of pages, the kind of cover and binding, the kind of typography, and the character of work in general. It is well also to specify the rate on extra work, such as proof correction and repaging. The contract should be in duplicate, signed by both parties, and sufficiently definite to stand the test of the law court.

Many printers prefer to set a lump price for the publication of a certain number of copies of certain size and make-up. This is especially true when they are bidding low; they hope to make up the difference on extras and additions. When the bid is attractively low, it is sometimes well to accept such a contract, but usually the small editor will find it best to sign a contract more favorable to himself and elastic enough to allow for growth. Such a contract needs to be divided into parts to correspond with the various operations involved. It should specify the rate per page for composition, the charge for additional runs on the press caused by increased number of pages, and the charge for folding and binding per 100 or 1,000 copies. In some cases the specifications cover the cost of composition per page (including additional press work) and the cost of "manufacturing" per 1,000 copies. Either arrangement allows for expansion in size or circulation at a proportionate rate.

Exercises

1. Plan a small publication—advertising booklet, periodical, student paper, house organ, etc.—after this method:

- (a) After choosing project, outline field and problems in writing, select best type and form of publication.
- (b) Work out the typography, selecting type from catalogues, and writing specifications.
- (c) Draw to scale a sample page, with complete type specifications and typical headlines.
- (d) Make a dummy diagram of complete publication.
- (e) Make a complete page dummy of entire publication with all specifications, rules, and schedules.

2. Work out type specifications and make-up schedules of various commercial magazines and booklets.

3. Plan organization of staff of student newspaper.

4. Make a plan for financing a small publication.

5. Write a detailed criticism of typography and dummying of some amateur publication—perhaps a student periodical.

6. Make up some rate cards, working out sliding scale.

7. Make up schedule of dates for a monthly publication.

8. Work out page sizes from various standard paper sizes. Do some arithmetic on determining number of pages.

9. Study paper samples obtained from printer—fold up dummies.

10. Design some title and cover pages of various kinds.

11. Cut up a small publication and repage it for better effect.

APPENDIX I

LIST OF SIGNIFICANT DATES IN THE HISTORY OF THE ART OF PRINTING AND THE DEVELOPMENT OF THE NEWSPAPER

Dates in History of Printing are in *Italics*.

1418 *Disputed date of earliest piece of printing—Brussels wood-cut of the Blessed Virgin.*
1450 *First book printed from movable types—by Gutenberg in Germany.*
1454 *Small type first used—in Pope Nicholas V. Indulgence.*
1457 First newspaper—*Nuremberg Gazzette*—in Germany.
1465 *Roman type appeared—cast at Subiaco, Italy, by two German printers.*
1475 *Approximate date of first English book—by William Caxton.*
1480 *Printing was well established throughout Europe.*
1501 *Italic type invented by Aldus Manutius, Venice.*
1534 First regular newspaper—*Neue Zeitung aus Hispanien und Italien*—Nuremberg.
1550 *Typefounding established as a separate business.*
1550 *Metal screw introduced in hand press by Danner of Nuremberg.*
1588 First English newsletter—*English Mercurie*.
1615 First daily newspaper—*Die Frankfurter Oberpostamts Zeitung*—by Egenolf Eurmel—Father of Newspapers.
1620 *First real improvement in the hand press, by W. J. Blaew, Amsterdam—he devised a spring to raise the platen.*
1621 First newspaper in England—*The Weekly Newes*—told of German wars—was beginning of "newsbooks" or "relations."

373

NEWSPAPER EDITING

1622   First advertisement in English periodical—a book advertisement in Thomas Archer's *Corantos*.

1626   First newspaper with a name—Archer's *Mercurius Brittanicus*.

1631   First regular French newspaper—*Gazette de France*—by Theophraste Renandot.

1637   *Decree of Star Chamber limiting number of English printers.*

1638   *First printer in America—Stephen Daye of Cambridge, Mass.*

1641   First English journal of domestic news—Thomas' *Diurnall Occurrences in Parliament*, later called *Perfect Diurnall*—its writer, Samuel Peck, is called Father of the English Newspaper.

1650   First official journal—Marchamont Needham's *Mercurius Publicus*, issued for Cromwell.

1657   M. Needham published a newspaper entirely composed of advertisements—*Publick Adviser*—rate not based on space.

1659   *Joseph Moxon, first English typefounder, began letter cutting.*

1660   *Leipsic Gazette published.*

1660   The word "advertisement" began to be used by English editors.

1665   First official organ, in form of newspaper, to reprint laws and proclamations—*Oxford Gazette*—later called *London Gazette*—it appeared after suppression of licensed "newsbooks" and marked end of age of pamphlets.

1681   Beginning of lists of prices and reports—*Merchants' Remembrancer*—English.

1690   First newspaper in America—Benjamin Harris's *Publick Occurrences*, printed in Boston—to be monthly—suppressed after one number. Harris was exiled English editor.

1692   First magazine—*Gentlemen's Journal*, London—monthly.

1693   First woman's newspaper—*Ladies' Mercury*, London.

APPENDIX 375

1695 Beginning of free press in England—ban on parliamentary report removed—licensing of books and newspapers stopped—*Post-Man, Post-Boy, Flying Post,* then appeared.

1695 Appearance of "editors," rather than "authors," of newspapers.

1700 First comic newspaper, *Merrie Mercury,* London.

1700 Approximate date of end of "news-letters" in England.

1702 First (?) daily in England—*Daily Courant*—morning.

1704 First regular newspaper in America—*Boston News-Letter,* by Nicholas Boone—it lived 72 years.

1704 First example of real reporting—in *Boston News-Letter* —a hanging.

1704 Appearance of Daniel Defoe's *Mercure Scandale*—or *Weekly Review of the Affairs of France Purg'd from the Errors and Partiality of Newswriters and Petty Statesmen.*

1706 First penny paper—*The Orange Postman*—half-penny or 1 cent.

1706 First evening paper—*The London Evening Post.*

1706 First provincial paper in England—*Crossgrove's Gazette* at Norwich.

1709 Steele's *Tatler* appeared.

1712 Establishment of Stamp Act—half-penny per half-sheet in red stamps—a shilling for each advertisement—tax of a shilling on every copy of more than one sheet killed magazines.

1719 *Boston Gazette* appeared—a postmaster's newspaper.

1719 *American Weekly Mercury* appeared in Philadelphia, edited by Andrew Bradford, postmaster—contained "Busy Body" articles by Benjamin Franklin.

1721 *New England Courant* started in Boston by James Franklin, later edited by Benjamin Franklin—first rebel newspaper.

1725 *New York Gazette,* weekly, started by William Bradford—later called the *Post-Boy*—was a government organ.

1725 *Plaster-of-paris stereotyping developed by William Ged of Edinburgh.*
1727 *Annapolis Gazette* appeared.
1728 *Pennsylvania Gazette* appeared in Philadelphia—later edited by B. Franklin—merged with *North American* in 1845.
1728 London coffeehouse men proposed a scheme of syndicating news and advertisements.
1731 *Charleston Gazette* appeared.
1731 *Boston Weekly Rehearsal* started by Jeremy Gridley—very literary—later became *Boston Evening Post.*
1733 *Rhode Island Gazette* started at Newport by James Franklin.
1733 *New York Weekly Journal* started by John P. Zenger—lived until 1752.
1734 Diagrams of Battle of Phillipsburg printed by *American Mercury.*
1734 First newspaper libel suit in America—against Zenger of *New York Journal*—Andres Hamilton, defending editor, secured acquittal by demanding that jury find on fact.
1736 *Virginia Gazette* started at Williamsburg.
1737 *First point system of type measurement worked out by Pierre S. Fournier, French typefounder.*
1742 *Pennsylvania Journal and Weekly Advertiser* started war on Stamp Act.
1748 *Independent Advertiser* started by Samuel Adams, one of first rebel newspapers.
1752 *New York Mercury* started by Hugh Gaine—ran until 1783.
1753 *Boston Gazette and Country Gentleman* started as real organ of revolutionary party.
1755 *Connecticut Gazette* started at New Haven.
1756 Founding of oldest living continuous newspaper in America—*The Portsmouth* (N. H.) *Gazette.*
1758 *Poor Richard's Almanac* published by Benjamin Franklin.
1762 *New York Royal Gazetteer* founded to combat revolutionary ideas.

APPENDIX

1764 *Connecticut Courant* started at Hartford—still published under same name.

1765 "Join or Die" motto, with device of snake divided into eight parts, first used by *Constitutional Courant* (Burlington, N. J.)—editor was William Goddard.

1767 *New York Journal & General Advertiser* started by John Holt as revolutionary organ.

1767 *Connecticut Journal & New Haven Post-Boy* started—now known as *New Haven Journal-Courier*.

1768 First typefounding in America.

1770 *Massachusetts Spy*, tri-weekly revolutionary paper, started—carried "Join or Die" motto in 1774—still published as *Worcester Spy*.

1771 There were twenty-five newspapers in America.

1775 There were thirty-seven newspapers in America.

1776 First paper to print the Declaration of Independence was the *Virginia Gazette*—carried a synopsis on July 19 and the entire document on July 26.

1777 First daily in Paris—*Journal de Paris ou Poste au Soir*.

1767 *Boston Chronicle* founded as Tory organ—ran until 1770.

1784 First daily paper in America—*American Daily Advertiser* of Philadelphia—later merged with *North American*.

1785 Second daily paper in America—*New York Daily Advertiser*.

1785 *London Times* founded by John Walter of logotype fame—known as *The Daily Universal Register. Printed Logographically*—name changed to *The Times or Daily Universal Register* in 1788—became *The Times* three months later.

1786 First newspaper west of the Alleghenies—*The Pittsburg Gazette*.

1787 First real reporter was Joseph Gales who covered first meeting of Congress at Philadelphia.

1791 *National Gazette* started in Philadelphia as Democratic organ.

1792 *State Gazette* started in Trenton, N. J.—still is published.
1793 First paper in Tennessee—*Knoxville Gazette.*
1797 Oldest paper in New York City started—*The Minerva,* founded by Noah Webster, attacked slavery in one of its first numbers—later became *Commercial Advertiser & New York Spectator.*
1798 *First iron hand press, built by the Earl of Stanhope, England.*
1799 *Sciota Gazette,* Chillicothe, O., started by Nathaniel Willis, "Father of the Press of the Northwest."
1799 *Fourdinier papermaking machine invented by Robert Louis, Paris.*
1800 First official government paper in America—*National Intelligence & Washington Advertiser*—dubbed the *Court Paper*—printed debates of Congress as reported by Gales and Seaton.
1801 *New York Evening Post* started by William Coleman—oldest paper in city that has continued under same name.
1803 First paper in New Orleans—*The Moniteur.*
1804 *First papermaking machine in England erected at Frogmoor Mill, called the Fourdinier machine.*
1804 *Plaster stereotyping developed by Earl of Stanhope.*
1806 First paper in New Orleans after Louisiana Purchase—*Louisiana Courier*—part French and part English.
1806 First American market reports—*Prices Current* in *United States Gazette* of Philadelphia.
1807 *Patent granted on plunger idea on which modern typecaster is based.*
1808 First paper in Indiana started at Vincennes.
1810 *First power press, built by Frederick Koenig—modified hand press.*
1811 Expression "Gerrymandering" invented by *Columbia Centinel,* Boston.
1812 *First cylinder press, built by F. Koenig in England.*
1813 *National Advocate* started in New York by Tammany Hall—James Gordon Bennett became its editor in 1825.

APPENDIX

1813   *First stereotyped book in America—by John Watts, New York.*

1814   First newspaper in Illinois—*The Intelligencer* at Kaskaskia.

1814   *Steam press used for first time to print London Times—it was a Koenig cylinder press.*

1815   English Stamp duty raised to four pence per copy on newspapers.

1816   *St. Louis Enquirer* founded.

1816   Largest newspaper in New York, *Mercantile Advertiser*, had 2,250 circulation—there were then six dailies and two weeklies in the city.

1816   *First steam papermaking machine in America, erected at Pittsburg.*

1816   *Clymer-Columbian hand press with lever instead of screw invented.*

1817   *First cylinder papermaking machine—built by Thomas Gilpin at Brandywine, U. S. A.*

1817   *Detroit Gazette* founded—suspended 1830.

1820   *Lithographic printing developed—approximate date.*

1820   *Machine-made paper supplanted hand-made paper about this time.*

1821   *Date of first attempt to set type by machinery.*

1822   *Papier-mâché stereotyping invented in France.*

1822   *Hand press with toggle-joint instead of lever brought out by Peter Smith in America.*

1822   *Daniel Treadwell built power press in Boston—modified hand press.*

1822   *Type-casting and composing machine patented in England by Dr. William Church of U. S.*

1822   *First attempt at uniform system of type measurement in America—by George Bruce, N. Y.*

1825   First Sunday paper in America—*New York Sunday Courier*—published on Sunday only.

1826   *Philadelphia Public Ledger* started—as a penny paper.

1826   *Youth's Companion* started in Boston—as a religious paper.

1826   First printing in Wisconsin—1,000 lottery tickets at Green Bay.

1826 William Cullen Bryant became editor of *New York Evening Post.*

1827 First woman's magazine in America, *The Ladies' Magazine,* Boston, by Mrs. Sarah J. Hale.

1827 The Wall street "Blanket Sheets" appeared in New York —*Courier & Enquirer* and *Journal of Commerce*—6 cents per copy—the latter was founded as an abolition paper.

1827 Applegate & Cowper perfecting cylinder press adopted by London Times.

1827 Washington hand press perfected by Samuel Rust, N. Y.

1828 Grippers to handle paper on cylinder press invented by Napier.

1828 First attempt to cast type by machinery—by W. M. Johnson, U. S.

1829 First American sporting paper—Porter's *Spirit of the Times,* N. Y.

1830 *Washington Globe* started—part of "Kitchen Cabinet."

1830 *Boston Transcript* founded.

1831 Humor column originated in *Boston Daily Morning Post.*

1831 First railway passenger train—Mohawk & Hudson Railroad.

1831 *Louisville* (Ky.) *Journal* started—merged with *Courier* in 1868.

1831 New York papers established news schooners to meet incoming vessels.

1831 *Boston Liberator,* abolition paper, started by William Lloyd Garrison—published for 34 years.

1831 *Democratic Free Press & Michigan Intelligencer* founded —later *Detroit Free Press.*

1832 First independent penny paper, *New York Globe,* started by James Gordon Bennett in opposition to "Blanket Sheets"—failed at once.

1832 First cylinder press in America—built by Robert Hoe.

1832 Papier-mâché stereotyping introduced into England.

1832 First illustrated journal in England—*Penny Magazine.*

1833 Second attempt to publish penny paper in New York— *Morning Post*—lasted twenty-one days—by Shepard.

APPENDIX 381

1833   First newspaper in Chicago—*The Democrat*—merged with *The Tribune* in 1861.

1833   First successful penny paper in New York—*The Sun*—started by Benjamin Day—small size, much local news, no editorials.

1833   First newspaper in Wisconsin—*Green Bay Intelligencer.*

1834   Fifteen daily papers in New York at this time—population 270,000—largest had 6,000 circulation.

1834   *First steam press in Northwest—Cincinnati Commercial Register.*

1835   Date of the famous Moon Hoax.

1835   There were then about 1,258 newspapers in United States—none had more than 6,000 circulation.

1835   *Wood engraving developed in America about this time.*

1835   *First steam press in New York*—installed by *The Sun.*

1835   *New York Herald* founded by James Gordon Bennett on $500 capital, penny paper, marks beginning of Independent Press.

1835   Famous money articles begun by *New York Herald.*

1835   First regular stock quotations, published by *New York Herald.*

1835   Idea of news companies to distribute papers, by *New York Herald.*

1835   Cash system in advertisements and subscriptions, by *New York Herald.*

1835   New York papers had pony expresses to Washington and Philadelphia.

1835   Second paper in Chicago—*The American*—later became *The Express* in 1842.

1836   Regular news summaries begun by *New York Weekly Herald.*

1837   First real reporters employed by New York papers.

1837   *New Orleans Picayune* started—built on George W. Kendall's jokes.

1838   Express companies started—began to distribute newspapers.

1838   First steamship line between New York and Europe.

1838 System of foreign correspondence started by *New York Herald*.
1838 First successful typecasting machine patented by David Bruce, New York.
1839 *Philadelphia North American* started—eleven papers merged in one.
1839 *Papier-mâché stereotyping patented in America by Moses Poole*.
1840 Newspaper war against *New York Herald* because of its independent position—waged by *Courier & Enquirer* and the "Holy Allies." *Herald* had 51,000 circulation, *C. & E.* had 4,200.
1840 *First electrotyped engraving, published by London Journal*.
1840 *First American patent for typesetting machine—Frederick Rosenberg*.
1841 *New York Tribune* started by Horace Greeley as penny political organ.
1841 *Tribune Almanac* started by Greeley—first newspaper almanac.
1841 *Young & Decambre typesetting machine patented (American)*.
1842 *London Illustrated News* started—began illustrative journalism.
1843 *Old style type revived in England and America.*
1844 *First newspaper on Pacific Coast—Flumgudgeon Gazette or Bumble Bee Budget, edited by the Long-Tailed Coon—California.*
1844 Electric telegraph perfected—taken up by New York papers at once. First line between Washington and Baltimore, built by Congress.
1844 *Reporting of Sunday sermons begun by New York Herald*.
1844 Famous Roorback Hoax, concerning branded slaves, published by *Albany Evening Journal*.
1844 *Chicago Journal* founded.
1844 *Kronheim's improvement on papier-mâché stereotyping patented.*

APPENDIX

1844 First daily in Wisconsin founded—*The Milwaukee Sentinel.*

1845 Overland expresses to New Orleans run by *New York Herald* to cover Mexican war—beat mails one to four days.

1845 First war correspondents were engaged in covering Mexican war.

1846 *Alta California & San Francisco Herald* appeared—published by men from *New York Herald.*

1846 Washington and Baltimore telegraph line extended to New York.

1846 Stock company idea of newspaper ownership started by *New York Tribune*—the idea came from France.

1846 First Hoe type-revolving press erected.

1847 *New York Herald* had Henry Clay's speech sent from Cincinnati to New York.

1847 Last of the pony expresses—established jointly by several New York papers.

1847 *Springfield* (Mass.) *Republican* founded by Samuel Bowles.

1847 *New York Herald* eliminated illustrations and other display from its advertisements. Length of insertion limited to two weeks—later to one day. Editorial notice of ad stopped. Every ad reset each day.

1847 *Chicago Tribune* founded.

1848 Associated Press founded—first known as New York Associated Press. Harbor News Association combined with it—its growth into country-wide association came during the '60's.

1848 Applegate's type-revolving press built for London Times.

1849 First paper in Minnesota, *Minnesota Pioneer* (now *St. Paul Pioneer Press*).

1850 Idea of printing from curved stereotyped plates patented.

1851 *New York Times* started by Henry J. Raymond.

1851 There were then 3,000 periodicals in America—2,000 of them newspapers.

1852 First paper in Washington Territory—*Olympia Pioneer & Democrat.*

- 1853 English tax on advertisements removed.
- *1853 First successful American typesetting machine—William H. Mitchell.*
- 1854 *Chicago Times* founded—merged with *Herald* as *Chicago Times-Herald* in 1895—merged with *Record* as *Chicago Record-Herald* in 1901—merged with *Inter-Ocean* as *Chicago Herald* in 1914.
- *1855 Wood-pulp paper began to supplant rag paper.*
- 1857 *Harper's Weekly* founded.
- *1857 Hoe type-revolving press installed in New York Times office—two ten-cylinder machines were erected.*
- 1859 First verbatim interview—with Gerrit Smith at time of John Brown raid on Harper's Ferry—by *New York Herald*.
- 1860 End of war between newspapers and telegraph lines which resulted from establishment of the Associated Press.
- 1860 *New York World* started as a religious and moral daily paper—carried news, but no evil news.
- *1860 Paper made of esparto introduced.*
- 1860 End of "Blanket Sheets"—*Courier & Enquirer* merged with *World*.
- 1861 Tax on paper removed.
- 1864 Famous Lincoln Proclamation Hoax printed by *New York Journal*.
- *1865 First web press with stereotyped plates, built by William Bullock of Philadelphia.*
- 1865 *Chicago Republican* founded—Charles A. Dana first editor.
- 1865 *San Francisco Chronicle* founded.
- 1866 *Chicago Weekly News*, now *The Daily News*, was founded.
- 1867 *Harper's Bazaar*, fashion paper, started under woman editor.
- 1867 Steam news yachts used by *New York Herald* to meet vessels.
- *1867 Cropper treadle platen job press introduced.*

APPENDIX

1868 *New York Sun* purchased by Charles A. Dana for $175,000—introduced literary ideal in newspaper work—had 65,000 circulation.

1868 Stanley expedition into Anglo-Abyssinia sent by *New York Herald* to find Livingston.

1868 Club subscription idea started by *New York Tribune*—with premium engravings.

1868 *Walter rotary web perfecting press built for London Times.*

1868 *Atlanta* (Ga.) *Constitution* founded.

1870 About 1,508,548,250 periodicals issued in America.

1870 American Press Association organized.

1870 *First automatic folder for web press invented.*

1870 *Burr-Kastenbein typesetter built—required hand justification.*

1871 Directory of advertisers begun by *New York Herald*.

1872 J. G. Bennett refused to sell *New York Herald* for $2,200,000.

1872 *Chicago Inter-Ocean* founded—merged with *Record-Herald*, 1914.

1873 Associated Press had 200 members.

1873 Charge for marriage announcements begun by *New York Herald*.

1873 *Frank Leslie's Illustrated Newspaper* appeared with 70 wood engravings.

1873 First illustrated daily paper in America—*New York Daily Graphic*.

1875 *Tucker's rotating folding machine invented—15,000 an hour.*

1876 *Experiments on Mergenthaler linotype machine begun.*

1877 *Washington Post* founded.

1878 *Minneapolis Journal* founded.

1878 *Chicago typefoundry began making type on point system after being burned out in great fire—Marder, Luse & Co.*

1880 *Photo-engraving came into use about this time.*

1880 *Thorn typesetter invented—required hand justification.*

NEWSPAPER EDITING

1881   *Los Angeles Times* founded.
1882   *New York Journal* founded—purchased by W. R. Hearst in 1895.
1883   Joseph Pulitzer bought *New York World*—beginning of sensational journalism.
1884   *Offset printing developed.*
1885   *First punch-cutting machine for typefounders.*
1885   *London Times installed its first folding machine.*
1886   *Point system of type measurement adopted by American Type Founders' Association.*
1886   *Mergenthaler linotype machine placed on the market.*
1887   *First quadruple press built—for New York World.*
1888   *Automatic typecasting and trimming machine patented by Henry Barth—100 to 140 per minute.*
1888   *Hoe built first three-page-wide rotary press.*
1890   *First successful machine to set, justify, and distribute type—Paige machine.*
1890   *Photo-engraving becoming established commercially.*
1890   *Chicago Evening Post founded.*
1891   *First sextuple press built—for New York Herald.*
1892   *Three-color engraving process becoming established commercially.*
1892   *Chicago Record* founded as morning edition of *Daily News*—merged with *Times-Herald* as *Record-Herald*, 1901—merged with *Inter-Ocean* as *Chicago Herald*, 1914.
1895   *Rembrandt photogravure process introduced.*
1895   *New York Journal* purchased by W. R. Hearst—beginning of ultra-sensational journalism.
1899   *Lanston monotype placed on market.*

APPENDIX II

TYPICAL STYLE SHEET

This Style Sheet is one that was prepared by the Course of Journalism of the University of Wisconsin in coöperation with Madison newspapers. It is in general a "down" style and is representative of the tendencies of the average American newspaper of today. While it is not ideal in many ways, it is inserted here as a means of emphasizing *accuracy in details*. Strict attention to typographical style assists the journalism student and young newspaper man in developing habits of accuracy. Rules are numbered for reference.

STYLE SHEET

Accuracy Always

Capitalization

Capitalize:

1. All proper nouns, months, days of the week, but not the seasons.
2. Principal words in the titles of books, plays, lectures, pictures, toasts, etc., including the initial "A" or "The": "The Man from Home."
3. Titles denoting official position, rank, or occupation, when they precede a proper noun: President Wilson, Judge John R. Holt (but John R. Holt, judge of the circuit court). Avoid long, awkward titles before a name, such as State Superintendent of Public Property Jones.
4. Distinguishing parts of names of associations, societies, leagues, companies, roads, lines, and incorporated bodies: Louisiana State university, First National bank, Union Trust company, Northwestern line, Epworth Methodist church, First Wisconsin volunteers.

5. Common nouns when they precede the distinguishing parts in names of associations, societies, companies, etc.: University of Wisconsin, Association of Collegiate Alumnæ, Bank of Wisconsin.
6. Only proper noun in geographical names, except when the common noun precedes: Rock river, Fox lake; but Lake Michigan, Gulf of Mexico.
7. Only the distinguishing parts of names of streets, avenues, boulevards, buildings, houses, hotels, theaters, stations, wards, districts, counties, etc.: Pinckney street, Northwestern station, Grand hotel, Third ward, Second district.
8. Schools, colleges and other main divisions of a university, but not departments: College of Agriculture, Law school, but department of astronomy.
9. Names of religious denominations, and nouns and pronouns of the deity.
10. Names of all political parties: Republican, Bolshevist, Socialist.
11. Sections of the country: the North, the Middle West.
12. Abbreviations of college degrees: M. A., LL. D., Ph. D.
13. Names of sections of a city: the East side; and distinguishing parts of nicknames of states and cities: the Buckeye state, the Windy city.
14. Distinguishing parts of names of holidays: Fourth of July, New Year's day.
15. Names of all races and nationalities: Indians, Caucasian, Negro.
16. Nicknames of athletic clubs and teams: the White Sox, the Gophers.
17. **Avoid all capitalization not absolutely necessary.**

Do Not Capitalize:

18. Names of national, state, and city bodies, buildings, officers, boards, etc.: congress, senate, assembly, department of justice, tax commission, budget committee, postoffice, city hall, common council, capitol.
19. Points of the compass: east, northwest.
20. Common religious terms: bible, scripture, gospels, heathen.
21. Names of school or college studies, except names of languages: biology, French.
22. Titles when they follow the name: Henry Wilson, Professor of Greek.
23. Abbreviations of time of day: a. m., p. m.; but 12 M.
24. Names of college classes: sophomore, senior.

APPENDIX

25. College degrees when spelled out: bachelor of arts: but B. A., Ph. D.
26. Seasons of the year: spring, autumn.
27. Name of offices in list of officers, as in election of officers: The new officers are: John C. Walter, president, etc.
28. The following nouns after a proper noun: street, avenue, boulevard, place, building, depot, hotel, station, theater, ward, county, district, etc.

Punctuation

29. Omit period after "per cent" and after nicknames (Tom, Sam, Will).
30. Use a comma before "and" in a list, red, white, and blue.
31. Punctuate lists of names with cities or states thus: Messrs. Arnold Woll, Racine; R. G. Davitt, Beloit; etc. Punctuate list of names with offices after a colon thus: J. S. Hall, president; Henry Stoltz, vice-president.
32. Use a colon after a statement introducing a direct quotation of one or more paragraphs, and begin a new paragraph for the quotation. Use a colon after "as follows."
33. Never use a colon after viz., to wit, namely, e. g., i. e., except when they end a paragraph. Use colon, dash or semicolon before them and comma after them, thus: This is the man; to wit, the victim.
34. Do not use a comma between a man's name and "Jr." or "Sr."
35. Use an apostrophe with year of college classes: Class of '87, John White '01.
36. Do not use a hyphen in "today" and "tomorrow."
37. Use a hyphen in compound numbers: thirty-two.
38. Use no apostrophe in making plurals of figures and letters: early 90s, three Rs.
39. Use no apostrophe in such abbreviations as Frisco, varsity, phone, bus.
40. Use an em dash after a man's name placed at the beginning in series of interviews: Henry Keith—I have nothing to say. (Use no quotation marks with this form.)
41. Use no comma in "6 feet 3 inches tall", "3 years 6 months old", etc.
42. In sporting news punctuate thus: Score: Wisconsin 8, Chicago 3. 100-yard dash—Smith, first: Hanks, second. Time 6:10 1-5. Peters ran thirty yards to the 10-yard line.

Quotation

Quote:

43. All verbatim quotations when they are to be set in the same type and measure as the context, but not when they are to be in smaller type or narrower measure.
44. All testimony, conversation, and interviews given in direct form, except when name of speaker, or Q. and A., with a dash, precedes, as: John Keith—I have nothing to say; Q.—What is your name? A.—Oscar Brown.
45. Names of books, dramas, paintings, statuary, operas, songs, subjects of lectures, sermons, toasts, magazine articles, including the initial "A" or "The": "A Man Without a Country."
46. Nicknames used before surnames: "Al" Harris, ("Slim") Hall.
47. Use single quotation marks for quotations within a quotation.
48. Use quotation marks at the beginning of each paragraph of a continuous quotation of several paragraphs, but at the end of the last paragraph only.

Do Not Quote:

49. Names of characters in plays: Shylock in "The Merchant of Venice."
50. Names of newspapers or periodicals: the Springfield Republican.
51. Names of vessels, horses, dogs, automobiles.

Figures

Use Figures For:

52. Numbers of 100 or over, except in the case of approximate numbers, as "about a hundred men."
53. Numbers under 100 only in the following cases:
54. Hours of the day: 7 p. m., at 8:30 this morning.
55. Days of the month, omitting d, th, st: April 29, 1913; July 1.
56. Ages: he was 12 years old; 2-year-old James.
57. All dimensions, prices, degrees of temperature, per cents, dates, votes, times in races, scores, etc.: 3 feet long, $3 a yard, 78 degrees, 95 per cent.
58. All sums of money (with dollar mark or cents): $24, 5.06, 75 cents.
59. Street and room numbers: 1324 Grand avenue, 67 University hall.

APPENDIX

60. When used in close connection with numbers over 100: 133 boys and 56 girls.
61. Do not begin a sentence with figures; supply a word or spell out.

Abbreviations

Abbreviate:

62. The following titles and no others, when they precede a name: Rev., Dr., Mr., Mrs., M., Mme., Mlle., Prof. (before a full name only: Prof. E. G. Hunt, but Professor Hunt), and military titles, except sergeant, corporal, and chaplain. Never write Pres. Coolidge, Vice-Pres. Dawes, or Sen. Jones.
63. Names of states, only when they follow names of cities: Madison, Wis. (but never "a citizen of Wis.").
64. "Number" before figures: No. 24.
65. Saint and Mount in proper names, but not Fort: St. John, but Fort Wayne.

Do Not Abbreviate:

66. Railway, company, street, avenue, district, etc.: Chicago and Northwestern railway, State street, A. B. Hall company. (Railway and railroad may be abbreviated when initials are used: C. M. & St. P. Ry.)
67. Christian names like William, Charles, Thomas, John, Alexander.
68. The titles, congressman, senator, representative, president, secretary, treasurer, etc., preceding a name.
69. Names of months except in dates and date lines.
70. Years ('97 for 1897), except in referring to college classes, etc.
71. Christmas in the form Xmas.
72. Per cent: 15 per cent (not 15%).
73. Cents: 75 cents (not 75 cts. or 75 c.).
74. Avoid colloquial abbreviations like "prof.," "libe," "agrics."

Dates and Date Lines

75. In dates, write Jan. 12, 1914 (not the 12th of January, or 12 January).
76. Punctuate date lines thus:
    MADISON, Wis., Feb. 11.—Fire destroyed the, etc.
    Omit state after names of prominent cities. Abbreviate months of more than five letters. Omit year and d, st, th (after figures). Begin the story immediately after dash on same line.

Addresses

77. Write addresses thus:
    Frank D. Miles, 136 Gilman street. Hiram Swenk, Cuba City Wis.
78. Omit "at" and "of" before address. Do not abbreviate or capitalize street, avenue, etc. Spell out numbered streets up to 100th.

Titles

79. Always give initials or first names of persons the first time they appear in a story.
80. Never use only one initial; use both or first name: J. H. Ward, John H. Ward, or John Ward (not J. Ward). Do not use nicknames except in sporting news or in the form—John ("Spike") Brown.
81. Never use Mr. with initials or first name: Mr. Ward (not Mr. John Ward).
82. Give first name of unmarried woman, not initials only: Miss Mary R. Snow (not Miss M. R. Snow).
83. Always use the title Miss before unmarried women's names and Mrs. before married women's.
84. Begin list of unmarried women with "Misses," and one of married women with "Mesdames," giving first name of unmarried women, and husband's first name or initials with married women's names. Begin lists of men's names with "Messrs."
85. Supply "the" before Rev.; supply Mr. if first name is omitted: the Rev. S. R. Hart, or the Rev. Mr. Hart (not Rev. S. R. Hart, the Rev. Hart, or Rev. Hart).
86. Write Mr. and Mrs. Arthur S. Miles (not Arthur S. Miles and wife).
87. Write Prof. and Mrs. Henry Wilton (not Mr. and Mrs. Prof. Henry Wilton).
88. Give the title professor only to members of faculty of professorial rank: use "Mr." when necessary with names of instructors and assistants.
89. Avoid long titles, such as Superintendent of Public Instruction Moore.
90. Never use the title "Honorable" or "Hon."

APPENDIX

General Directions

Preparation of Copy:

1. Write legibly; use a typewriter whenever possible.
2. Never write on both sides of the sheet.
3. Double space your typewritten and longhand copy.
4. Use 8½ x 11 soft white copy paper for all your work.
5. Begin your story about the middle of the first page.
6. Number sheets at the top of the page and enclose the numbers in a circle.
7. Put the end mark (#) at the close of every complete story.
8. Enclose all quotation marks in half circles.
9. Underscore "u's" and overscore "n's" in longhand copy.

Paragraphs:

10. Indent each paragraph about two inches.
11. Remember that the length of paragraphs in newspapers does not normally exceed 100 words, and generally ranges from 25 to 70 words.
12. Put an important idea at the beginning of the first sentence of each paragraph.
13. Avoid beginning successive paragraphs with the same word, phrase, or construction.
14. Don't put important details in the last paragraph where they may be cut off in make-up.
15. Make separate paragraphs of introductory statements like "He said in part," "The report is as follows," and end them with colon.
16. Set off as a separate paragraph a direct quotation of more than one sentence without explanatory material, at the beginning of a story.

Sentences:

17. Make evident the construction of every sentence so that it may be read rapidly.
18. Avoid choppy, disconnected short sentences.
19. Don't overload the first sentence of a summary lead, by crowding in unessential details.
20. Put an important idea at the beginning of every sentence.

Words:

21. Avoid words that are likely to be unfamiliar to the average reader, unless you explain them in your story.
22. Don't use trite phrases.
23. Use superlatives sparingly.
24. Use slang only when circumstances demand it.
25. Find the one noun to express the idea, the one adjective, if necessary, to qualify it, and the one verb to give it life.

Accuracy:

26. Remember that the truth and nothing but the truth, interestingly presented, makes the best news story.
27. Don't try to make cleverness a substitute for truth.
28. Don't forget that faking is lying.
29. Realize that every mistake you make hurts some one.
30. Remember that what you write for newspaper publication is read by thousands and helps to influence public opinion.
31. Be especially careful about names, initials, and addresses.
32. Get all the news; don't stop with half of it.
33. Don't give rumors as facts.
34. Be fair and unbiased; give both sides of the case.
35. Don't misrepresent by playing up a statement that, taken from its context, is misleading.
36. Don't make the necessity for speed an excuse for carelessness and inaccuracy.

APPENDIX III

BOOKS ON JOURNALISM

Reporting and News Writing

BLEYER, W. G., *Newspaper Writing and Editing* (Houghton Mifflin), 1913; Revised, 1923.
BLEYER, W. G., *Types of News Writing* (Houghton Mifflin), 1916.
CUNLIFFE and LOMER, *Writing of Today* (Century), 1915, 1922.
HARRINGTON and FRANKENBERG, *Essentials of Journalism* (Ginn), 1912; Revised, 1924.
HARRINGTON, H. F., *Typical Newspaper Stories* (Ginn), 1915.
HYDE, G. M., *Newspaper Reporting and Correspondence* (Appleton), 1912.
HYDE, G. M., *Handbook for Newspaper Workers* (Appleton), 1921; Enlarged, 1925.
MILLER, O. W., *Practical Exercises in News Writing and Editing* (Heath), 1922.
ROSS, C. G., *The Writing of News* (Holt), 1911.
SPENCER, M. L., *News Writing* (Heath), 1917.

Copyreading, Headlines, Proofreading

BASTIAN, G. C., *Editing the Day's News* (Macmillan), 1923.
CONVERSE and BRYSON, *Copyreading Exercises* (Iowa State College, Ames).
HENRY, F. S., *Printing for School and Shop* (Wiley, London), 1917.
HYDE, G. M., *Newspaper Editing* (Appleton), 1915; Revised, 1925.
RADDER, N. J., *Newspaper Make-up and Headlines* (McGraw-Hill), 1924.
SMITH, A. M., *Exercises in Proofreading* (J. C. Winston, Philadelphia), 1904.

Editorial Writing, Collections of Editorials

Casual Essays of the [N. Y.] *Sun* (R. G. Cooke), 1905.
CRANE, FRANK, *War and Government* (Lane), 1915.
Editorials from Hearst Newspapers (International), 1906.
FLINT, L. N., *The Editorial* (Appleton), 1920.
HEATON, J. L., *Story of a Page* [N. Y. *World*], (Harpers), 1913.
KROCK, A., *Editorials of Henry Watterson* (Doran), 1923.
MACKAIL, J. W., *Modern Essays* [London Times], (Longmans), 1915.
MAHIN, H. O., *Editorials of William Allen White* (Macmillan), 1923.
National Floodmarks [Collier's], (Doran), 1915.
NEAL, R. W., *Editorials and Editorial Writing* (Home Corres. School), 1921.
POLLAK, G., *Fifty Years of American Idealism* [Nation], (Houghton Mifflin), 1915.

Special Feature Articles

BLEYER, W. G., *How to Write Special Feature Articles* (Houghton, Mifflin), 1919.
CUSHING, C. P., *If You Don't Write Fiction* (McBride), 1920.
WILDMAN, E., *Writing to Sell* (Appleton), 1923.

Country Weekly and Community Newspaper

ATWOOD, M. V., *The Country Newspaper* (McClurg), 1923.
BING, P. C., *The Country Weekly* (Appleton), 1917.
BYXBEE, O. F., *Establishing a Newspaper* (Inland Printer), 1901.
HARRIS, E. P., and HOOKE, F. H., *The Community Newspaper* (Appleton), 1923.
MUNSON, A. J., *Making a Country Newspaper* (Dominion Co., Chicago), 1899.

Descriptions of Newspaper Work

DIBLEE, G. B., *The Newspaper* (Holt), 1913.
GIVEN, J. L., *Making a Newspaper* (Holt), 1907.

APPENDIX

HEMSTREET, C., *Reporting for Newspapers* (Wessels), 1901.
LUCE, R., *Writing for the Press* (Clipping Bureau, Boston), 1907.
SHUMAN, E. L., *Practical Journalism* (Appleton), 1903.
SYNON, J. D., *The English Press and Its Story* (Seeley Service), 1914.
WARREN, L., *English Journalism* (Cecil Palmer, London), 1922.
WILLIAMS and MARTIN, *Practice of Journalism* (Stephens), 1911; Revised, 1922.

Personal Experiences in Journalism

BANKS, E. L., *Autobiography of a Newspaper Girl* (Dodd, Mead).
BLYTHE, S., *Making of a Newspaper Man* (Altemus), 1912.
COBB, IRVIN, *Myself—To Date* [Stickfuls], (Doran), 1923.
GIBBS, P., *Adventures in (English) Journalism* (Harpers), 1923.
RALPH, J., *Making a Journalist* (Harpers), 1903.
RUSSELL, C. E., *These Shifting Scenes.*
STONE, M. E., *Fifty Years a Journalist.*
WATTERSON, H., *Marse Henry* (Doran), 1919.

History of American Journalism

HUDSON, F., *Journalism in United States, 1690-1872* (Harper), 1873.
LEE, J. M., *History of American Journalism* (Houghton Mifflin), 1923.
PAYNE, G. H., *History of Journalism in U. S.* (Appleton), 1920.

Histories of American Newspapers

DAVIS, ELMER, *History of N. Y. Times* (N. Y. Times), 1921.
NEVINS, A., *The [N. Y.] Evening Post* (Boni & Liveright), 1922.
O'BRIEN, F. M., *Story of the [N. Y.] Sun* (Doran), 1918.
The W. G. N. (Chicago Tribune), 1922.

Biographies of American Newspaper Editors

GODWIN, P., *William Cullen Bryant* [N. Y. Post], (Appleton), 1893.

HARRIS, J. C., *Life of Henry W. Brady* [*Atlanta Constitution*], (Cassell), 1890.
LINN, W. A., *Horace Greeley* (Appleton), 1903.
MAVERICK, A., *Henry J. Raymond* [*N. Y. Times*], 1870.
MERRIAM, G. S., *Life and Times of Samuel Bowles* [*Springfield Republican*], (Century), 1885.
NELSON, W., *Story of a Man, a Newspaper, and a City* [*K. C. Star*], 1915.
OGDEN, R., *Life and Letters of E. L. Godkin* [*N. Y. Post*], (Macmillan), 1907.
PARTON, J., *Life of Horace Greeley* (Houghton Mifflin), 1896.
(PRAY, I. C.), *Memoirs of James G. Bennett* (Stringers), 1855.
WILSON, J. H., *Life of Charles A. Dana* [*N. Y. Sun*].

Journalism as a Vocation

LEE, J. M., *Opportunities in Newspaper Business* (Harper), 1919.
LORD, C. S., *Young Man and Journalism* (Macmillan), 1922.
SEITZ, D., *Training for the Newspaper Trade* (Lippincott), 1916.
WILLIAM, T., *The Newspaper Man* (Scribner), 1922.

Journalistic Writing in High Schools

DILLON, C., *Journalism in High Schools* (Noble), 1918.
FLINT, L. N., *Newspaper Writing in High Schools* (U. of Kansas).
HARRINGTON, H. F., *Writing for Print* (Heath), 1922.
HYDE, G. M., *A Course in Journalistic Writing* (Appleton), 1922.

Law of the Press

HALE, W. G., *The Law of the Press* (West Pub. Co.,), 1923.
HENDERSON, W. G., *Newspapers and Libel* (Chemical Bank Note Co.,), 1915.
LOOMIS, W. W., *Newspaper Law* (Citizens Pub. Co., LaGrange, Ill.), 1922.

Principles, Philosophy, and Ethics of Journalism

ANGELL, N., *Press and Organization of Society* (Labour Pub. Co., London), 1922.

BLEYER, W. G., *The Profession of Journalism* (Atlantic Mon. Press), 1918.
CRAWFORD, N. A., *The Ethics of Journalism* (Knopf), 1924.
FLINT, L. N., *The Conscience of the Newspaper* (Appleton), 1925.
HAPGOOD, N., *Ethics of Journalism* [Every Day Ethics], (Yale U. Press), 1910.
HOLT, H., *Commercialism and Journalism* (Houghton Mifflin), 1909.
LIPPMANN, W., *Public Opinion* (Harcourt, Brace), 1922.
LIPPMANN, W., *Liberty and the News* (Harcourt, Brace), 1920.
Report of First National Newspaper Conference (U. of Wisconsin), 1912.
ROGERS, J. E., *The American Newspaper* (U. of Chicago Press), 1909.
SALMON, L., *The Newspaper and the Historian* (Oxford U. Press), 1923.
SINCLAIR, U., *The Brass Check* (published by author, Pasadena, Cal.).
THORPE, MERLE, *The Coming Newspaper* (Holt), 1915.
VILLARD, O. G., *Some Newspapers and Newspapermen* (Knopf), 1923.
YOST, C., *The Principles of Journalism* (Appleton), 1924.

Freedom of the Press, Censorship, Etc.

BROWNRIGG, SIR D., *Indiscretions of Naval Censor* (English), (Cassell), 1920.
CHAFEE, Z., *Freedom of Speech* (Harcourt, Brace), 1920.
COOK, SIR E., *The Press in War Time* (English).
LYTTON, N., *The Press and the General Staff* (English).
SALMON, L. M., *The Newspaper and Authority* (Oxford U. Press), 1924.

Advertising, Circulation, Publishing

BLANCHARD, F. L., *Essentials of Advertising* (McGraw-Hill).
CHASNOFF, J. E., *Selling Advertising Space* (Ronald Press), 1913.
HALL, S. R., *Writing on Advertisement* (Houghton Mifflin), 1915.
HALL, S. R., *Advertisers' Handbook* (Inter. Corres. School).

HERROLD, L. D., *Advertising for the Retailer* (Appleton), 1923.
ROGERS, J., *Newspaper Building* (Harpers), 1918.
ROGERS, J., *Newspaper Making* (Author), 1922.
ROGERS, J., *Building Newspaper Advertising* (Harpers), 1919.
SAMPSON, E., *Advertize!* (Heath), 1918.
SCOTT, W. R., *Scientific Circulation Management* (Ronald Press), 1915.
STARCH, D., *Advertising* (Scott, Foresman), 1914.
STARCH, D., *Principles of Advertising*, 1923.
TIPPER, HOTCHKISS, HOLLINGWORTH, PARSONS, *Principles of Advertising* (Ronald), 1921.

Fiction Dealing with Journalism

ABBOTT, W. J., *Philip Derby, Reporter* (Dodd, Mead), 1922.
ADAMS, S. H., *The Clarion* (Houghton Mifflin), 1914.
ADAMS, S. H., *The Common Cause* (Houghton Mifflin), 1919.
ADAMS, S. H., *Success* (Houghton Mifflin), 1921.
COURLANDER, A., *Mightier than the Sword* (Unwin, London), 1913.
DAVIS, R. H., *Gallegher and Other Stories* (Scribner), 1892.
FERBER, E., *Dawn O'Hara* (Stokes), 1911.
GEORGE, W. L., *Caliban* (Harpers), 1920.
GIBBS, P., *The Street of Adventure* (Dutton), 1919.
JORDAN, E., *Tales of the City Room* (Scribner), 1898.
MONTAGUE, C. E., *A Hind Let Loose* (English).
O'BRIEN, H. V., *Thirty* (Dodd, Mead), 1915.
SMITH, H. J., *Deadlines* (Covici-McGee, Chicago), 1922.
WHITE, W. A., *In Our Town*.
WILLIAMS, J. L., *The Stolen Story* (Scribner), 1899.

Bibliographies

BLEYER, W. G., *Profession of Journalism* (Atlantic Monthly Press), 1918.
ELY, M., *Some Great American Newspaper Editors* (H. W. Wilson), 1916.
PAYNE, G. H., *History of Journalism in the United States* (Appleton), 1920.
STOCKETTE, J. C., *Masters of American Journalism* (H. W. Wilson), 1916.
WIEDER, C., *Daily Newspapers in U. S.* (H. W. Wilson), 1916.

INDEX

Abbreviation, 31, 41, 44, 175, 391; in headlines, 123, 144.
Accuracy, 33, 46, 156, 176, 387, 394.
Active voice, 68, 122, 133, 136.
Adams press, 307.
"Add" catchline, 14, 88, 92, 238.
Addresses, 33, 44, 392.
Addressing machines, 366.
Adjectives, 40, 61, 153
Adverbs, 36, 61, 122, 135
Advertisements, 191, 210, 211, 346, 360.
Advertising, contract, 364; headlines, 99, 162, 188; manager, 6; rates, 361
Agate, 267, 269, 361.
Alignment, 182, 185, 292.
"All in hand," 92, 195.
"All up," 92, 195.
"Alleged," 75.
Allegorical headlines, 122, 141.
Alliteration in headlines, 122, 140.
Almanacs, 53.
Ambiguity in headlines, 123, 151.
Analysis of newspaper, 22.
Anonymous headlines, 123, 151.
Antecedents, 35.
Antique, paper, 339; type, 273.
Apostrophe, 41, 143, 174, 389.
Applegate press, 309.
Aquatint etchings, 324.
Art department, 11, 91, 164, 326.
Articles, 122, 139.
Assignment, 9, 11; book, 250.
Associated Press, 233.
Associations, press, 232.
Automobile page, 219.

Autoplate, 16, 300; junior, 300.
Auxiliaries, 36.

Back page, 189, 211, 215, 219.
"Backing in," 227.
Balanced page, 206.
Bank, 104, 109, 123, 146; men, 7, 14.
Banner headline, 99, 162, 200, 209, 316.
Beat, 9, 91, 227.
Ben Day shading, 223, 323.
Bibliography, 395.
Bill head, 365.
Binding, 344.
Biographical syndicates, 244.
Black-face type, 272.
Black-letter type, 273.
Blaew press, 305.
Blanket, head, 163, 217; sheet, 189.
Block paragraph, 61.
Bodge, 265.
Bodoni, 109, 199, 273.
Body, of type, 271; type, 197, 267, 272.
Bogus, 91, 195.
"Boiled" story, 249, 252.
"Boiler plate," 242, 302.
Boiling, 65, 80.
Bold type, 31, 173, 198, 272, 279.
Books, on journalism, 395; of reference, 47, 53; style, 42, 142, 387.
Borders, 275.
Bourgeois type, 197, 267, 270.

INDEX

Box, 198, 275, 279; headline, 167; in type case, 276.
Break, line, 104; over, 16, 91, 160, 193, 203.
Brevier type, 197, 267, 269.
Brilliant type, 267, 269.
Broken type, 173, 182.
Bug, 167.
Bulletin, 95, 99, 100, 163, 200, 238.
Bullock press, 311.
Bureau, 235.
Business manager, 6, 359.
"Butchering copy," 79, 80.
By-lines, 90, 167.

Cable, 10, 25, 239.
Calendered paper, 338.
Canon type, 267.
Capitalization, 31, 33, 43, 44, 109, 123, 125, 146, 173, 179, 198, 272, 276, 279, 387.
Captions, 27, 166, 223.
Caret, 32, 175, 179.
Cartoons, 11, 205, 215, 326.
Case of type, 276.
Caslon, 109, 199, 273, 280.
Catchlines, 12, 87, 238.
Centered, 104.
Chalk plates, 317.
Chase, 15, 190, 185.
Chemical pulp paper, 337.
Cheltenham, 109, 100, 273.
Church text type, 273.
Circulation, 6, 101, 200, 215, 266.
Circus make-up, 207.
City, editor, 9, 25, 192; press association, 241.
Civil War, 98, 233.
Clean copy, 92.
Clippings, 3.
Closed up, 195.
Clymer-Columbian press, 307.
Coinage of words, 66, 95.

College newspapers, 329.
Colloquialisms, 68, 122, 139, 202.
Collotype, 324.
Colon, 40, 142, 173, 389.
"Color," 62, 152, 156.
Color, engraving, 321; in paper 336; printing, 312.
Coloroto, 324.
Columbian type, 267.
Column, rules, 180, 274; width, 189, 210, 269, 279, 340.
Combination desk, 26.
Comics, 220, 223, 326.
Comma, 39, 44, 142, 173, 389.
Comment, 34, 61, 152.
Complex sentence, 39.
Composition, 7, 184, 275, 283, 297, 343.
Compound sentence, 39.
Condensed type, 271.
Condensing, 80.
Conference, editorial, 192.
Conjunction, 35, 39.
Constructive journalism, 20.
Contractions in headlines, 122, 139.
Contracts, 364, 370.
Copperplate, 324; paper, 339.
Copy, 122, 277, 352, 393; "butcher," 79, 80; cutting, 7, 14, 80; desk, 10, 25; preparing for printer, 85; record, 354.
Copyholder, 172.
Copyreader, 9, 12, 19; record, 12, 27.
Copyreading, 24, 354; sample, 32; signs, 29.
Copyright, 346.
Correspondent, 123, 150, 232.
Cost of printing, 329.
Counter punch, 284.
Counting headline letters, 122, 124.
Courtesy, 71, 150.
Cover, 344.
Credit line, 245.
Crossline, 104, 112, 118, 126.
Cut-off rule, 163, 196, 204, 275.

INDEX

Cuts, 166, 244, 317, 321, 331, 343; lines, 166, 167.
Cutting in make-up, 34, 60, 128.
Cylinder press, 307.

Dandy roll, 338.
Dangling participles, 35.
Dash, 40, 143, 145, 174, 275, 389.
Date, 33, 44, 52, 391; line, 10, 44, 237, 391.
Deadline, 195.
Deckle-edge, 339.
Decks, 97, 102, 126, 199; combination or interrelation, 108, 122, 129.
"Dele," 175.
Department, 1, 189, 213; editors, 9, 10; headlines, 87; men, 9.
Desk men, 9, 19, 25.
Diagram of make-up, 190, 340, 355.
Diamond type, 267, 269.
Diction, 34, 62, 122, 137.
Digest, news, 166.
Dignity, 34, 69, 139, 150.
Digraph, 38.
Dingbat, 167, 275.
Dinky dash, 167.
Dirty, case, 183, 277; proof, 177.
Display, 104, 142, 188, 198, 200, 212; type, 267, 272, 279.
Dissymmetrical page, 207.
Distributing type, 277, 289.
Division of words, 123, 146.
Divisional heads, 165.
Double, English type, 267; leaded, 274, 299; measure, 198, 279; octuple press, 313; pica type, 267; rule, 275; sextuple press, 313; supplement press, 312.
"Down" style, 43, 45.
Dragon's blood, 317.
Dramatic critic, 11, 73, 218.
"Dress up" page, 163, 201.

Drop, head, 167; line, 104, 112, 126, 200.
Dummy, 15, 91, 191, 348, 356.
Duodecimo fold, 333.
Duplex press, 301, 313.

Ears, 195.
Ease of reading, 60, 101, 188, 199, 201, 224.
Editions, 114, 193.
Editor-in-chief, 8, 192.
Editorial, 96, 159, 160, 214, 215, 220, 340; department, 7; writers, 8.
Electro, 171, 304, 344; electrotype, 303.
Em, 174, 270, 274.
Emphasis, 34, 55, 225, 252; headline, 138, 147; paragraph, 64; sentence, 63.
Enameled paper, 338.
End mark, 13, 14, 32, 89, 237.
English, language, 21, 27, 71, 217; type, 267.
Engraving, 204, 222, 317; department, 7, 331, 343.
Envelopes, 366.
Errors, in editing, 23; expression, 33; grammar, 33; proofreading, 182; punctuation, 33, 40; spelling, 37; style, 33, 43; various sets, 185.
Esparto paper, 337.
Estimating space, 84.
Ethics, 5, 20, 66, 69, 96, 142, 156, 201, 217.
European press associations, 234.
Evidence, 49.
Excelsior type, 267.
Exchange editor, 10, 11, 91.
Exclusive, 91.
Expanding stories, 82.
Extended type, 109, 271.
Extra-condensed type, 109, 271.

INDEX

Face of type, 197, 263, 271, 284.
Facts, 48, 157.
False quotation, 158.
Families, type, 273.
Fashions, 218.
Fat headlines, 116, 124, 127, 263.
Feature, in stories, 12, 33, 55, 57, 59, 102, 129, 250; non-news, 215, 227, 246.
Figures, 31, 33, 44, 51, 123, 145, 175, 248, 390.
Filing editor, 236.
Fillers, 91, 195, 220.
Fillet, 273.
Filter, 321.
Flag, 163, 167.
Flash, 91, 238, 239.
Flat bed press, 308, 315.
Flong, 299.
Flush headline, 104, 107.
Focused page, 207.
Fold, 167, 196, 200.
Folding, 311, 332, 344.
Folio, 333; head, 342.
"Follow," catchline, 14, 88, 92, 238; copy, 91; leader, 55; story, 57, 92, 129, 150, 165, 248, 254.
Font, 173, 276.
Foreign news, 234.
Form, 195, 261, 333; proof, 171, 359.
Fractions, 40.
Franklin, 307.
Frisket, 306.
Front page, 189, 193, 196, 203, 205, 211, 226.
Fudge, 16, 195, 316.
Furniture, printing, 274.

Galley, 14, 170, 276; proof, 170, 190, 276.
General manager, 5.
Generalities in headlines, 123, 148.

German text type, 273.
Gothic type, 109, 199, 273.
Government, 45, 70, 73, 76.
Grammatical errors, 33, 34, 62, 122, 129.
Great Primer type, 267.
Gripper, 308.
Guide lines, 13, 27, 87, 238.
Gutenberg, 307.

Hairlines, 184, 275, 292.
Half, measure, 279; stick, 91.
Half-tone, 205, 223, 299, 318, 336, 344.
Hand press, 305.
Hanging indention, 104, 106, 126, 142, 218, 279.
Headline, 9, 13, 58, 87, 95, 195, 342, 358; banner or streamer, 99, 162, 200; building, 110; jump, 109, 160, 193; readers, 95, 200; schedule, 87, 103, 110, 126, 129, 278; spread, 99, 164, 201.
Hearst services, 234.
Heel nick, 263.
Height of type, 264.
Hell-box, 277.
Helter-skelter make-up, 207.
High-school newspapers, 329.
Hints, headline diction, 138; style sheet, 46.
Hoe presses, 309, 311, 312.
Hold for release, 91.
Hooked, 91.
Humor, headline, 123, 153.
Hyphen, 40, 174.

Ideals in newspaper work, 5, 20, 66, 69, 96, 142, 156, 201, 217.
Illustrations, 11, 204, 222, 343.
Imperative headline, 122, 136.

INDEX

Inaccuracy, 33, 46, 156, 176, 387, 394.
Indention, 126, 174, 198, 218, 274, 279.
Index of news, 44, 166.
Infinitive, 36, 122, 135.
Inserts, 30, 77, 88, 173, 175, 179, 181, 184.
Intaglio, 315, 323, 324.
International news service, 234.
Intertype machine, 297.
Interviews, 49, 50, 95.
Iron hand press, 307.
Italic type, 31, 173, 272, 279.

Jargon, headline, 70, 122, 141, 144, 155.
Jim dash, 167.
Job press, 314.
Journalese, 69.
Journalism, books, 395; school, 328, 387.
Jump head, 109, 160, 193, 211.
Junior, autoplate, 300; linotype, 297.
Justification, 180, 195, 267, 274, 286, 357; linotype, 181, 290; monotype, 185, 293.

Key address, 360.
Kill, 91.
Koenig press, 307.

Label headings, 97, 123, 149.
Laffan Press service, 234.
Laid paper, 338.
Lanston monotype, 292.
Lap line, 104.
Laws, 76.
Laying the foundation, 249.
Layout, 164, 201, 326.

Lead of story, 27, 33, 55, 56, 95, 99, 128, 250, 256.
Leaded, 175, 179, 191, 195, 198, 266, 271, 274, 299.
Leaders, 217, 275.
Leased wire, 227, 235.
Leaves, 333.
Length, headline, 122; paragraph, 64; sentence, 62; story, 220.
Letter-spacing, 174, 274.
Libel, libelous, 19, 26, 34, 51, 72, 160.
Librarian, 11.
Ligature, 174, 276.
Line engraving, 223, 317.
Lining series, 268.
Linograph, 297.
Linotype, 7, 181, 184, 198, 279, 288; junior, 297.
List, punctuation of, 39.
Lithograph, 309, 313, 324.
Loaded paper, 339.
Local, news field, 49, 52, 225; staff, 9, 90.
Locking up, 195.
Logotype, 276.
Long primer type, 267, 270.
Loop, telegraph, 237.
Lower case, 31, 110, 125, 173, 199, 276.

Machine-finished paper, 338.
Magazine, 24, 171, 187, 245, 313.
Mailing machine, 7, 366.
Major headlines, 109, 200.
Make-ready, 171, 315, 320.
Make-up, 60, 87, 128, 160, 171, 187; diagram, 190, 340, 355.
Managing editor, 9, 15, 190.
Margins, 30, 85, 172, 176, 279, 339.
Market, editor, 11, 26; section, 89, 214, 219.
Masthead, 167.
Mat, service, 301; stereotype, 299.

INDEX

Matrix, 293; grid, 293; linotype, 289; service, 244, 301; stereotype, 16, 299; type, 284.
Mechanical pulp paper, 337.
Mergenthaler linotype, 288.
Mezzotint engraving, 325.
Microscopique type, 267.
Minion type, 197, 267, 269.
Miscellany, 91.
Misrepresentation, 49.
Missal type, 273.
Mo, 333.
Modern type, 273.
Monotype machine, 185, 292.
"More to come," 13, 14, 89, 238.
Morgue, 11, 54, 244, 302.
Morkrum telegraph printer, 237.
"Mr.," "Mrs.," and "Miss," 45, 71, 144.
Multiplate, 300.
Multiple rotary press, 312.
Music, critic, 11; engraving, 326.
"Must" copy, 91.
Mustang mailer, 367.
Mutton quad, 274.

Nameplate, 167, 195.
Names, use of, 50, 123, 150.
Neatness, 77, 177.
Negative, photo, 317.
News, 5, 213; digests, 44, 166; editor, 10, 16, 190; staff, 8, 9; story, 54, 98; values, 54.
News contents bill, 100, 162.
Newsboy or stand sale, 101, 162, 189, 200, 209.
Nick in type, 263, 276.
Nicknames, 34, 69, 70, 150.
Non-news features, 215, 227, 246.
Nonpareil type, 197, 265, 267, 269.
Nouns, 34, 40, 42, 66, 131, 153.
Number, of columns, 209; of lines per inch, 280; of pages, 210, 332, 334; of stories, 202;

220; of words per inch, 280; of words per line, 280.
Nut quad, 274.

Obituaries, 11, 135, 144, 214, 219, 227.
Oblique lines, 31, 179.
Octavo, 333.
Octuple press, 313.
"Off its feets," 195.
Office style, 26, 42, 52, 180.
Offset, 310, 314, 324; printing, 314.
Old English type, 273.
Old style type, 273.
Opinion, 34, 61, 152.
Opposition paper, 55, 224.
Originality, 142.
Overlays, 309, 315.
Overlines, 166.
Overplaying news, 158, 163, 188, 201.

Page, back, 189, 211, 215, 219; diagram, 190, 340, 355; dummy, 15, 91, 191, 348, 356; front, 189, 193, 196, 203, 205, 211, 226; proof, 171, 359; size, 331.
Paging, 171, 356.
Paper, 331, 336; making, 337; size, 331.
Papier-mâché, matrix, 16, 299; stereotyping, 310.
Paragon type, 267.
Paragraphs, 31, 34, 55, 60, 64, 78, 175, 393.
Participles, 37, 122, 135.
Passive voice, 68, 122, 133, 136.
Patent insides, 242, 317.
Pearl type, 267, 269.
Pelt balls, 305.
Perfecting, 308, 310.

INDEX

Perforating rule, 275.
Period, 41, 142, 173.
Personal journalism, 90.
Photo-engraving, 204, 317.
Photograph, 11, 205, 222; syndicate, 205, 222, 243.
Photogravure, 323, 325.
Pi, 277.
Pica type, 265, 267, 269, 270.
"Pick up," 91.
Planing down, 195.
Plaster stereotyping, 298.
Plate, matter, 242, 302; paper, 339; service, 242, 301.
Platen, 305.
Playing up feature, 12, 55, 59, 226, 227, 250.
Point system, 266.
Policy, 80, 96, 142, 156, 159, 203, 212.
Pony service, 234, 236.
Postal rates, 368.
Power press, 307.
Prejudices, stock, 49.
Press association, 90, 217, 232.
Press, 210, 304; box, 238; men, 7; work, 171, 232.
Printing presses, 16, 210, 304; processes, 282.
Privilege, libel, 73.
Pronouns, 35.
Proof, 15, 276, 353, 359, 364; marks, 173; reading, 7, 28, 170.
Pulling proof, 170, 276.
Punch, 63, 285.
Punctuation, 33, 38, 123, 142, 143, 173, 389.
"Put to bed," 15, 195.
Pyramid, deck, 104, 106, 119, 126, 142; page, 212; story, 55; top deck, 108.

Quad, 274.
Quadruple press, 312.
Quarto, 333.
Query, 175.
Questions, in headlines, 123, 143, 154.
Qui êtes-vous?, 53.
Quoins, 195.
Quotation marks, 31, 44, 50, 58, 174, 390; in headlines, 123, 144, 158.

Radio, 219.
Rag paper, 337.
Railroad editor, 11.
Rate, advertising, 361; card, 362.
Ready-made advertisements, 242.
Ready-prints, 242, 317.
Real estate editor, 11.
Ream, 336.
Record, copy, 354; copy cutter's, 14; copyreader's, 12, 27.
Red ink, proofreading, 179.
Reference books, 47, 53.
Register, 323.
Reglet, 274.
Rehash, 249.
Relative clause, 36.
Relay, 236.
Release, 91, 237.
Relief, relievo, 315, 324.
Rembrandt photogravure, 325.
Renaissance photogravure, 325.
Repetition of words, headline, 122, 138.
Replate edition, 195.
Reporter, 9.
Reprint, 91.
Retouching, 223.
"Rev.," 44.
Reversed letters, 173, 183.
Revising, 28; proof, 15, 30, 170, 173, 276; type, 290, 296.
Rewrite, man, 248; story, 248, 250.
Rhyme, headlines, 122, 140.

INDEX

Ribbon, 163.
Rim man, 26.
Ripped open, 194, 195.
Roman type, 173, 272.
Rotary press, 16, 210, 311.
Rotogravure, 323.
Rounce, 306.
Routed out, 223, 319.
"Rubber stamp" writing, 69, 142.
Rule, 274.
Run around, 91.
Run-in line, 32, 78.
Runs, 9; on press, 332.

Safeguards against inaccuracy, 52.
Schedule, 91, 103, 114, 192.
Scheme of type, 276.
School of journalism, 328, 387.
Scoop, 91, 227, 233.
Screen, half-tone, 223, 319.
Script type, 273.
Second-class postal rate, 346, 367, 368.
Second day story, 57, 67, 92, 129, 150, 227, 255.
Semicolon, 39, 173, 389; in headline, 143.
Sensationalism, 99, 101, 159, 188, 201, 203, 216, 219.
Sentence, 34, 39, 62, 393.
Serial, numbers, 44, 391; story, 67.
Series of type, 273.
Serif, 273.
Set-width, 264, 268, 285.
Sextuple press, 312.
Shank, type, 263.
Shoulder, type, 263.
Show window, 58.
Silhouetted cut, 222.
Size, page, 331; type, 197, 267.
Sizing, paper, 338.
Skeletonized, 239.

"Skinned" cable, 239.
Slang, 34, 70, 91, 122, 139, 144, 167.
Slant, 95.
Slot man, 26.
Slug, 27, 184, 274, 288.
Slugged, 87, 190.
Small, capitals, 31, 173, 198, 272, 279; pica type, 267, 270; publications, 328.
Smith press, 307.
Society, editor, 11, 89; section or page, 193, 213, 217.
Solid, set, 198, 266, 274.
Sorts, 277, 286, 296.
Source, news, 57.
Space, 174, 274; justification, 180.
Spanish war, 99.
Specialty, 53.
Specifying type, 277.
Speech reports, 50, 59.
Spelling, 33, 37; simplified, 122, 140.
Spiked, 91.
Split-line, 104.
Sporting, department or page, 89, 213, 216; editor, 10, 25, 142.
Spread headline, 99, 164, 201.
Squared-up type matter, 195, 274.
Standard, line, 267; paper sizes, 331; width type, 271.
Standing, heads, 167; matter, 91.
Stanhope press, 307.
Stapling, 331, 345.
Star-box, 275.
Starter page, 193, 195.
Steam table, 16, 299.
Steel plate engraving, 325.
Stencil address, 367.
Step or stepped line, 104.
Stereotyping, 7, 16, 242, 298, 310.
"Stet," 91, 175.
Stickful, 84, 275.
Stipple work, 323.
Stone, 92; engraving, 324; make-up, 195.

INDEX

Stop cylinder press, 308.
Stop-press news, 195.
Story syndicates, 245.
Straightline press, 313.
Streamer headline, 99, 162.
Street sales, 101, 162, 189, 200, 209.
Student publications, 328.
Style, 34, 62; headline, 142; type, 272; typographical, 33, 42, 142, 387.
Style book or sheet, 42, 52, 142, 387.
Subheads, 27, 165, 202, 217.
Subordinate headlines, 109.
Subscription, blanks, 367; lists, 367.
Summary lead, 27, 33, 55, 56, 95, 99, 101, 128, 250, 256.
Sunday, magazine, 245; supplement, 11, 224, 322.
Suppression of news, 80.
Symmetry, 205; headlines, 123, 156; make-up, 164.
Syndicate, 217, 221, 227, 231, 241.
Synonyms, headline, 122, 138, 140, 155.

"Tacked on" ending, 58.
Table, 91; type, 279.
Takes, 14, 91, 165, 236, 277.
Tandem press, 313.
Teacher-adviser, 329.
Telegraph, editor, 9, 10, 25, 123, 150, 192, 227, 231, 236; Morkrum printer, 237; room, 9, 10.
Tense, 36, 122, 135.
Terminology, 91.
Tests, of lead, 56, 58; of libel, 75.
"That" beginning, 58.
Thin-faced type, 272.
"Time" copy, 91.
Title page, 345.

Titles, 33, 40, 43, 44, 61, 71, 167, 387, 392.
Toggle-joint, 306.
"Tombstone" headlines, 200.
Tooling, 223.
Top heads, 167.
Transposition, 31, 36, 174, 179.
Treadwell press, 307.
Trial by headline, 159.
Trim, 331, 345.
"Trimming" copy, 80.
Trite words, 68, 142.
Tudor type, 273.
Turn story, 92, 211.
Turned rule, 14, 275.
Tympan, 306.
Type, caster, 294; casting, 285; founding, 284; making, 284; setters, 7, 275, 283; setting machines, 286.
Type, kinds of, 173, 261; black letter, 273; body, 197, 272, 339; bold, 272; directions, 27, 86; headline, 109, 199; high, 264; measurement, 264; sizes, 197, 268, 265; specifications, 277, 343.
Type-revolving press, 309.
Typographical style, 33, 42, 142, 387.

"U. & L. C.," 110, 125, 199.
Underlays, 315, 320.
Underlines, 167.
Underscoring, 31.
Units in headlines, 122, 124.
United News service, 234.
United Press service, 234.
Unitype, 286.
Universal desk, 26.
Universal News service, 234.
"Unskinned" cable, 239.
Upper case, 31, 73, 110, 125, 199, 276.

"Up" styles, 43, 45.

Verbs, 34, 61, 67, 102, 122, 134.
Vignette, 223.
Voice, 68, 122, 133, 136.

Walter press, 311.
Want-ad, 5.
War's effect on newspapers, 99, 163.
Washington hand press, 307.
Waste of space, headlines, 155.
Watermark, 338.
Web paper, 310.
Weekly syndicate service, 245.
Weight, paper, 236; type, 275.
Wer Ist's, 53.
White space, 198, 299.

Who's Who, 51, 53, 83.
Witness, 49.
Woman's page, 193, 194, 218.
Wood, cut, 204, 317; fiber paper, 337; pulp paper, 337.
"Wooden" headlines, 123, 149.
Word Diet, 69, 142, 155.
Wordiness, 34, 65.
Words, 34, 62, 394; headline, 137.
World War, 99, 163, 200, 210.
Wove paper, 338.
Wrapper, 212, 219, 366.
Wrong face, 173, 183, 277.

Yellow journalism, 101.

Zinc etching or engraving, 318.

CPSIA information can be obtained
at www.ICGtesting.com
Printed in the USA
LVHW051054270821
696246LV00001B/8